Abandonment Nightmares

&

The Honeysuckle Dream

Robert Ernest Bach

ISBN-13: 979-8-9928494-2-4

Cover Concept by Robert Ernest Bach

Cover Design by Pear Ink Design

RE Bach

PO Box 1823

East Greenwich, RI 02818

RobertErnestBach.com

Dedication

For Mom and Dad

-

Thank you for bringing me into this world and setting up all the experiences that were a part of our time with one another. I imagine this was no easy feat to carry out and I'm confident that these experiences you had individually and collectively will have a lasting influence, seen and unseen, for decades to come. I know deep within my soul that you loved us but couldn't love us in the way that we wanted or needed you to.

For my wife, best friend, and life partner Mia

-

You have made me "want to be a better man" since the first time I set eyes on you. You have taught me what it means to love another without condition, with reckless abandon, and without fear. Your patience and tolerance as I journeyed through experiences, and the understanding of these experiences, to get to this book have indeed always been inspiring to my at times weary soul. You pushed me to freedom and never gave up on me. You have always said that I was your "Knight in Shining Armor" but indeed your armor was far stronger and held more luster than my beaten wear ever did.

For my daughter Madison

-

Your arrival in my life changed my course in ways you might never truly understand. You taught me how to be a father when I had very little to draw upon in experience. Without knowing it you pushed me in powerful ways and still do. I imagine that you always will. You have always had the grace of Winnie the "Pooh" when it came to me and more importantly our relationship.

For my daughter Demetria

-

You added depth in me on how to be a parent and showed me that we are not limited to the parenting of those related by blood. You always held me in the palm of your hand as I tried to hold you in mine. Indeed, we are so nearly alike. I could not have asked for a better teacher in how to love unconditionally than in the lessons we have experienced together.

For my son Hans

-

This book is born out of you, me, and us. The reason I found the courage to share every single bit of this rests gently on your broad shoulders. As my son, you have been the lightning rod that fired up my desire to transcend *all* my "story." My only hope is that we get to have far more as father and son than what I had in the way of a relationship with my father.

For my family - close and estranged

-

I thank you for all the experiences you were a part of, became a part of, and remain a part of, in my life. I wholly believe that every single one was absolutely necessary not just for me but for you. Please know that this writing was done from a place of full acceptance, from a place of love. And that it was all done with one thought at its base. To be of help and service to others who might benefit from it and of course to be of help and service to God.

For You

-

My hope has always been that the telling of my story would reach at least one person and inspire them enough to be able to trudge through the mire that can be not only the family trauma and drama but life in general. That at least one person might say to themselves "I can do this, I can move on, I can let go absolutely." That you might be able to find the peace, ease, and comfort and rise out of the ashes as I have.

Perhaps this *will* be you.

CONTENTS

CONTENTS

CONTENTS

CONTENTS

Acknowledgement

To the countless men and women who I have crossed paths with, who became a part of my story and allowed me to become a part of theirs. To all who have made this journey with me as I wrote this narrative and supported me by giving me input without reservation as you reviewed it.

Introduction

"Make visible what, without you,
might never have been seen."

Robert Bresson

"Hi Mom."
"Hi Honey Bunny, whatcha doin?" I loved it when she called me "Honey Bunny." It told me she was in a good space. She sounded hopeful, upbeat, alive.
"Not much. I'm writing. In fact, I believe it's turning into a book."
"Am I in it?" she asked with a hint of fear in her voice. She knew I always wanted to write "*the book.*"
"Yes. Yes, you are."
The dreaded moment of silence I intuitively knew would be there as the conversation unfolded.
"Is it bad?" with a bit of defeat in her voice.
"It's truthful."
More of that painful silence.
"Do you think it will help someone?" now with a glint of hope in her voice.
"I really do. Even if it helps only one person then it'll be a success."
Another moment of silence.
"Then you be as truthful as you have to be."
She offered this with a level of confidence I had never heard before in her voice.

"Thank you, Mom. Thank you so much for that, I so appreciate it."

From a telephone conversation I had with my mother a short time before she passed away as I was writing my first book.

We all have a story. And it's authentically ours. To love, or to hate. To move from hating it to loving it. Or to move from loving it to hating it. No matter where your station is it will always be authentically yours. Would you believe me if I told you that there was an Infinite Design that held sway over it? Would you believe me if I told you that your story, no matter how big or small you think it is, is your most powerful possession? That indeed it can be used on so many levels? To encourage? To love? To be instrumental in another's "story," their station?

I have found that it is so.

Although there were long periods of time that I wished to hide my story, to run from my story, to evade my story, I have come to believe in its power. I have moved from loving my story to hating my story then back to loving my story. And this is where I am at this moment. Total ease and comfort with the *entire* design of it.

When I share with you that it took decades to reach this place I am not exaggerating. Although I've always worn my heart on my sleeve, I never wanted you to know my story. I didn't want you to know what was buried deep down inside of me. The guilt. The shame. The remorse. The sense of being lost. The feeling of never being a part of or the feeling of never fitting in. I always felt like a square peg trying to fit into a round hole. But I've come to believe, to see, and to feel, that we are all very much the same. People, places, and things may be different for each of us but at our core we are all the same. It makes no difference what our color is, what our creed is, what our race is. Deep down within we are one and the same and truly connected by God. And therefore, connected to one another.

Since arriving at loving my story, in essence fully accepting my story, I have wanted to shout it from rooftops. Not in a vain manner but in a way that might resonate. Resonate with you. But I was blocked. The greatest variable to writing my story without reservation has been fear. Actually, quite a few fears. The fear of what you might think perhaps heads the list. Most certainly followed by the fear of my family, fear of what they might think, fear of how they might react to it. I must share that it doesn't matter anymore at this point. I am free from these fears. This allows me to make what has always been held within "visible." And perhaps by making it all visible then another might be inspired to do the exact same thing. And perhaps with this more and more will be made visible thereby creating the two things that face fear head on. Faith and Hope.

My story began long before I arrived here, and it began with my family. Generations and generations of persuasions and philosophies passed down from generation to generation. Guiding forces created by varied experiences that allowed many of my relatives, many I did not know, to pass on their ideas, their attitudes, and their emotions. As a species who is in a constant state of evolution there seems to be no escaping the passing on of generational trauma for us. This is the part of my story I held in contempt for so many years. The trauma is the part of my story that I felt so powerless over. Powerless over accepting and powerless over changing. My story has always been tied into my family's story, individually and collectively.

As you read it is my hope that you might identify, relate, to a better part of it. I really hope you can relate to every aspect. The joy. The pain. The love. The hate. All of it. It is the greatest of my hopes that you might find what I have found in the way of an Answer.

I ask two things of you. If you throw the writing across the room, go pick it up and dust it off. And if you begin to experience awareness's perhaps never felt or long abandoned, please embrace them and know this. You are not alone. We are never alone.

Here is my story. I am ready to make it visible and ready to take you on a magical mystery tour.

One

I Gotta Go

I finished my day at the floral studio with the same level of dread as the previous day. The hopelessness and uselessness I felt deep in my core couldn't be escaped. I simply didn't have the energy to go on anymore but there was something inside that remained. Something that had been preventing me from making the supreme sacrifice of ending it all.

The cocktail of medications prescribed by my doctor for depression and anxiety were no longer working. I don't think they ever worked. I arrived at a place that might. I wanted out, I wanted to be free from the pain and sadness. I was thoroughly exhausted and could no longer function under the weight of heavy emotions that I was now fully weary of shouldering. Darkness permeated every part of my soul and being, it seemed to cast a shadow over everything in my life. I arrived at a decision.

With my pistol in my pocket, I loaded my Labradors into my truck and made the short ride home to my wife and son. I could see the exhaustion and pain in my wife's eyes when I entered the house. I didn't want to see it anymore; I didn't want her to feel pain anymore. I wanted to take the pain away from her as much as I wanted someone to take the pain away from me, but I knew I couldn't. I knew no one could take the pain away from us. It was like a wet T-shirt firmly attached to us.

As a worn-down couple we exchanged the obligatory pleasantries as we sat before the kitchen counter to eat dinner while our son languished in his own personal hell upstairs. He and I had long been disconnected from one another. I couldn't wait to get out of the house, couldn't wait to bring the pain to an end. I wanted to break free from that elephant in the room that she and I were always trying to evade, ignore.

After a short time, I said goodbye to Mia. I told her I loved her. With the same obligation that forced our pleasantries she responded in kind. I went upstairs and said goodbye to my son wholly believing that these would be the last words I said to him. I told him I loved him. He barely replied.

I left our home and headed to one of those AA meetings. I had my pistol in my pocket and my plan was set. Tonight was the night the pain would end. I would be free, and my family would be free of the madness that I put them through over the years. I drove the distance out to the northern part of the state along the same route I always took. The route that included each of the telephone poles I dreamed about wrapping my truck around.

I knew that if I could get up enough speed and create the perfect impact that it would work. I reasoned that if I used my pistol at near the same time as the impact that an ending to the pain would be guaranteed. I knew that there would be no chance of survival or rescue as this road is barely travelled in the dark and the likelihood of being found in time was near zero. I had been practicing this scenario, literally and figuratively, for weeks.

As I drove north my thinking fell into a review of sorts. My mind brought forth a fast-paced replay of images of my life that held so much pain with only a weak scattering of images that were pleasant. It felt more bitter than sweet. The pleasant memories didn't hold the power to squelch the painful ones. The darkness couldn't be escaped. No amount of effort on my part could relieve the absolute despair I was feeling.

I drove through the winding roads and turned onto Route 116. As I made the turn, I felt a sense of relief that it would soon be over. The pain would finally end. As I drove the first stretch of road my decision became solid. I felt there were no other options, it seemed there was no other solution. I had tried everything in my power.

I crossed Route 14 at the flashing light and began the next stretch of road that held the longest straight-aways which would allow me to gain the most speed. I took the gun that I had been dry firing into the roof of my mouth and up the side of my head for the past three months out of my pocket. The shiny piece of metal was already in battery. I held it in my hand and noticed it wasn't cold to the touch. The warmth of the metal brought a sense of comfort, a sense of relief.

I stepped on the gas pedal and watched the needle on the speedometer move up. I could hear the noise created by the speed of my Rover as it smashed through the cold and dark dead calm air outside. The sound of it was more noticeable than the music that was playing. My senses seem to heighten even more. I could have heard a pin drop. I could hear the increasing pace of my blood flow and feel the pressure in my temples. I could feel my heart in my chest along with the tightness that was gripping me. I felt resolute. Relief began to wash over me; I felt something inside of me begin to relax.

The quickened pace of the carousel of images that were flashing before me began to slow as I was brought to images of my wife and children. Tears began to stream down my face blurring the road before me. I wiped them away with my sleeve. With the sudden arrival of anger born out of the powerlessness I felt I punched the button on the radio to turn it off. The radio would never play another song after that like I would never see another look in the eyes of those closest to me. The ones that I hurt the most. The ones I was about to hurt for the last time.

I just couldn't go on. I couldn't deal with the pain anymore.

As I drew closer to the set of poles that I knew would do the job, I pushed the truck as hard as I could. I held the gun tighter. One hundred. That was the number I was looking for on the dashboard and it had reached 90 when I looked down. I raised the gun to my head. I could still hear the air smashing against the truck, could still feel the coldness creeping in from outside.

I began sobbing and my body began to shake uncontrollably. The fear that I would fail at this like I had failed at so many other things in life quickly gripped me. I tried to calm myself. I was fast approaching the set of poles I knew would work as the truck flew at a hundred miles an hour. My finger tightened on the trigger. Absolute relief would soon be had.

"Stop. I am not done with you yet."

This was *not* one of the familiar voices in my head. This voice was *different*. It was *powerful*. Surreal. Though I immediately moved to protest the suggestion it was far too commanding to allow that to happen. There was no negotiating with it.

My finger eased up on the trigger as my foot let up on the gas pedal.

Was it odd? Or was it God?

Two

The Honeysuckle Dream - Lost

I stood in the sunlight and felt absolute peace, nothing but a comfortable emptiness. Not the eerie emptiness associated with trauma or pain or a bottoming out. It was a real peace. The kind that so many of us long for in life, right? There wasn't a cloud in the sky and the heavens were as blue as can be in New England.

I was in the backyard of my childhood home. The place my family called home. Mom, dad, sister, and myself - this was my family. The grass was as green as it could be, and it was a hot summer day. I remember the feeling of the sun's warmth and the warmth in the air as the breeze picked up. It was a perfect day if there is such a thing when you're six years old.

There was no noise in the neighborhood outside of nature's symphony of birds and the rattling of leaves in that warm breeze. No scents save for the ones that are natural; the grass, and the mint growing along the back edge of the foundation of the two-bedroom home, and one other.

I stood along the back fence of the yard along the row of overgrown shrubs that lined it. To the right in the corner of the yard behind the dog kennel was the old crabapple tree that always produced, and over my left shoulder was the old apple tree that dropped its fruit on the ground through the summer and into the fall providing for the bees. Before me was my favorite scent of all, my favorite space in the yard. I was standing before the wild-looking honeysuckle.

I loved to stand there and drink in deep breaths. The scent was intoxicating to me. It was so sweet that you could taste it on the back of your tongue as you inhaled. The flowers were so unique, they were inviting. Bold orange color. Their foliage created the perfect backdrop for them.

As I stood before the flowers there was something deep within me that felt wholly connected. I knew deep within that there was far more to life. I intuitively knew there was Something, a Higher Power, at work about me and within me. I knew it was God, yet I couldn't verbalize it, I couldn't express it. I just knew it. This is what brought me that overwhelming sense and feeling of peace, ease, and comfort as I stood there. It felt like a dream. It became my Honeysuckle Dream.

It wouldn't last long. Its Power wasn't strong enough to hold me or sway me. My faith wasn't fully arrived at and wasn't fully understood yet. It was weak and ineffective.

In a flash I was ripped away from it all.

The peace, ease, and comfort would dissipate like a faint wisp of smoke.

The intuitive nudge I had been experiencing would soon be buried by fear and resentment.

The fundamental idea of God and this Power that was so evident yet undefinable at a young age would be tossed aside as a consequence of unwitting calamity.

I was about to be tossed into the stream of life without a life jacket as so many of us are at such a young age. I had no oars to steer my vessel. I was not prepared for it. That infantile navigation of faith would be snuffed out and would remain like that for a great many years until I returned to the dream. The honeysuckle flowers, and dream, quickly withered.

Three

Two Levels of Separation

I didn't know that the course of my life would be set in a downward-spiraling motion as a result of a violent separation from what little faith I had at an early age. I didn't know that I didn't know. It was a compounded ignorance to say the least. I was simply too young to have any other reaction or experience. By a Grand Design the course of my life had been set, and I was about to be introduced to a part of the self that I have to describe as the lower self. It certainly wasn't the part of me that felt and understood at limited levels the faith within as I stood before the honeysuckle. A darkness was introduced to my being, perhaps even awakened.

My violent separation from God seemed to activate this part of me that would produce the most colorful parts of my constitution. I'll have to describe it as wicked. I'll attach the word decrepit. It was dark and insidious. It seemed to grow and build into this description. In hindsight it appears as if there were a split in myself. There was this innocent little guy filled with an infantile faith who was basically at ease and comfort with everything and everybody around him much like any young child, and then with a single spark there was this other little guy.

Perhaps we can use the analogy of Dr. Jekyll and Mr. Hyde as a blanket to better understand what I came to see so many years later in life as a weary adult. I didn't understand it at the time. How could I? How would you be able to? When we are so young without the benefit of life experiences to guide our understanding(s) it is nearly impossible to decipher reality most times. We have that benefit of living in the Honeysuckle Dream and then we are ripped away from it. For me the Honeysuckle Dream was a bubble of sorts free from the natural irritants of life.

I describe it as a violent separation for a great reason. The violent way in which I was moved from one reality, almost a dream state, to another reality, an actual nightmare, was caused by an injurious and destructive force. Again, wholly unbeknown to me, and to those about me.

While I do not have the full benefit of knowing every nuance of my mother and father's relationship, I will share what I do know, what I was able to gather from them, and most certainly what I have felt, seen, and come to believe by experience. After all, isn't this what many of us are left with? Our experiences? Their "story" became my story as their parents' stories became theirs and so it has been for all of us.

Mom and Dad were married out of high school. They were forced to get married as my mother was pregnant with me. I arrived on the scene in March of 1968 and my mother always described me as a happy baby. An "all he does is sleep and eat baby." My sister arrived a year and two days later. Our younger brother didn't make it.

We moved into my childhood home before I could recall my earliest memories. To me it was my first home. It was a small two-bedroom house my parents rented on a street lined with homes more generous in size. The neighborhood was host to family after family with many children. There weren't any broken homes on my street, the families were all intact.

Though my happiest and fondest memories at times can become clouded by those that are darker in nature there were brief moments of happiness between my mother and father. I was indeed told of this later in life by them, told this by other family members. I also had the benefit of living some of them for a bit of time.

There were those moments when we were all gathered in the living room before that big ass 70's television set that seemed to be the size of a couch watching Sonny and Cher and a host of sitcoms. (Later on, these sitcoms would become a babysitter and even a parent to me. Most times handing me lessons in life.) The times that our Disney albums spun on the turntable set atop the mammoth-sized piece of furniture. The trips in the old Chevy's and Pontiac's to the local Mister Donut for a dose of sugar and return to the television for the stimulation of Saturday morning Warner Bros. cartoons where my appreciation for classical music was stoked by a rabbit, a pig, a duck, a Martian, and a gun toting fellow.

What I didn't know was that there was a storm brewing between my parents and there would be no stopping it or the resultant damage it would cause. The cause and effect wouldn't be fully understood by me for a great many years.

My sister and I were in our bedroom at one end of the house. My mother is in the kitchen cooking dinner at the other end of the house. My father is sitting in his chair in the living room smoking Camel cigarettes listening to music while playing with our cat Ramy. The music was loud. I could hear my mother and father speaking over it at the other end of the house. It seemed like it was in the far distance, not just the short walk down the hallway. I can't recall what they were talking about.

I can remember that our shared bedroom was bathed in sunlight as the sun set on that side of the house. It was the end of the day (dream) but the beginning of the evening (nightmare). It was warm. It was the same type of day I had experienced before the honeysuckle, but it wouldn't end on the same sweet note.

As I went about whatever I was doing their voices at the other end of the house began to get louder. As I said the music was already loud to begin with. I felt something within that I didn't recognize, something new to me. I now know it was fear. I could not define it, nor could I justify it in this moment. I was simply too young, simply without life experience. I didn't know what to do with it and I believe I let it take me. What other choice did I have?

As the fear built the voices got louder and louder and as the voices got louder and louder so did the clamors within my mind. My heart began to wrench. This was also something new to me. It felt foreign. Like it didn't belong there.

My mother and father were having an argument, it was the first that I remember. It was the first of many that would take place from this moment forward. Their voices kept getting louder and louder and it seemed like the music would match them in strength. I recall the beginning of the argument. My mother asked my father to turn the music down and he did not. This escalated the argument, and my mother responded with yelling that quickly turned into screaming. She had this uncanny way of moving from a quiet casual conversation to an explosive volume in yelling then deeper into screaming. It was the sudden escalation that roused me from my dream state of being a child thinking child things doing child things. It was the screaming that activated the fear. Instinctively I didn't want my mother to feel pain, to be bothered, to be hurt. I felt the innate need to reciprocate the protection my mother always extended to me.

The fuse had been lit between them and what I didn't know was that it had been lit long before this moment. This was simply the explosion. My mother finally screamed two words at the top of her lungs.

"Get out!"

That was it. In a flash it was done. I wholly suspect that my father was waiting for these words to arrive, that he couldn't wait to hear them. As if he was waiting for permission or sufficient reason which he would use as an excuse or justification for years to come. A cowardly way of placing blame at another's feet instead of taking full responsibility for his own intent and resultant consequence.

And with this the volume of the music was lowered. In fact, it was turned off much like my parents' marriage was at this moment. My father left our home. Before he did, he walked down the hallway and into our room. He gave my sister and I a kiss goodbye. The next time he would be inside our home would be nearly ten years later as he raised his fist to my face.

Here's the piece I didn't know about. My mother was pregnant. It was a boy. He would have been my younger brother. I also didn't know that the effect of what just happened would be the beginning of so, so many endings.

My sister and I never had a chance. Like so many children at a young age we simply didn't have the strength, knowledge, or faith to withstand the tidal wave that just landed on the shore looking to annihilate us.

Four

The Harsh Decision

Here's what I didn't know and what would become the impetus for the core of our lives as a broken family. As quickly as my mother said the words "Get out" a resentment was placed at her feet. She would use it as a sword - she would wield this weapon around without any discipline because of the deep levels of pain it brought to her. I believe she experienced her own violent separation from God and faith as I did as a child, yet she was an adult when it happened. This holds an instructive lesson for me even to this day. The idea that a resentment has the power to kill us. It has the power to kill not only faith but our God-consciousness. The power to create a separation from God, to create a wider space between us and God. At its core resentment is about re-feeling something over and over and over again. Sometimes they lose their power over time, yet at other times they just hang in there without mercy. And as long as I am in this state, as long as my mother was in this state, all things worthwhile are easily set aside or tossed aside. To a great extent it causes many to just give up. God-consciousness and faith being the driving force in our lives is supplanted with a deep level of defeat. This is indeed what unbeknownst happened to me when my father walked out of the door, and what happened to my mother when my brother was taken.

My mom was in her third term with her third child when my father abandoned us. By all accounts, hers included, she absolutely loved being a mom. She loved the idea of having a family with more than one child as she grew up as an only child. She always said that she loved my father's family because it was larger than hers. Even as I watch the videos I had transferred to DVD from the old reel to reel cans I can see the spark in her eyes. I can feel the power in her smile that backed the spark. I can see the deep levels of satisfaction in her body language while she was surrounded by not only her son and daughter but the family. Hers and my father's. She seemed to be whole. She seemed to be at ease. She seemed to be content. I do have memories of her in this state and when my mind falls upon them, they are sweet and very touching.

As my mother and father separated my mother held the hope that they would get back together, that her dream of a family would be restored. My father had different ideas. He found another woman and began seeing her.

The decision to abort my brother at such a late term was not my mother's. It was my father's decision to make. She left it up to him. She gave her power to my father and without a conscience he absolutely annihilated it. Why my mother ever posed the option for continuing their marriage and relationship upon the fate of an unborn child and handed this decision to my father will be forever lost on me. It became the greatest regret and guiding force in her life from that point forward. It was a decision she would come to wholly regret and a decision that would lead to her own defeat. She began to give up and perhaps rightly so.

I didn't know what was happening at the time though later

in life I recall the exact day it happened. The entire family was well aware of what was going on and what was going to happen. Later in life I would reach out to my aunt, my father's sister, and simply request if I could ask her some questions about my mother and father. Abruptly, without any hesitation at all, she said "No. Ask your father." I believe she knew exactly what I was going to ask about and she didn't want any part of it. As if this denial would continue to add more cement to the wall I think she used to continue to block it from her memory. She followed the refusal by unfriending me on social media.

On another one of the not a cloud in the sky filled with sunshine days my sister and I had just walked the twelve or so blocks home from elementary school with our friends who lived on our street. We came into the house through the side door at the driveway and Mom wasn't there. My aunt was there, which awakened an awareness in me, a suspicion of sorts, that I wasn't used to. I don't remember where my sister fit into the scene, I don't remember what she was doing. I remember standing in front of the big ass 70's television, the turntable and stereo now removed from the top of it, in the same manner my father was removed from the house. The front door was wide open. The front door was rarely open, and I remember thinking this was odd. It fit the scene's awkward nature.

I looked up into my aunt's eyes. I asked her where Mom was, and she refused to answer the question much like she refused to answer any questions later in life. I remember her *energy.* I instinctively knew something was amiss. Something was seriously wrong, and I knew deep within it involved my Mom. She answered by telling me "We have to go." We left our home, and I do not remember anything else about that day. I time traveled. I checked out.

The idea of "time-traveling," the blocking out of reality, the evasion of reality, would become a part of my nature. My insistence on denying the reality of my senses began at a very young age. As quickly as I became aware of my surroundings this ability to evade awareness's arrived. At times it can be a healthy reaction of sorts, creating a level of protection, survival, but I've found that most times it is the opposite. It creates more damage and clearly indicated my inability to process hard truths, reality.

Mom wasn't home because the decision to abort my brother was being followed by the action of making it happen. Although I don't have the benefit of answers to the questions I've always wanted to ask my aunt, I believe deep in my heart she was angry. Maybe it even hurt too. She herself would have three children. As a nurse I believe she didn't agree with any of it and her participation in it by looking after my sister and I that day perhaps haunted her.

My mother would never be the same after this. The spark in her eyes was extinguished. Her body language began to match the dimness. Her soul was cut to the core, and the scars would exacerbate the deep resentment that became the rudders in not only her life but in the lives of my sister and me. She was now broken and by extension my sister and I were too.

My brother was to be named the opposite of mine, a play on my name. He was to be Ernest Robert, but he didn’t make it.

Five

"Bye Mommy"

When "Big Bob" walked out of the door he was "gone." Whatever was there in the way of a rudimentary relationship, father to son, son to father, was immediately destroyed. It wasn't squelched, its infantile nature was simply put to death.

The same can be said to a smaller extent for the relationship I had with Mom. I "time travelled" the day my aunt was at the house to pick up my sister and I and cannot recall the rest of the day. It's amazing how at some level our consciousness can move us to a state of protection all in an effort to only give us what we can handle. My grandmother, Nana, my mother's mother, always commented that "he's the sensitive one" when speaking of me. She never tried to hide the words; she knew there was nothing wrong with speaking the truth.

Over the years I would become skilled at time travelling, evading the reality of situations and my senses and when I couldn't muster this without little effort, I would find ways to make it happen whether it was by substances, alcohol, or the like.

That morning that we left for school all was as good as could be expected in our home. My mother was trying to manage as best she could. She managed to get us to school. We managed to arrive home after school. But something changed at levels I could never understand at that young age. I knew my father was gone. I was feeling the beginnings of abandonment, and my nature quickly began to match this rough force. My nature was only at the beginning of becoming very colorful.

Mom was gone now too. At times I think there is nothing more baffling than having a parent but not having a parent. They are there but they are not there. In thc physical sense they are in your life but in all other areas they are not. Mentally, emotionally, and spiritually they are empty shells. They are unable to be nurturing in a positive manner. My father was always like this to a great extent, but my mother was not. From day one all she wanted was to be the best wife and mother that she could be. She wanted better than what she grew up with. Don't we all want this most of the time?

What my mother went through literally killed her. As her unborn child was destroyed so was her spirit. So was her will to live. It was a slow and painful death. It was a death by a thousand cuts. The cuts being lashes against her consciousness and she suffered from this until the day she died.

She tried. She tried with all the strength that she could muster to rise above this traumatic experience and at times she only seemed to surmount it. But for the better part she spent her days and nights in a deep slumber, in a deep sleep. She tried to time travel, to evade the reality of it, but most times was not successful. She learned to wear a mask and put on a happy face.

I recall the presence of my family all about us, but I cannot recall my father being anywhere at all. I remember my mother's parents, Nana and Papa, always being there in a constant manner. They became the "Rocks" in my life. My father's mother, we called her "Moo," was also there but to a lesser extent. I would find out exactly why later. My father's brother, Rick, became a greater part of our lives. These would be the family members who would step in and act as our parents because Dad refused, and Mom gave up to a certain extent.

Nana and Papa were the bedrock throughout the course of my life until the day each of them died and growing up we spent nearly every weekend with them. Though I cannot recall who it was that we stayed with while Mom was "away" I know it was Nana who took us to visit her.

Shortly after my brother was taken, my mother was brought to Butler Hospital, one of our state's mental institutions. I remember walking the grounds on another one of those not a cloud in the sky sunny days and there were people gathered all about. It was like a scene out of a movie where "people went to rest." I believe it was a Saturday or Sunday and there was almost a carnival-like atmosphere to it all. It wasn't what you typically see today in these institutions. In hindsight it *felt* as though hope was something they put at the forefront of treatment.

On the grounds outside they had these giant washing machines that were modified. The agitator, the impeller, was removed and you could attach a thick cardboard square to the bottom of the inside. They would start them up and then you would drip different colored paints inside creating a splash pattern on the card. I remember making one and giving it to Mom. She wasn't there. She had this faraway look in her eyes, and it terrified me. I instinctively knew my father was gone and didn't want my mother to leave me too. I never wanted to be abandoned.

But she did leave. She experienced a violent collision with her faith and would spend her life trying to surmount the guilt, shame, and remorse in an effort to recapture her connection to God.

Six

"Little Bobby"

With every single fiber of my being, I grew to absolutely despise this moniker affixed to me by my family. "Little Bobby." I know it was simply a natural consequence of having the same first name as my father but there was so much more to it for me.

Though I couldn't fully recognize it or even understand it I quickly grew to despise my father from the moment he left us. I would carry this hate most of my life and even today I suppose there are moments when the smallest vestiges can be felt if I drift too deeply into a gloomy reflection that rubs the scar tissue.

I came to know that it is somewhat natural to hold someone in contempt when they have wronged you. It is a part of our human nature, a *lower* part of our human nature. It certainly isn't a part of our Higher Nature, that which is fully connected to God. Resentment simply cannot exist in the latter.

The more my father drifted away from us the more resentful I became. The more I witnessed how he was and what he did, his demonstration, the more I blamed him, held him to account, for the station my mother, sister, and I were left at.

"Little Bobby" came to life the day my father left. The split in my personality, the arrival of what I will call an alter ego, brought with it a myriad of colorful parts to my nature. He wasn't the little guy that stood before the honeysuckle who enjoyed the ease and comfort of an undefined faith. This person, this other half of me, was entirely different. He wasn't that carefree "all he does is eat and sleep" little guy. This fellow was unknowingly the victim of circumstances.

He was a chameleon.

At his core was a level of selfishness and self-centeredness that would propel me for a great many years into adulthood. I became sick with this self. Spiritually sick. So spiritually sick that it permeated not only every aspect of my life, the people and the places, but my physical, emotional, and mental state as well.

I became a self-seeking person. If I became resentful, I retaliated and when I did, I outdid what you did to me. There were still other times that I became resentful and simply walked away. I did the same thing as my father did. I would abandon you and act as if you were no more. If I became fearful, I ran away. And other times? I tried with all my might to muscle my way through it, but most times found myself right back at being resentful. It was a vicious circle of what I would describe as uselessness and when I arrived at this point, I simply wanted to give up. I wanted to throw in the towel and end it. I didn't want to be here in this world anymore. It was confusing for me as a child.

Of course, I couldn't express even a bit of this to you because I was afraid you'd abandon me for not being perfect before I could abandon you. Or worse, I was afraid I'd end up in the same place as Mom. As much as I didn't want to let you in, I wanted you to know what was happening within me and wanted to let you in. But I was afraid that you might see the "ugly" part and run. I became a people pleaser.

In other words, I grew into a spiritually sick person, disconnected from God. I had varied traits. If circumstances called for me to be nice, kind, or even considerate to get what I wanted, so it was. If circumstances required the opposite to get what I wanted then indeed I was not kind. I became mean and nasty. *Always* to get what I wanted.

When I was growing up Mom never held back on her honesty with me, never held back on her honest opinion and assessment of me. She once called me a "self-centered, manipulative bastard" and she so hit it out of the park with that one.

Being abandoned by a parent, or parents, on any level whether physical, mental, emotional, or spiritual has a profound effect on one's soul. On one's thinking. On one's emotions. Even on one's physical well-being.

The message is loud and clear and for someone like me who was already ultra-sensitive. The message was vile. It became an insidiousness within me that few can recognize or even speak of, or handle. The message was that I was expendable. That I was garbage. That I was not worthy. That I was defective. That my existence was useless, and I am undeserving of love, or even relation, with others.

The abandonment precipitated so many troubles in my life. Most of which I was indeed the cause of and most of which were the direct extension and result of becoming a selfish and self-centered person, a self-seeking individual.

"Little Bobby" watched "Big Bob" whenever the opportunity presented itself. My father had the typical visitation with us, the one night during the week just long enough to grab a bite to eat where he spent most of the time dragging heavily on a cigarette and then the obligatory five hours on a Sunday. Except for two occasions, we were not allowed to stay at his place overnight.

My father's first apartment after leaving us came with a new girlfriend, the woman he began seeing when he left, and her three children. His spirits were buoyed. They were high as he began anew while mine were buried with wildly misunderstood resentment and fear that included mountains of confusion. I felt left behind, not a part of.

"How can my father just toss us aside with a smile on his face?" was the question I found myself asking somewhere deep within. I couldn't verbalize it, but it was there in a very raw and painful form.

I watched my father through the lens of fear.

We had already been tossed aside, and he barely spoke to our mother. It was as if he had shut the door on her. Like she was dead to him. Though I was pissed off I still wanted my father to be my father. I wanted a Dad. My fear was that he would abruptly and completely shut the door on my sister and I as he did on my mother. Though I didn't know the details of the abortion at the time, in hindsight I can see how he easily decided to abort my brother. In hindsight I can see where my sister and I rated.

With a heightened sensitivity at the core of my own fast-changing emotional arrangement I read messages differently. When I was introduced to my father's soon-to-be second wife the lesson I took away was that you could trade people in like they were some kind of commodity. My Mom had been switched out for a different model. Again, I couldn't verbalize this, but it was there.

When we were introduced to her three daughters the message squarely hit the mark. When the fear that my sister and I could be replaced presented itself it brought about a deepening of all the colorful characteristics of "Little Bobby." He didn't want to become totally irrelevant. He wanted to hold onto his position as a son by any means.

I just wanted to be loved. I didn't want to be tossed aside. My greatest fear as a child? That one day my Mom or Dad would stop loving me.

We spent only one night at my father's new place, and it was pretty cool. Something new always brings heightened senses with it. Colors are brighter. Scents are stronger. Taste is more pronounced. You hear things differently. And of course, you feel things at deeper levels. It was cool - until the morning.

The ingredients for the meatballs we mixed by hand while standing on chairs before the kitchen counter felt cool to the touch. The smell of my father's cigarettes as he smoked reached deep within as I breathed. The Beatles album "Magical Mystery Tour" sounded ethereal and mystical while it spoke of a walrus. The feel of the Fruity Pebbles against the roof of my mouth felt sharp but not as sharp as my father's words as we got ready for the day after breakfast.

In the short span of time through the night I mustered the courage to ask him a question. Something I would regret for quite some time. As my sister stood in the mirror in the bathroom brushing her teeth, I looked up at him as he and I stood outside the door in the hallway. He seemed like a giant. With all the seriousness I had in me to act as the adult I found my courage.

"Dad why did you leave Mom?"

Asking the question and being the observer I am, a most natural part of being a child, there wasn't too much that went unnoticed by me. I absorbed details wherever I was and at times they became embedded within and sometimes this happened unknowingly.

My father's place was a two-bedroom apartment. Of course, he had a bed in his room and there was a bed in the spare bedroom but here's the thing. That bed was never made up. It was a portable bed with a frame that was folded up, and banded so it wouldn't fall flat. Like it was prepared for storage. As a child the message that landed on me as I looked into this room was harsh and abrasive.

The bed spoke to my father's basic attitude toward his children. That they were not welcome. That there was no place made up for them in his life. That they were not a part of his life but rather guests. There was no place for them to feel safe with him, only a place to be stored much like all the other stuff that was stored in the spare bedroom.

He didn't hesitate to answer the question. He didn't waver or falter. His response was immediate and when it landed on me it felt like someone dropped a bag of cement mix on my chest. I lost all the air in my lungs, and I imagine the color washed out of my face. I held back tears because I didn't want to appear the weakling.

"Because I stopped loving her."

I didn't hear another word. I time travelled again as I felt my soul sink into an abyss.

If he could stop loving her then he could stop loving me, stop loving my sister. This bolstered my effort to not only become the chameleon but to perfect it. I learned not only from his demonstration of what had already happened with my mother, my sister, and I but through his words that we can turn love off. It would take me decades to learn how to undo this. To turn this fight or flight mechanism off and discard it.

The one evening my sister and I spent at my father's new apartment had the profound effect of putting me in a place of never wanting to ask questions. I learned to fear the answer, the truth. It was the perfect setup for my mind to set itself on creating false narratives. The stories we make up at times. Most times when we do this it is simply a method of protection, a part of our survival mode.

“Little Bobby” would become “Big Bob.” And I grew to hate him as much as I did my father. The level of self-hatred and self-harm knew no bounds as I tried to navigate the reality of these guiding forces that were set up in me and in the end my own family hated the person they unknowingly had a hand in creating. Later in life I would become an escape artist.

Seven

Teachers

Each lesson placed before me was not limited to a person as the conduit when I was a child. Most times the lessons arrived in the form of circumstances or what seemed a happenstance. Most times their arrival and presentation were pronounced with force and still others were in the background to be collected and reviewed at a later time, an intermezzo if you will.

As Mom and Dad were living the experiences they *had* to live I didn't have the benefit of knowing at such a young age that indeed I was *supposed* to be living the same. I didn't know anything about divine design. Not the twists of fate but perhaps the happenings that are indeed meant to be. I didn't know that there was more to all of this living life than met the eye. How could I?

Don't we all spend a better part of our lives asking "Why?" To some extent, aren't we searching for this answer from the day we arrive here? I have come to see and believe that we are placed in this position from the day we are born. Perhaps we are here simply to learn. To learn from one another all the nuances of living. The nuances of living a *spiritual* life.

Perhaps each circumstance placed before us, whether we judge it to be good, to be bad, to be indifferent, is divinely designed to bring forth all of the best within us. No doubt the best within us is a lengthy list. I believe Faith is at the top of this list.

The stream of life is not easy but then again it *can* be easy. The conditions vary. Vary dramatically. The currents can be strong and at times graceful. The surface of life can be tumultuous and choppy and *seem* unmanageable. At other times the surface can remain smooth, easy.

When the split between Mom and Dad happened I immediately began to ask the question of why on an almost constant basis. I may not have been fully conscious of this, but it was at the forefront of my mind, and it was always backed by charged emotion. Not only was I asking the question as it related to my parents and the state of the stream, but I also began to ask the question as it related to everything. This I believe to be natural as well.

If we look about us and rest our gaze at the younger children as they move through the stream, they still have something that each of them loses as they get older. They have their innocence, something we let go of as a consequence of the stream, that flow of life. Their nature has yet to be corrupted. They are free of fear. They are free of resentment. They have no need to feel self-pity or to be dishonest. They are simply explorers full of a natural and still connected wonderment.

And then something happens. The awareness of the *self* arrives, and we are shown the depth of the stream for the first time. A lot of times we are without a life jacket and begin to sink but never fall below the surface for to long. And still at other times we are forced to learn how to swim, to learn how to navigate. While doing this we leave behind our innocence. We leave a piece of our faith behind on the shore.

From the start I made the declarative statement that we are all one and the same. Perhaps you wanted to argue with that and that is perfectly fine. I've come to believe that deep down inside of us is this amazing barometer of sorts. This amazing compass. It's *installed* deep within. It is the basis of our lives. It is an essential part of us. A vital part of us.

It is the *idea* of God.

It's a thought, a conception, a notion. It is there. We are all born with it and maybe it is at its strongest when we are young children. It guides us from day one and remains there giving us comfort and peace. Call it intuition or sixth sense. Call it whatever you want but know that deep within each of us is this amazing Light.

The stream offers us so many varied experiences, teachers, as we navigate our senses and responses to lessons placed before us. With this comes that faith within, a spirituality and trust in God, *and* our humanness. Our humanness, perhaps a lower self at times, seems to be the problem. As this lower self presents, most times as we break from the innocence of being a child and most times because of a resentment or even a fear brought about by others, it becomes the dominant part of our being with only one desire. Survival. It has arrived and now that it is here it begins its constant and incessant collision with our spirituality. It's like there is a war taking place within and we are there trying to decide which side we want to fight for. Naturally we don’t even know it's happening. How would we? No one has explained it to us. No one told us about it because they're too busy fighting their own war. Everyone is paddling their canoe through the stream of life upstream against headwinds. I had this mode of survival, coupled with a fast-growing mode of survival that was being built in me, that was needed to be a part of my family.

Perhaps the greatest reason for all these lessons, profoundly *all,* is to come to this realization. To return to the faith and innocence abandoned. To flip the scripts and learn to move with healthy and nourishing tailwinds instead.

Nana and Papa became my greatest teachers and the greatest constant in my life. This was so as far back as I can remember. They picked up the pieces when the house came crumbling down and tried to reassemble it as best they could. My father was gone and now my mother was off to navigate her own storm. Nana and Papa stepped in and, in many respects, became parents to my sister and me.

Though we did not live with them they were always there. We lived on one side of the city and they on the other. It was a short distance between the homes. We were with Mom during the week at our place and we were with them at weekends at their place. We had a place created for us and were always welcomed in each of their worlds. We had bedrooms in each home.

Nana and Papa became the rocks. They were solid. They always, without fail, remained steadfast. They were firm in their faith and acceptance of all the lessons they had learned from the stream, from their storms in life.

Arriving at their place on Friday nights for the weekend allowed Mom to work as a waitress through the weekend. This also allowed her to be home most of the week with us. I remember the Friday nights going out for a bite to eat with Nana and Papa or accompanying Nana to the Big G as she did her shopping. I remember waking up on Saturday mornings without a care in the world, without an agenda, and watching the Saturday morning cartoons. The big mugs of hot tea with sugar and milk added.

I would spend Saturday afternoons with Nana hitting the yard sales where she would buy me the most foolish things after grinding the price down. She spoiled me rotten as they say. Or the times when I would tag along with Papa as he did the chores around the house. The cutting of the lawn, the checking of fluids in the Nova or Rambler wagon, or the burning of the garbage in the fireplace. We would end the day with a dinner prepared by Nana in her kitchen which was simply cozy. Though the kitchen was at the rear of the house it was the center of their home.

What they brought to me in their teachings was consistency. It was stability in the face of a storm. They were the eye in the hurricane that became my life when Mom and Dad split. They were the calm as the storm raged all around me. As the water became choppy in the stream, they became the sails and rudders that remained as strong as can be. Rocks. You couldn't break them. They became my greatest hope for a better future. To this day and after all these years I still value this lesson the most. Nana and Papa were that powerful and time spent with them was equally powerful.

There was always time to go to mass at Nana's church. We went on Saturday afternoon or on Sunday morning, depending on her mood. She was Irish Catholic and had the deepest of faith. She tried, mostly by example and demonstration, to pass this along to me. She rarely used words as she was a quiet person. She chose her *way* as the instrument to pass along lessons. This had a resounding effect on me. It was the classic lesson that actions speak louder than words.

Her patience was indeed something to be admired. How she arrived at it, perhaps through her own experiences within her family growing up at a truly different time than what we are in now, is not known. She never spoke about her experience of growing up save for the occasional mention of a family member here and there. Most notably "Pa." As I look back, I think she spared me the facts of her life and her own lessons because she knew how fragile my sensitive arrangement was. I don't think she wanted to add any more weight to my shoulders. I believe she wanted to pass on the lesson of faith. She wanted to *teach* this to me. Like she could glimpse the future, like she knew I was going to need it, or even return to it one day.

We attended mass each weekend and like most kids in church I was restless. How could I not be? She always had me drinking her tea. I was a wired puppy! I would sit in awe of her church; it was truly magnificent. It was huge. It wasn't a cathedral by any means, but it was a larger church compared to most. Especially compared to the church we would be introduced to on our side of the city as we attended catechism classes.

There was something that happened to me each time I went to a mass with her outside of her way of being a teacher. I enjoyed the service. They resonated with me. I *knew* there was something there. Safety. Nana's church, while enormous in scale, was comparatively humble to others. Its walls and trappings were simple. The stone structure had a very bland grey tone with the obligatory stained-glass windows but even these were simple in nature. The pews a natural wood while the altar held the same freedom from complexity. Perhaps it was all this simplicity that resonated with me as well.

The scent of patchouli touched my soul and even carried me away from the stream of life. It seemed to wash away the cares I had. Nana was trying to teach me that indeed there is a God. That if I could accept this then life would be an easy row through the stream. She didn't lecture, pontificate, or speak down to me from some kind of higher morality or spiritual mountain. She did it with grace, and humility. While I didn't fully see this at such a young age the lesson was embedded in me at very deep levels creating a rudimentary foundation, or even an addition, for and to that faith we are all born with and carry as a child before we experience a separation. A separation that occurs most of the time at the hands of others about us. My separation was caused by Mom and Dad, and I truly believe that although Nana could never verbalize all of this to me, she was always trying to show me the facts about this moment in time.

Lessons taught to me always had a deeper value and meaning when shown rather than passed on with words. I watched everything as a kid and either drew inspiration from it or a distaste. I am very much the same way today.

Nana and Papa grew up in a different time and I'll always be grateful for all they shared with me about their own recollections even if it was limited. These memories held lessons as powerful as the way they carried themselves. Their demonstrations were always guided by the lessons they were exposed to, by the teachers in their lives, as they moved into adulthood. And so it was with their parents before them and still their parents' parents and so on and so on. We all benefit from the generational lessons passed on to us.

We also experience generational trauma that is passed down to us and perhaps a greater purpose for us while here is to surmount these irritants and traumas, these lessons, and return to a faith that truly binds us all together. I couldn't see this lesson when I was a child tagging along with Nana on the weekends as she moved through her never-ending "to-do lists" or when Papa would take us to the local zoo and park to see the animals, to ride the amusement rides.

The stream of life took me in a violent manner in a quick way. It was like a band aid was ripped off and my soul exposed. Every nerve was on fire. But Nana and Papa stepped up as parents offering the best protection wherever they could. They truly honored us and respected us and what we were experiencing. They tried to shield us.

On Sundays, after a hearty breakfast with all the fixings prepared by Nana, I would begin to grow restless and irritable. My inner compass, my intuition, would begin to wretch back and forth within me. It happened each week without fail.

My father would pick us up at Nana and Papa's house and take us for the Sunday visitation thing. From the start I wanted to go with him. Of course I wanted to be with my father. I also wanted to be the people pleaser; I didn't want to cause any waves in the stream by not going.

But then that changed. Sundays began to include his soon-to-be wife Pat, and on occasion her three children. I didn't want anything to do with her. I didn't want anything to do with her children. In my ripped-apart heart and mind that felt like it was constantly being bent they appeared to be substitutes for my mother, my sister, and myself. It felt as though we had been traded in. The worst thing was that I felt my father wanted to keep kicking the tires on his old vehicle. That he was trying to fulfil an unwanted obligation. Deep within the message I always heard was that my sister and I were spare parts.

I didn't want to return to the abrupt change in reality that was thrust upon us and didn't want to leave the stability of faith and love demonstrated by Nana and Papa. I wanted to remain in the *safety* of it all.

Nana became a fierce defender for me. She took the place of my mother on so many occasions as Mom went about her descent into her personal hell and travelled to her oblivion. Nana also knew what I was thinking and always feeling, much like God does. Nana and I had this amazing connection between us that carried me for years.

She knew I didn't want to be with my father on Sundays anymore, that I didn't want to be with him when Pat and her children were involved. I would protest each Sunday, and she would pump me up as best she could before I left. Then one Sunday there was absolutely nothing she could say or do to convince me to let go of her. I refused to go with my father, and she supported this. She placed a call to him explaining I would not be going but that my sister would.

As I look back it was from this point that I tried to communicate to my father just how unhappy I was, just how angry I was. I tried to do this my entire life, and it always fell on deaf ears as they say. He never listened, never cared to listen. He simply wasn't available at any level. He could not see beyond his own world, didn't notice all that was orbiting around him and the state of the bodies that were in motion around him because of his actions.

My father arrived to pick up my sister and I simply refused to speak with him. I didn't say a word as he tried to convince me that I "had to come with him." This infuriated me at levels I could never understand at the time. How could I? I believe I was six years old, just one year into my hyper awareness of everything in and around me.

Nana stepped in and asked him to stop and then asked him to leave with my sister. I time travelled again after this. I suppose this happened for a few reasons. Of course, there was the emotional tidal wave that I was being tossed around in, but the larger reason was at the heart of it. I tried to communicate with my father from a base of absolute terror and fear, not with words. I tried it with action, with a demonstration, and it failed to bring forth what I really craved.

I wanted my father to stop. I wanted him to stop the madness like my mother always wanted him to stop the madness. I wanted him to say something to the effect of "I've been wrong, and I will fix all of this and put us all back together." It didn't happen.

So, I time travelled. I fell into my own story land where I was the narrator and could create a world that would bring peace and comfort. Would keep me safe. I began to live a life of delusion and something else happened on this day in my mind, in my eyes, in my heart.

Nana moved from the place of introducing me to God and fostering faith in God from within me to becoming a God in my eyes. I placed her on a pedestal. I believe rightly so. In the space of one morning she became the most powerful force in my life. She became everything to me. She always called me "Pet" and my heart would swell when I heard her say this.

I always wanted to be with her and became open to learning anything she would pass on to me, even the God part. I was just north of twelve years old, just a quick six years from this point in time, when she passed away. And when this happened it was as if God died too. All faith was tossed aside and my descent into hell would quicken.

Eight

"I Have A New Family"

The dust seemed to settle a bit after Mom re-engaged to a small extent with the daily chore of living. I suppose we all began to pick up the pieces as best as we could and tried to move on as best as we could but to a greater extent it never happened. Mom simply couldn't move on. She became fiercely bitter and resentful. It was a natural reaction to all that had happened and with it came a great deal of retaliation. My sister and I would be a better part of this, and I would feel all of it at deep levels. I took on and even supported her resentments and efforts to retaliate a lot of times. How could I not do this? I quickly became that people pleaser and was working from a place of fear. The fear of being abandoned. I didn't want to be abandoned by Mom the way Dad had abandoned us. Her resentments mixed with my resentments and my resentments mixed with hers. Slowly I became my mother and took on her trauma. I learned to take on the trauma of everyone in my family.

At one point Mom spoke of changing her name back to her maiden name. As we drove in the old Pontiac, my sister and I in the back seat with our arms flung over the back of the front seat, we bolstered the idea by saying we wanted to change our names too. We were too young to resist going with her flow. Later in life when Papa spoke of me to Mom he would include "your boy" to point out the fact that I was very much like her. It drove Mom nuts when he pointed out this truth.

It was far easier to take on trauma than to take on the faith Nana had been trying to teach me about. Out of the cast of characters that made up my family Nana was the only one who was totally open about and forthcoming with God, prayer, and faith. Everyone else seemed to keep that stuff locked up in a closet. They didn't wear it on their sleeve like Nana. You had to pry them open like a closed pistachio shell if you wanted a glimpse of what was inside them.

My father got remarried in a short time and there was no way in hell that my mother was going to allow my sister and I to attend the wedding though my father wanted us there. It just wasn't going to happen. My sister and I were grounded for something petty which I cannot even remember. This was how Mom prevented us from seeing our father most times. We spent the day in our room while she spent her day depressed and angry. We were shamed by my father's side of the family for not going to the wedding as if it were our decision not to attend.

My father left his apartment and moved in with Pat and her three children. His life moved on while ours entered and remained in this never-ending holding pattern that was a constant reminder of the bomb my father dropped on all of us. We were in this new home only a handful of times.

As much as I do want to tell you about Pat here, I will remain reserved for a bit. But let me share this one bit. She never wanted a thing to do with me and my sister. She didn't have it within her to even be a friend to us. We were an imposition to her and later in life she would tell me this without reservation and without a bit of emotion.

In time Dad and Pat bought a new home and moved to another city with her three children. All their lives changed while ours became static. My father bought this long-ass Pontiac station wagon to better accommodate all of us when we were together, the two of them, my sister and I, and Pat's three daughters. I still remember how happy he was that it had air conditioning. I remember how it felt like a sealed submarine as it filled with cigarette smoke when the windows were closed.

They planned a trip to Niagara Falls and my sister and I were to be included. As they prepared my father spent a Sunday working on the station wagon changing out the water pump. When we were supposed to return home by 5, he had not yet finished the repair. Pat had to drive us home.

My father's friend Vinny, a native New Yorker who looked like, spoke like, and had the same mannerisms as Father Guido Sarducci, was helping him work on his car. His wife Dimity was at the house too. To this day I believe Pat wasn't capable of spending time alone with my sister and me. When Pat drove us home, she asked Dimity to take the ride with her. My sister and I bounced around the backseat all the way home.

As we made the final few turns to get to our neighborhood, I became aware of my surroundings as if I was supposed to hear what was going to be spoken to. I stopped bouncing around the back seat and began listening to Pat and her friend as they spoke. I caught just enough of the conversation where Pat was telling her that she didn't know why she had to take us home and that she didn't want anything to do with us, didn't want to be a part of our lives.

Though I was only a child these words and declarative statements cut me like a knife. As I took on the role of people pleaser there was no one else that I tried to please more than my father's wife. I tried to act and speak in a way that might gain her love and approval when in her company. When I wasn't in her company, I would spend time ruminating on just how much I despised her. There would never be a chance for her to abandon us as she never even opened the door for us to be a part of her life. What's the saying? When someone shows you or tells you who they are, believe them? In truth I did believe what was being shown to me by her both by words and certainly by demonstration.

We weren't allowed to go on the trip to Niagara Falls. Mom wouldn't let us go. We were grounded again. My father and Pat took two friends of my stepsisters with them in our place. I remember being shown the pictures from their trip by my stepsister. She had that same contemptible look on her face for us as she showed them to me that her mother had.

Dad's mother was an only child like Mom. She and Mom had this in common. She also had three children; my father had a sister and a brother. Mom would have had three children. My mother adored her, adored the idea of having a family like she did. My mother looked up to her and it was easy to see why.

My grandmother, Moo, had a free spirit and lived without bounds. She had this amazing way of taking a bad situation and making it better, downright amazing is how I would describe it. Perhaps this came from the way she was brought up. She made the best of everything. She was wildly independent, and her level of confidence and self-reliance was resilient, at times to a fault. She had no fear as she lived a full life. She always stood tall in the face of adversity. She was strong. Strong enough to mask her own fears.

She was a nurse by trade and managed this place in the south of Providence. It was called Saint Elizabeth's. I can lend a few words describing what this place was like but the easiest way to do it would be to liken it to a scene from "One Flew Over the Cuckoo's Nest." This is what it seemed like seen through the lens of a child. We would visit her there on occasion as she was that charge nurse fully dressed in whites with the white millinery and white shoes to compliment. You might think that I would be freaked out by the scene there, but I wasn't. I felt safe there because I was with her. She didn't hold the same place as Nana, but she was indeed one of my grandmothers and we were close.

Although she didn't have the opportunity to share time with me in the manner Nana did when I was young, she did so later in life. Nana was the early teacher, and Moo was the later teacher. There was a reason for this. Not only on a divinely inspired level but also on the human level. The latter part is where we will go but I should explain her name first.

Moo's name was Wilma. Growing up my father would call her "Bill." It was short for Wilma. It also sent me the clear message that there was very little in the way of a relationship or love between the two of them as he chose to speak with her by a different name rather than the term of endearment "Mom." I called her "Bill" once and it felt so foreign and off that I never did it again. It felt heartless. I called her "Moo."

Moo was Swedish and could be as hard as nails, a real blockhead as we said of one another in the family at times. The Swedish name for grandmother is "Mormor." Being the eldest of her six grandchildren I was encouraged to call her this but couldn't say it. I landed on "Moo Moo" instead. It stuck. Her five other grandchildren, my sister and four cousins, would call her the same. Eventually we all landed on "Moo." Our friends even called her "Moo."

She was as unique as this term of endearment that I had for her. Like Nana and Papa, she didn't share much about her past or how she grew up. She was really reserved about this. She was not as reserved when it came to sharing her opinion though. Especially when it came to my grandfather, the father of her three children. I never met him but was indulged with the horror stories of his drunkenness and violence over the years. She was missing one of her small toes and when I asked her where it was, she pointed to the fireplace and told me her ex-husband had cut it off and threw it into the fire.

During many of the visitations with Dad we were also with Moo. It was like my father needed help and support just to be around his children. I didn't mind it at all as I was always acutely aware of the space between us and Dad and that never-ending feeling of awkwardness.

After my father got married and we began to spend time with his new wife and her children Moo was with all of us a lot of the time. She had this way about her that didn't deviate from the Moo that I knew and loved. But there was this other side to her that I was introduced to that was ice cold. I didn't know where it came from and why it was so. It would be revealed to me later in life after spending years hidden away like many of the family secrets. In fact, all that was going on at that time in my life was validated and spoken to plainly between her and I leading up to her death. We had the wonderful experience of being able to speak to the truth of what we had both experienced in life. Her teaching, as profound as the teaching from Nana, was indeed reserved for a later time in my life.

A great deal was revealed to me as I mustered the courage to ask her hard questions about the family as I began to have children, as I began to create my own family. As I looked in my daughters' eyes, I wanted to know more with the intent of trying to get it right. To perhaps flip the script, that family curse, if this was even possible.

Moo walked away from us. She walked away from my mom, my sister, and myself. One day she was there and then one day she was not. Naturally she was at family gatherings and holiday celebrations, but she was removed on an emotional level. Even on a spiritual level. She became aloof when it came to my sister and I. Mom, too.

When she came to our house she always came inside and then one day she stopped. She would approach the house at the front door rather than the familiar side door we all used, and she would speak to us through the door. She would bring gifts for our birthdays and drop them at the door without coming in. When Mom was in retaliation mode using my sister and I as a weapon and refusing to even let us go to family gatherings at Christmas Moo was the one to bring us our gifts. Again, leaving them at the door with a hurried spirit and a need to get away from us as quickly as she could.

The message received was sent at its highest volume setting. We were somehow defective. When she left Mom would fight this message by criticizing the gifts. She would then lapse into criticizing the family on my father's side.

Moo was close to Mom and Mom was close to Moo. When I watch the old films, I can see their combined chemistry and it's simply beautiful. They had this extraordinary and visible connection with one another. This carried on even after my father left. It was explained to me later that she, Moo, not only felt horrible about the split but about the taking of my younger brother. She said it was a regret she always carried with her. But there was something else that took place.

As my father moved on with his life, with his new family, he told his mother that she wasn't allowed to be with my mother anymore. That he "had a new family" and he wanted her to be a part of it. Not one of us knew this until it was revealed to me later in life. It certainly explained layers and layers of confusion I was constantly trying to sift through the most of which being the idea that I wasn't only abandoned by my father but by his mother too. Her abandonment added more credence to my closely held belief that I was somehow defective, that my mother and sister were somehow defective. It also bolstered the newly forming idea that people were expendable, easily tossed aside without plausible cause or reason, or even explanation.

Moo gave my father her power much like my mother had. To this day I cannot understand how this could be yet there it was. Thankfully each of them would reclaim this power later in life and the day Moo did she said to me "Your father is a wimp."

Nine

Where Are My Purple Socks?

In many ways it seemed as though time stood still after Dad left. But the funny thing about the word "seem" is that it simply means appears. It isn't necessarily so. It really *seemed* like time stood still but indeed it did not. Time never stands still. In fact, it moves lightning fast while we are mired down in the complexities of emotion and when this happens it feels like everything grinds to a sudden halt.

It was so with me as the reality of my senses guided by my parents' split took on some heavy nuances. I quickly became the chameleon and would change into whatever the setting or situation called for and this was always guided by fear. Abandonment began to destroy my spirit, and the resultant decay would last for years with evidence of it visible to this day. The reality of it became difficult to endure without the proper tools or even faith to withstand the violent currents in the stream of life.

I began to dream and imagine. Dream and imagine a different reality that might come to be. I began to lie to myself. I would tell myself that none of what was happening was real. Of course I did not know this at the time. How could I? It was only after sifting through the rubble decades later that I came to see all that had happened for what it was. Letting go can be a monumental feat, but it can be done. It must be done. I believe it's a necessity while we are having a human experience. The difficulty for me with the emotional arrangement I had was this. It was impossible to let go. I was caught up in the absolute trauma of it all. Again, I didn't know it.

By the time I let go of anything it is typically covered with deep claw marks. Chances are good that I have spent every ounce of my energy trying to figure out a way to *not* let go. To keep it close to me.

There was this *before*. And then there was this *after*. The time that was before the split held its own reality. And then the time after the split held its own reality. The previous was bliss, and the latter was the polar opposite for me. And the more distasteful and hurtful it became the more I tried to convince myself that things would return to normal, return to their previous state. Again, I couldn't see this at the time. In other words, I began lying to myself and by extension lying to others. Though they could see that I was lying, telling stories, I believed my lies so deeply that I couldn't tell, couldn't fathom, that they knew I was lying. That's how much I invested in my false narrative. No one ever called me on this.

There were indeed two of me and the deeper I sank into the stream of life it became impossible to differentiate between the two. I couldn't differentiate between the true and the false. It was as though I was standing in the middle of train tracks with one on the left, the false, and one on the right, the truth. As I gazed ahead of me the two tracks, the true and the false, became one and the same to me as the vision of them merged. The deeper I sank the more difficult it would be to recover all that was authentic, the real me. The one that just happens to indeed be a spiritual being having a human experience.

I always had two stories going on in my mind and the fantasy of the false narrative became a method of surviving the damage resulting from the causation of abandonment issues and ensuing fears. It became a source of protection for me but in the end would become my undoing. It took serious effort to see everything for what it is. It surely took help from others and more importantly from the God that I turned my back on.

My belief and faith in God weren't near strong enough to withstand the humanness of all that was happening and what I came to see was that *I* was the one who turned my back on God. This was not a conscious thing. Indeed, it was a reaction to circumstances. I believe many of us have this reaction and perhaps one of the greatest lessons while here is to recognize our failure, to repair the resultant loss of faith, and to return to God. Perhaps this is why we have these varied experiences that seem, appear, to be distasteful. They're designed to bring us back to God and perhaps this must happen *while* we are here. We are born with something, then it is lost to some degree, and then we are to recover it. Then we are certainly placed in a position of being able to pass on a different lesson. Perhaps even placed in a position to flip the script.

As I shared, I have this inability to let go. I leave claw marks on everything. When I was the "all he does is eat and sleep" baby I had this blanket. It was the typical security blanket that I took everywhere with me. Covered in dirt, grime, saliva and whatever else I dragged it through. I always had it in my hands and against my face as I sucked my thumb. My mother had to wash it at night while I was asleep. That is how attached I was to it.

As I got older, and the blanket became worn, it shrank. It wasn't a natural shrinking. Mom cut it into four pieces. It was easier for her to wash it that way as it was always being dragged through everything much like I was being dragged through the circumstances around me against my immature will. Eventually the blanket disappeared. Eventually I got over it and moved on. Nonetheless I felt this loss at some level.

My favorite color is purple. Always has been and after all these years I suppose it always will be. Before Mom and Dad split, when I was in kindergarten and the first grade I had this pair of purple socks. They weren't thin, they were a bit thicker. They weren't dress socks, and they weren't sports socks either. I would have to describe them as being like a polyester. I think they became the replacement for the blanket.

My mother had to do the same thing with the purple socks as she had with the blanket. They were washed constantly so that I could wear them constantly. I loved them. I loved them so much that throughout my life when a family member gave me a gift a lot of times it was tied to the color purple. The color became a signature of sorts and even today it is the dominant color in the logo for my business.

Back in the late sixties and seventies there were these thin wooden cutouts that you would hand paint. They were ornaments for a Christmas tree. The three wise men, a Santa figure, a snowman, Christmas tree, elves, etc. They had outlines in black on them and you would choose the colors you wanted to paint within the lines. A string was attached so they could be hung from the tree branches. We had these ornaments for years.

Dad was the one who painted all of them and when he painted the elf he painted his feet, his socks, purple. It was my ornament, and it hung from the tree every year for quite some time as did all the others he crafted. They all became a part of the "time stood still" aspect of life.

My elf became the purple socks when one day they

vanished as did the turntable on the television and my father. Naturally the socks became worn with time and even had these white lines on them from the time bleach splashed on them. I believe the elf became the solution to substituting that which needed to be discarded. Pretty metaphorical when you think of the fact that many of us do just this with so many things in our lives. People, places, and things. Replacements. I'll get to this bit later on.

Each year after Dad left, we would put the Christmas tree up and I would lapse heavily into my false narrative. I would look at Mom and without words ask her if he was coming back and without words, she would painfully answer that he was not. I was afraid to ask the question, afraid of that bag of cement landing on me.

I would see the elf on the tree and wonder where Dad was. What he was doing. Who he was with. Was he thinking of us? Did he care? Did he want to come home? Was he coming home? When was he coming home? Would he ever return to loving us again? Everything in my false narrative answered these wonderments in a positive way and each time I let these answers solidify in my mind I became sicker. As the false narrative didn't play out the way I tried to make it play out I grew more and more resentful. My level of resentment began to match the strength of Mom's resentment.

I was too young to decipher what was happening to me, so I kept going deeper and deeper into survival mode. The deeper and deeper I went the farther I was moving away from God. The deeper and deeper I went the greater the disconnect from the idea of Him that was deep down inside of me, the intuition if you will. As my faith weakened, I began to rely more and more on myself and my infantile and finite power to process reality. Ultimately this all failed, and I didn't see the sense of it until I was a grown adult.

Dad was an artist, as are many in my family, and he was

into needlepoint for a bit. He created these pieces and mounted them on cardboard and had them framed. They hung in our home. After he left, not much changed in the house. These pieces remained on the walls along with the braided carpets on the floors until the day Mom moved out. The walls, except for one bedroom, remained wallpapered with the same look that was there when we moved into the house. Even the canary yellow appliances, the stalwarts of the seventies, stood in place and stood the test of time that seemed to grind to a halt in our house.

Later, as we moved Mom out of what became her prison cell of a home, I would take these needlepoint hangings off the walls that had hung there for better than twenty years. I didn't take them with us. I didn't throw them away. I remember taking them in my hands like a Frisbee and throwing them through the air with such anger that they bent under the force when they connected with the wall. The resentments I had, the resentments that I carried were powerful. And as resentment is simply the re-feeling and re-living of a previous injury I could see as I closed the door for the last time in this house that I was ruled by them. I was a young adult at this point, yet I was still trying to sift through the ashes of my childhood.

I took the elf with me and kept it for a great many years as an adult. I couldn't let it go. It was covered in claw marks and wrapped in a false narrative. It was bathed in the false hope that one day my father would return to me and be just that. A father. This day never came but the day did arrive when I wanted to be free of the resentments. I wanted to be free of the fears. I wanted to be free to live my life without the drag of the past. As I look back, I really think I just wanted to return to the innocence I had before the split. I wanted to return to the Honeysuckle Dream.

The day came when I took the elf into my hands and

caressed it. I could feel the grains in the wood and the sharp edges along with the sharp memories attached to it. I could see the clear distinction between the colors and of course the purple socks. I noticed the marked change in its size, how it seemed so big to me in my small hands as a child, and so small to me in my larger hands as an adult. When I looked upon it, I came to the realization that this piece was indeed created with thought. It was created with love. There was a moment in time when my father was there. Was there wholly, however brief it was. I came to realize that at some level he had the capacity to be a Dad but couldn't find a way to fully embrace it. He simply couldn't do it. His own generational trauma would not allow it to happen, and he didn't have the strength to surmount his own resentments and fears. He chose to run. He chose to evade reality. He chose to time travel.

I made a clear decision to never be like that. To fight. To be better. To be a better husband, to be a better father. It would require some serious action on my part following this decision. I would have work to do, and this would take some time. It would require me to move away from resentment and back to God.

I snapped the elf in half and tossed it across the room.

It was an ending of sorts that opened the door to a new beginning.

Ten

Seeking Refuge

I moved to a place of *trying* to rely and trust upon others as the storms raged, even though I was already feeling the pain of having the same trust and reliance I had on my parents trounced upon. Even though I was moving through life with a false hope born out of the false narrative there was a space for real hope that not everyone was like my Mom and Dad. This feeling was validated by those about me who could be, and remained, present. Nana, Papa, Moo, and even my father's brother Rick. I sought refuge in all of them as well as in anyone else I *felt* was safe whether it was a teacher in school or a friend's parents.

In many respects Papa took on the role of being my father, as did my uncle. And there was a vast difference between these two men. Papa fought in World War II and had all the experiences of being in the Pacific theater. He always said this shaped him and you could see by his demonstration that indeed it had. He was also shaped by his childhood, his own generational trauma.

He had two sisters, and his father was a violent drunk. Ironically my father had two siblings, and I'm told his father was a violent drunk as well. Maybe you could say my mother married her father. My mother always had difficulties as an only child, and with her father, Papa. She said she hated him while growing up. That he was tough with her. Not very loving and very demanding. She rebelled and by the time she met my father, and his family, she was looking for an escape. Although there were times when Papa had visible difficulties with alcohol, I didn't see them as she did and remained unaffected by them on a deep level. I only felt them topically. Both Nana and Mom experienced these difficulties, and I only experienced them secondhand through them.

Nana was the teacher of faith and brought the lessons in God to me, Papa's lessons were different. They were real-life lessons far removed from the dimension of spirituality. They were about work, and work ethics. They were about being responsible and getting things done and enjoying the satisfaction that comes along with this. They were about achieving and then looking upon the achievement with pride. He always had a "to do" list.

The lessons were wrapped in the hard mechanics of life and how things worked. Whether it was applying the right amount of pressure to the back end of a screwdriver as you tried to put a screw into the wall or knowing just how tight to screw on an oil filter. The lessons were always offered in a way that inspired one to be as frugal as possible and he was exactly this when it came to his feelings and emotions, though he would soften quite a bit as he aged.

He was the epitome of the hard reality that he lived in and the reality of the times he grew up in. In many respects as I watched "All In The Family" while lying on the floor in their home swirling my spoon around a bowl of ice cream turning it into mush, I was watching him on the screen in the character of Archie Bunker while he was sitting behind me in his recliner smoking Chesterfield cigarettes. My sister once commented that his heavily calloused hands with nicotine-stained fingers and thumb from years of hard work and smoking reminded her of the safety he provided. The safety he provided for all of us.

He was as much of a rock as was Nana. He was consistent, and solid. He was a deeply principled man and tried, mostly through his own demonstration of principles, to teach me the same. Unfortunately for a great many years I wouldn't have the capacity to see or learn these lessons from him.

What I've come to know is that once I experienced the split in my personality there was this darker side of me that came to the forefront of my being. Perhaps it was always lying in wait. While this part of me moved further away from God it brought about not only a delusional way of thinking but a sense of selfishness and self-centeredness that wouldn't allow me to see not only the truth but the lessons in principles Papa brought. It was impossible for me to grasp the lessons. Even if he had placed me in a school-like setting and stood before a chalkboard bullet-pointing and explaining a higher set of principles they would not have permeated the shield, the wall, I had quickly formed around myself.

Deep in my heart, and even unknowingly, I was utterly disappointed in my mother and father though I didn't fully understand this. They had let me down and at some level even though I placed some trust and reliance on others, Nana and Papa, I wanted to trust and rely only on myself. I would only ask for help after a complete failure of my power and most times I didn't want to ask for help because if I did it meant that there was a deficiency in me and if someone saw this, they might want to leave me, might want to walk away, might want to abandon me. I simply couldn't endure more of that.

In this respect I think I know what my mother experienced with her father. She was always in a constant state of fear of failing him which led to this exact thing within me in many ways. I was afraid of failing him and as he was, in essence, my father, I was terrified that he would leave me, would toss me aside. I was afraid to make waves. I was afraid to disturb this vessel in the stream of life.

Here's something I have never shared with anyone in my life until now. Try to imagine this if you've never been in this position. You have been tossed aside like an old rag by one of your parents, or by both to some extent, and you arrive at a place where you're deathly afraid to be alone and not only that, you’re also afraid that everyone else will leave. You feel defective on every level and are constantly questioning your worth. Questioning where you fit into the scheme of things or where you fit into your family. This is where I was when this happened to me. I was in a state of constant bewilderment and terror and my young mind couldn't differentiate between the true and the false. I was six or seven years old.

It was a Saturday, another one of those not a cloud in the sky sunny days and as usual I was at Nana and Papa's house for the weekend. The place I felt the safest. Their house had one bathroom like ours did. Papa went in to take a bath. They didn't have a shower; they had a bear claw tub.

I had to go to the bathroom, and it wasn't just a "piddle" as Nana called it. I really had to go to the bathroom. I had to poop. My fear of being defective permeated me so badly that I didn't want to disturb Papa while he was in the bathroom. I remember dancing around like kids do when they have to go to the bathroom while trying to hold it. This lasted for what seemed an eternity. The dancing. So didn't the time that Papa was in the bathroom. I was gripped with fear, and it intensified the more I danced around trying to keep myself from having an accident. And then it happened. I crapped my pants! Imagine being wrapped with, and gripped with, so much fear that you crap your pants!

I wanted refuge so badly in my life that once I saw that it was there in a person, in this case my grandfather, I would do or wouldn't do anything to place that protection in danger of being taken away from me. Oh, how I wish I could tell you that I fully understood all of this as it was happening, but it was impossible to understand and that's the thing about a false narrative that is created and the attendant delusion that comes with it. It is impossible to understand anything.

These understandings wouldn't come to me until years later as I learned to sift through them one at a time. The principles that Papa tried to pass on to me also wouldn't be understood until years later. It was only after the delusions and false narrative were exposed to the Light that I could clearly see all that he tried to pass on to me. That I could finally embrace and live by the exact principles that create real sustenance.

I do not remember the rest of this day, or the weekend for that matter, after I crapped my pants. I time-traveled again.

Eleven

Cheers

As I stood before the honeysuckle there was this feeling, this knowing, deep within me. The feeling that everything, profoundly everything, was going to be good and that everything is as it was and will be as it must be for very specific reasons. I felt this peace deep within that guaranteed that no matter what the circumstances I would never be left alone. Naturally I couldn't verbalize or fully understand this. How could I? I was indeed far too young to decipher or interpret those sometimes-loud messages from within that emanate from the voice of Spirit, from God. They were there though, and I would carry this small piece, this mustard seed-sized fragment of peace and comfort, God-consciousness, with me always. It would remain there in every storm that arrived to churn up the mud at the base of the stream of life. Even in those moments when I felt alone within a crowded room but most especially in the presence of my own family, somehow, I knew that I was never alone. Never.

Even when those about me, people much like me, sometimes lost, sometimes found, felt far and distant. When I felt alone, I was not. I never was and I never will be. I knew this as I stood before the honeysuckle, but it was only a fleeting suspicion. Today I know this with every fiber of my being. God is always here. I just needed to turn back to Him with a willingness to meet Him and when I did make the decision to do this, He met me halfway. More than halfway.

A secret shared is a secret halved and there are many that we carry with us. We even want to carry some of them to the grave. What I've found is that they're like acid. Their corrosive nature eats away at us and the resultant breakdown of our spirit does not happen quickly. It is a slow and painful deterioration that dulls the senses. The greatest secret that I began to carry as I turned from the honeysuckle and let the stream of life and all its nuances dictate to me how to think, how to feel, and how to act was that I not only began to dream and think about not being here at some level I also began wishing for the end. I became acutely aware of the fact that I didn't want to be here, didn't want to be alive.

It was a few of those about me in my family who seemed to have a numbing effect on this position, a position that would place itself front and center before me later in life as I seriously contemplated ending my own life. Nana and Papa seemed to have this calming effect on my spirit. As I said they became the rocks in my life. Most times I looked upon them as Gods. They were my Higher Parents and thankfully so.

As my mother entered her own dream state, her exit from reality, and as Nana and Papa became the center in the lives of my sister and I, my mother grew more and more angry with a sincere desire to retaliate against my father anyway that she could. This included using my sister and I as a weapon against him. She had not one kind word for him or about him and I'm confident that if she could have kept us from ever seeing him again, she would have.

As I developed the need to make everyone feel okay,

especially Mom, I quickly became a people pleaser. Watching television on one of those not a cloud in the sky sunny days while kept home from school, while my mother slept well into the early afternoon, I saw a commercial for an Elvis album. If you sent $4.10 to the address listed, they would send you the album.

I took the money from my mother's pocketbook and stuck it in an envelope and wrote the address on it. I didn't know anything about stamps but they mentioned that you needed to send a self-addressed stamped envelope with the money so my immature reasoning led me to draw a stamp on the outside of the envelope in the place where you would put the postage to get the piece mailed successfully. I walked to the top of the street and put the envelope in the mailbox with the excitement that this might put a smile on Mom's face, might bring her back to us.

It didn't happen. I don't recall how she found out what I had done but remember her reaction. I believe this coincided with the weekend that my father was going to take us to the circus that was in town. Mom grounded me. She kept me from going. She also included my sister in her effort to use whatever she could to hurt our father. We spent nearly the entire weekend in our bunk beds in our shared bedroom.

Nana and Papa never verbally bashed my father in front of me when I was young. They never put him down, never criticized him. Never spoke to his actions or character save for the one-time Papa made a comment that resonated with me deeply. Later in life Papa would openly share his honest opinion of Dad much like Moo would do with me.

My father was twenty years older than I and between us, almost equal in distance in age, is his brother. His name is Rick. In many ways he was the older brother I never had, yet he was my uncle. And in many more ways he stepped up much like Nana and Papa and assumed the role of father.

Papa's lone criticism of my father while I was younger came in a direct observation that he made about Rick.

"I don't where you kids would be without your Uncle Rick, he has been more of a father to you than an uncle." was the enlightening statement he made. This was Papa's way. In his humility he was dismissive of the powerful role that he had been playing while complimenting another's. Papa could see and speak to things plainly. Always. And I believe this was the result of all he had experienced in his own stream of life. He learned the lessons that would move him from a space of understanding to even deeper places of understanding. This would be part of the role that Rick would take up in my journey.

As I navigated the new realities of my life and the changes thrust upon me, I vacillated from clear thinking to the colorful delusional thinking brought on by the false narrative that I had quickly formed, the false narrative I was adding layers to daily. Instead of draining nourishment from experiences by way of sound reasoning I began draining energy from the false narrative, the delusion, and it was bringing what seemed to be infinite layers of guilt, shame, and remorse and along with-it boatloads of self-hatred and self-doubt that were always trying to sink my vessel. Nana, Papa, and Rick would be the three that always brought me back to sound reasoning. They spoke plainly and honestly. They were the buckets constantly removing the water that was trying to sink or drown me, and my vessel.

Rick not only landed in age between my father, his brother, and I, he also landed in the middle of the vast space between us. While he played the role of younger brother to his brother he was playing the role of older brother to his nephew. While he was playing the role of father to me, he was also playing the role of diplomat. There were many times when he was also working from the place of generational pain and had the incessant need to keep up the many destructive forces that were always lurking at the base of our family. While he recognized that he was playing the role of my father he would defend my father in ambiguous ways. I suspect he wanted to protect the unhealthy persuasions that held sway over the family. I believe we all do this, most times unknowingly, to some extent within the dynamics of our family.

My wife and I, and he and his husband, went for dinner one evening a short time after Moo passed away. We often spent time together as couples. This particular evening was more difficult than others. Rick and I were older at this time and so much had changed over the years which I hope to make clear but at this point, at this time, a deep-rooted anger from within me was making its way to the surface and leaking from me at any opportunity without a filter or care for how and when it landed on others. Why wouldn't this be a natural consequence of what I had experienced?

The night before Moo's service I didn't sleep. I was going to see my father and his wife at the service and didn't want the opportunity to possibly be heard, to hold him accountable, to pass by without an effort on my part. This was always futile. I spent the sleepless night writing him the longest letter I have ever written. I burned through the entire catalog of Metallica while I wrote and edited it by hand. "Little Bobby" thought it was a masterpiece.

After arriving a bit late for the service, I sat there with every nerve in my body on fire. The family were all gathered up front, yet we sat toward the back of the church. I'm a "get there ten minutes early" sort and this day I was thankful for being late. I didn't want to sit with my father and those who supported his pain. I was filled with fear, like a dog crapping razor blades.

As we gathered in the rear of the church after the service in what became a receiving line my wife and I exchanged the obligatory "put on the show" pleasantries where my father announced that he and his wife were taking advantage of the time away from their home to spend the night at a local casino. They didn't have casinos in Massachusetts, and we were in Connecticut where they did. I held back my urge to verbally vomit my emotions on them in front of everyone and handed my father the twenty-page letter with the hope that his weekend would be ruined. I was all about retaliation at this point in my life.

Needless to say, the letter was not well received, much like the blistering letter that my father's wife wrote to my mother years before when I was young was not well received. My letter sent a shockwave throughout the family as did the blistering letter my stepmother wrote my mother had. The difference between the two letters was this. My letter landed on deaf ears against the backdrop of a dead conscience. The letter Pat wrote to my Mom, as equally poignant as the one I handed my father, was a heat-seeking missile that brought on a state of depression in my mother that mirrored what looked like the capsizing of her vessel in the stream of life. For quite some time she gave up at deeper levels than she had ever done before. She arrived at near full defeat. I suppose I was looking for the same effect.

My father responded to my letter with a phone call trying to plead his case. He was mostly upset that I gave it to him at his mother's funeral and ruined his weekend. He couldn’t see the content or messaging within it. I guess I was supposed to know the specific rules of engagement in the family when it came to these matters, yet no one seemed to have shared those with me. That's the rub about dealing with generational pain that is left mostly untouched or wholly ignored. When you poke it or prod it there is a built-in defense mechanism that is activated to ensure it remains intact. To ensure it survives.

Pat responded too. She wrote me a scorching letter in return trying to plead with my father's case. It became the only chance I was ever given to put down on paper exactly how I felt about her, so I returned the favor. Her reply to it was a card signed "Fair Winds." To this day I haven't any idea what she meant by this but suspect it meant touché.

As my wife & I and my uncle & his husband sat in that restaurant in Providence a short time after Moo's passing, enjoying dinner and laughing, out of the blue from over there in the left field, Rick turned to me with a raised voice and hit me with one line. I don't recall the exact words but can remember the looks on the faces of those at the tables closest to us. His voice and delivery commanded the attention of the other guests within earshot. The line was accusatory in nature, one that held me in contempt for writing the letter to my father. It was wrapped with his disappointment in me for the way in which I delivered it, when I delivered it. I understand this yet there was so much more. This moment was the equivalent to the verbal cement bag my father dropped on me that one time my sister and I stayed at his apartment twenty-five years before.

I had upset the apple cart as they say. I had disturbed the status quo. I always did this unknowingly, but I do know this. I became, and was, that "black sheep" in the family and still am today. The thing about this label and more importantly, assuming its nature, is that the black sheep typically sees more, understands more, and can even transcend all those things that were once thought impossible to surmount. We can burn it down and let it burn down. We can be comfortable in the ashes for a bit with some satisfaction but equally as important, we can rise from these ashes unafraid of letting others see the damage, unafraid of others seeing the cloak of black discoloration wrapped around us from the ashes. We *can* rise like a phoenix.

Rick became a respected and admired teacher in my life. Later, he would become a lamentable preacher of sorts. He was indeed one of the brightest spots in my life when there was nothing but darkness about me and on me. I placed him on a pedestal as I had done with Nana and Papa. Mom adored him.

He didn't live near us; he lived in the next state over. He became a constant in our lives. As a young child I would spend time with him and in those moments I felt as though I was standing before the honeysuckle. It was nourishing. He would come into town and would make the effort to include a visit to us while here. At times he and I would go off alone and these moments also became a bright spot in my life. Although he had learned to navigate his own stream, he indeed had difficulties that made him stronger. Again, isn't this why the difficulties are here? To help us to grow in understanding and effectiveness?

While Rick and Papa stepped up and played the role of Dad, they could not have been any more different from one another. As I mentioned they came from different times and places, from a different era, but there was more.

The first time I was allowed to travel alone to the next state by bus to spend the weekend with my uncle it was a very freeing experience for me. I was placed on the bus and instructed to sit behind the driver. The driver knew I was young and travelling alone. He agreed to watch over me until I reached my destination after numerous stops along the way.

I landed at my destination and began my weekend. It would be an enlightening experience on so many levels. Levels that would play out for years. I was taxied to the salon my uncle worked at and introduced to his people. I met his friend Lou. We left the salon at the end of the day and went to their home. We ate dinner with Lou's mother and played some video games. They put me up in the spare bedroom and when Rick and Lou retired to a bedroom together, I became confused.

When I returned home to Mom, I asked her why Rick and Lou had the same bedroom. She explained to me in the most gentle and loving way that my uncle was gay. Now I couldn't fully comprehend all this encompassed, but it made not one difference to me. He was my uncle, and I adored him as my mother adored him. It didn't faze me in the least.

Though I was already being taught by Mom, Nana, and Papa what unconditional love is to some extent, mostly by their demonstrations, individually and collectively, I learned this in a more pronounced manner by and from my relationship with Rick. The relationship I had with him was one of the most powerful in my life while growing up. He extended compassion and empathy to my sister and I when so many couldn't. I like to believe, and I think rightly so, that it was his own personal struggles of announcing that he was gay and going to live a gay lifestyle that brought forth this depth of admirable character in him.

When Nana passed away my sister and I were allowed to be at her wake and funeral. Nana, my God in human form, was laid out and it seemed so surreal to see her like this. Lifeless. Here's the small piece I want to share about it. It was six years after Mom and Dad split and Rick took on so much in addition to the position of being an uncle. His position extended to being a Dad to us. He simply wanted to comfort us as a Dad might do. He was at the service for the evening part and returned for the morning part. He was the bright spot for my sister and I during this unchartered experience.

He couldn't stay for the entire funeral and had to leave between the church service and the grave service. As my sister and I sat in the black limousine behind the hearse that carried Nana we looked out of the back window. Arrangements were made for Rick to drive behind us in his small orange MG. As we drove, he put his signal light on to let us know that this was where he had to get off, where he had to leave us.

He waved at us with a big smile with all the enthusiasm he could pass on to us from the distance between us trying to reassure us that we could get through the rest of the day. He returned to his life. We turned around in our seats and returned to our life.

Rick came out of the closet at a time when to do so might mean great harm to oneself. His personal experience placed him in the laudable position of wanting to help others. He also paid a price far outside of the spiritual realm. In the realm of human suffering. As we all do with experiences.

When he announced that he was gay there was a reaction within my family. I wholly suspect the generational trauma and pain carried on played a big part in this. His older brother, my father, reacted with violence. He punched his brother in the face. My father would attempt to do this to me as I got older, but I believe that this incident with his brother held him back just short of following through. I would see his fist and white knuckles in my face, but they would never fully connect.

His mother's reaction, Moo's reaction, was perhaps the harshest of them all. She stopped talking to him and wouldn't speak with him for nearly a year. He was tossed aside much like my sister and I were tossed aside. A parent turning out their child became the thing that Rick and I held the most in common with one another and the irony is that we never even spoke of this. It was just there. Perhaps this is what inspired him to take on the role of being my Dad as best he could even though he didn't live close by. To a great extent my father would come to resent this about him, about the two of us. The fact that Rick and I had a bond with one another that he didn't have with his own father, or his own son. Dad simply wasn't capable of it.

Throughout my life I believe I've always been looking for a father and they have shown up in the guise of many men. At the base of this search though has always been this never-wavering yearning to have a relationship with my father. To have him engage in the role of Dad. It never happened. Papa and Rick were the constants in my life trying to play this role for many years. Papa until the day he passed away and Rick until I reached early adulthood. Rick would come in and out of my life on numerous occasions over the years that followed.

My family had this uncanny way of telling one another to fuck off. At times it was done without words and at other times words were spoken. My way was to simply leave. My father taught me this. When I was done with something or someone I could just simply leave without a word, or an explanation. Rick had this way of ending a conversation with you or period of time with you. He did it with one word. My sister would pick up this trait as she got older, and it became their way of telling you they were done with you or a conversation. Not only that it became their way of telling you to "fuck off."

They would say or type the word "Cheers." I would get these "cheers" from Rick on numerous occasions in the years that followed. They typically arrived when I was upsetting learned family dynamics.

The men in my life when I was a child were merciful with me. The fathers of my friends, the fathers in the other families in the neighborhood I grew up in. They all knew the living situation in my home. I suspect they also knew what happened to and with my mother. They all stepped up to help. They helped my mother when she needed help around the house when I was too young to do things. They stepped up when I needed direction, when I needed guidance, when I needed help. And all of this was never lost on me. It left an indelible mark upon me and became a part of the principles I wanted to live by. Principles I would chase for many years. These principles always seemed to be just out of my reach though.

Although I had one father, I did not have a Dad. As a father myself I have come to know there is indeed a distinction between the two. One is simply a title while the other is an actual role that one is assigned but it is not only assigned. It is one that needs to be assumed and relentlessly engaged in. It needs to be earned.

I had two "Dads" growing up. Papa was a strong disciplinarian with principles he strictly adhered to always with the spirit of teaching. He was the harder of the two. Rick was gay and his nature was very spiritual. He displayed a never-ending level of compassion and empathy toward me as I grew up. He was the softer of the two.

It would be decades before I would come to see the Higher Parent.

Twelve

A Higher Parent

As I look back in reflection, I can see it all. Can see it all clearly. Isn't this the benefit of hindsight for us? In many respects isn't this the value that comes from our stories? The awareness's arrived at and born out of the pain we endure and experience? Aren't our stories our greatest asset? I have come to believe that this is so. Our stories can be used for a greater benefit, but we must come to terms with them and be willing to understand them for *all* that they are. And aren't. The *real* needs to be differentiated from the *false*. Delusions, false narratives, need to be smashed, need to be dissolved. Perhaps the only thing that can do this in truth is time.

I didn't know as I stood before the honeysuckle that I would be violently disconnected from God, disconnected from my infantile God-consciousness. I didn't know that all it would take was a resentment, a spark of fear and anger combined to explode, causing a propulsion from the sweet reality that is faith to the harsh reality of the stream of life that holds destructive storms within its currents.

It was impossible for me to hold onto that bit of faith. There was very little to no understanding of it. Though Nana tried to pass on the lessons of faith and God to me, the resentment and fear and darkness, were far too powerful and easily overshadowed any lesson I might have been open to seeing or learning.

There was the period *before*. The space of childish faith and trust and reliance on God.

Then there was the period of *after*. The space of self-propulsion with very little thought of God.

What I have come to know is that it is impossible for me to see, hear, or even feel God, or His Presence, when I'm in a state of anger or in a state of fear. My state of anger always had me living in the past in a constant state of reviewing what I perceived to be harm against me. Mom spent most of her life in this neighborhood, which I believe is a necessary part of the human experience. My state of fear always had me living in the future assuming and projecting what was going to be. It was always false. It was supported by the same energy as the anger, it was vile. It was not supported by facts. Both the anger, the living in the past, and the fear, the assumptions made about the future, pulled me away from the present. And God. And as long as I swung like a pendulum from these two harmful states I could not remain at the most nourishing and encouraging of stations. God-consciousness.

In many respects my journey home to God began the moment I was separated from Him. Sounds a bit weird but it's true if you really think about it. The moment I was abruptly separated from God, from God-consciousness, I wanted to go back to it. I wanted to return to the safety and bliss of it. There was a stirring within me that sent the message that I was in trouble. Deep within I could feel that if I returned to the *before* I would be okay again. As I journeyed away from God and used the most colorful of principles while trying to harness the power of resentments and fears to navigate the storms in the stream of life I was always trying to get back to God.

My humanness seemed to be a roadblock though. I went from placing a blind dependence upon God, something I was surely born with, something that was installed in me as I arrived here, to placing my dependence on things human, my parents, family, and others. The latter always has faults, is always susceptible to an unseen and unknown corruption. It is fallible.

I suffered as my dependence on God waned and dependence placed on things human took on deeper levels. I never knew this was at the *root* of all my suffering. I wouldn't come to know it for many years. I also didn't know that each time I suffered I was being called home to God.

I have come to see that each part of my life was divinely designed with one purpose. To get me *back* to God. I have come to see this as an absolute truth not only through my own experience but by those about me. I came to know that suffering is a calling from God to return to Him, a calling to seek refuge in Him. It is a call, a text message if you will, from Him.

All my life I've been searching for God, and I didn't know it until I found Him. I came to know that while we do have parents here, we also have a Parent in God.

I was brought up in the Catholic faith, inspired by Nana as I have shared, but the day came when all of that ended. I made my first confession but never finished the sacraments. (It would be decades before I would come close to making a true and heartfelt confession and the essence of it wouldn't be related to the religion at all.)

I was twelve years old when everything seemed to crash. It was about six years *after* my separation from God, six years after I left the Honeysuckle Dream behind me. While Papa and Rick took on the roles of "Dad" it was Nana who became the center of my life, the closest thing to God that there could be in my mind. She was the human form of God. If you've not gathered this, she was everything to me. She was the absolute center to *and* for me.

I didn't know she had cancer. I didn't know she was dying. I thought that all the work she was doing to her and Papa's home in the way of painting and papering walls and new carpeting was just a refresh. I didn't know she was preparing for her departure from here. Although I was curious as to why she was buying sets of dinnerware and glassware and warehousing them in the musty cellar I didn't know she was leaving things for us to use later as we grew into adulthood. The pantry at the rear of the kitchen was always stocked with canned goods, it was a natural reaction from a generation who lived through a World War who didn't want to be caught without provisions, but she was adding more to it. I didn't know that she was trying to ensure that we all had something to eat.

In the months leading up to her passing she began knitting furiously. She spent hours at it. She knitted bedspreads and afghans and made one for each of us. Mine is striped and every color of the rainbow. I still have it and use it in the colder months here in New England. I call it "Nana." The afghan is a pet magnet in our home, they love it.

She was trying to extend her care into a future that she wouldn't be here to witness. She was trying to pass on as much as she could before the cancer would take her. As I said I didn't know any of this at the time but in hindsight I can see it all clearly. She died when I was twelve and while she left many physical things behind whatever vestiges of faith that were still within me were taken with her.

God was dead.

I became fiercely resentful. Resentful toward God.

He did this. *He* took her away. This is what I believed, what I *wanted* to believe. I was wrong, it was a part of the false narrative.

The tragedy of my family, the divorce, the undercurrents felt and experienced in the stream of life before this, I could causatively link to my parents. While I still held the childish faith that was buried by anger and fears it seemed as though it was now gone. As if a sponge were used to soak up the last drops of it. And it left me dry and even more sour than I already was. I became dissociative. I withdrew. I wanted to escape. It became a pain I felt I couldn't endure.

From the day I lost my God-consciousness I began placing my dependence on things human whether a family member or even physical trappings. At times there would be satisfaction without irritability and annoyance, but this would be short-lived. Dependence on things human always led back to the disappointment I was feeling and when I arrived back at the disappointment I would seek to find the satisfaction again, and by any means. In other words, I wanted to escape. I wanted to escape the reality of life.

In addition to becoming a time traveler I became an escape artist.

The harder I tried to escape the more difficult it became and when I did achieve a reprieve from reality it was short lived. Each reprieve became shorter and shorter. The further I moved from God and the more I placed my trust and reliance on myself and things human the more disappointment and dissatisfaction I would experience. It was a vicious cycle that led to layers and layers of futility. I wanted to check out.

Nana was gone and I felt as though I had no one left to speak with, to find hope in. Then one day I got high with my friends.

Thirteen

Meow

The thing that is fiercely misunderstood about spiritual illness is that it’s wildly contagious. The same can be said about spiritual fitness but when it comes to spiritual illness, most can't or won't see it, can't or won't admit that it exists. As difficult as it is to "sell" someone on the benefit of spiritual fitness and healthy living, the fact of the matter is that most simply don't want it. Yet they will gladly accept spiritual sickness.

I never believed I would live past 50 years old. Quite frankly I have spent a better part of my life not wanting to live, not wanting to be here. I spent a great deal of time hoping and praying I wouldn't live past 50. I always had this welcoming spirit for the end’s arrival. I always wanted the suffering that comes with being abandoned to just stop. I've always wanted the darkness to go away. I imagine it will always be there even if it's in a very miniscule manner.

Consequently, I have paid a price for this. The neglect of my physical and mental wellbeing is near the top of the list. Whether it was the use and abuse of alcohol and drugs, nicotine use, the fascination and dependence on sugar and different foods, the allure of using sex as an escape, the power of money. On and on and on it has gone for me. Always with the effort to become the most efficient escape artist that I could be. That of the fully unconscious time traveler, not the blackout time traveler that I was when I was young.

After years of neglecting my teeth, a lack of care inspired by fear and our dentist Dr. Torgeon who had severe rheumatoid arthritis when I was a young kid, I am making the effort of seeking to repair the damage. (He really was a scary looking character with those twisted hands coming at me!) My last visit to the periodontist saw the removal of two molars because of bone loss caused by Paget's disease.

When Doctor Anu finished the procedure I asked the assistant, an absolutely high-energy, full of life young lady, if I could see my teeth. She rinsed them off and then held them in her gloved hand. Sophia pointed out a few things about them, not pretty at all, and then asked me one question. It hit me like that bag of cement. It became a part of the inspiration to finally sit and type this book.

"What happened to you?"

No adjectives or adverbs added to the string of words that formed the question. No fluff. No colorful or pretty words. There was no accusation or shame in her voice, or the inflection of it. It was just a question without any attachment that landed squarely on my soul. I wanted to fully answer it but knew we didn't have enough time, so I offered her the first thought that crossed my mind.

"I didn't think I would live this long, so I didn't pay attention to my teeth. I didn't think I'd be using them this long."

On my first visit when she asked me if I was allergic to anything I replied that I was allergic to "pain and bullshit." This is indeed the truth for many of us. The assault against our senses, especially those deep within tied directly to God and our faith in Him, can be likened to an allergy of sorts. Our abnormal reaction, allergy, changes our state. Our state of mind, our state of emotion, our physical state. All this having an effect on our soul. Most times we cannot see it happening until the change has become so dramatic that it cannot be *unseen*. Perhaps this is the best place to move us back to seeking God. To return to God. To return to God-consciousness.

I think when we are in the Honeysuckle Dream, we intuitively know that we are allergic to pain and bullshit. That it isn't necessary to be a part of it or participate in it. But then of course something changes, something shifts, and we get swept into that part of the stream of life that is torrid. Pain and bullshit burn into our consciousness, our God-consciousness. It damages us.

My lessons in human interaction, the harshest lessons, began with Mom and Dad.

Mom sought to retaliate against my father anyway she could, and she used my sister and I as weapons. She also falsely believed that she and Dad would get back together, even after my brother was taken from her.

As I bore witness to their treatment of one another I was being shown how to act, respond, and be as a human with others. This extended beyond my immediate family and into my life well into adulthood, into my friendships and even into my marriages. And sadly, into the relationships with my own children. It has all had a lasting effect on me and others.

There were times when my sister and I would act up as we quickly became latchkey kids. We became more than this as Mom withdrew more and more from life and reality, and as Dad wasn't there. We were in essence left to fend for ourselves most times during the week. Mom began to call my sister and I "partners in crime." It was a sugarcoated way of acknowledging that we were at most times unsupervised and prone to mischief.

On one occasion Mom took us to see my father when we got into trouble. She was looking for him to be a parent, something he could never be and would never be able to do. She wanted assistance, she wanted his help. She was seeking something that was not there, and this infuriated her. My father exacerbated this most times with his reactions or lack thereof. It became a never-ending vicious cycle charged with the base emotions born out of one person wanting to control another.

We were brought to my father's apartment this Sunday morning. There wasn't a cloud in the sky on this day and the sun seemed brighter than usual. As I look back it was by no coincidence that Pat showed up while my mother, sister, and I were there. I wholly believe my father called her and asked her to come over when he knew we were coming. It was too convenient to be anything else. I recall the cigarette smoke as it hung in the air in the basement apartment and the buzzer as it began to sound off when she arrived. It seemed to vibrate the walls. It seemed that powerful.

Before the buzzer sounded things were relatively calm in the apartment. Conversation without accusation, anger, or even the yelling that I quickly became accustomed to. This changed in an instant.

My father answered the buzzer and Pat announced that she was there. The volume in Mom's voice rose a few octaves as she hurriedly swept us to the door and into the hallway. We left the building and the three of us passed Pat as we walked down the hall.

I've always had a mind like a steel trap. Once a memory is embedded in there it doesn't budge. It is not like this with *all* of them though. It is precisely like this when it comes to emotion and energy, especially as it relates to relationships and interactions whether personal to me or outside of my sphere of involvement. I will never forget the energy that accompanied this day or those moments. It was just so damn dark, and despairing. I remember the desperation and exasperation on Mom's part. She only wanted to be heard, wanted to be supported, and wanted to be helped. Her fault was seeking this from the empty vessel that was my father. She simply couldn't see it through her false hope and attendant delusions.

As we passed Pat on our way out of the building she had this grin on her face. It was that "cat who ate the canary grin." But there was something more. It was a grimace of sorts. It held with it a contempt that would never subside. A contempt for not only Mom but for my sister and I as well. It was a criticism. And over time her criticism became and felt like an assault on me, like I was being cut open with a razor blade. A time would come decades later when she would verbalize it in a plain manner but until then she would demonstrate it at any moment's opportunity.

Every experience like this over the years would add to the space between me and God. Ironically it would one day also add to the depth of willingness required for me to seek Him at levels that can only be described as desperate. Until then I would remain adrift subject to the whims of the adults around me trying to stay afloat in the always changing stream.

About the only thing that didn't change in the stream was the derision passed between my mother and father which was constantly fueled by their need to retaliate against one another. Every layer of these retaliations and persuasions that each tried to set upon another became my lessons in growing up. Lessons in how to treat others and how to be treated. It was an ugly affair.

Naturally I was the chameleon, but I took these lessons to levels no one expected or could ever assume some responsibility for. In the way of roles I played or assumed in life I took these influences and practiced them to extremes whether it was by lying, being the storyteller, or by stealing, especially taking one's happiness or faith. I used to freely joke in an effort to cover up the pain that in many ways my family trained me to be a cat burglar. I wasn't that far off the mark. In fact, for many of the years I dreamt of writing this book the working title was "Becoming A Cat Burglar."

While I felt like I was dying by a thousand cuts that seemed to be the constant assault on my senses I would eventually arrive at a place of seeing that no matter how much of my humanness I threw at the pain I simply didn't have enough power to fix or transcend it. I needed another power. I would need God. The same God I held in contempt. He would have to be the One to cut me wide open. The One to perform spiritual surgery. In many respects something within me was going to have to die and then Something was going to have to be reborn. It would be my Faith. I was going to have to return to the Honeysuckle Dream.

Fourteen

Alien

I became a magnet attracting like things, feelings, and circumstances to myself as I went through life. The further away from God I travelled the sicker I became with the self. The sicker I became the sicker my life became in every area. Physically I abused my body, mentally my strength grew weary and thin. Emotionally I grew darker and darker. Spiritually I was dying.

I was sucked into the vicious cycle and circle of hate that became my parents' base line of interaction with one another. Mom went into full survival mode while Dad seemed to thrive and move on with his life. The only thing they shared in common was my sister and I, and their incessant need to keep trying to hurt one another, to retaliate against one another. And in many twisted ways the need to be victims to one another. We were recruited to participate in their war and weren't given any orders, we had to not only witness this conflict but had to be a part of it. We were used by them for their selfish needs born out of their body of pain.

I rightly imagine that this was the root cause of what would destroy any chance of a healthy relationship between my sister and me. We never had a shot in hell. We were oblivious to their whims while we were trying to hold onto the vestiges of being a child but that became impossible as we were forced to grow up almost overnight. As Mom and Dad became adversaries, they set upon the two of us by extension the same in marching orders. My sister and I eventually became our parents and would turn on one another. We went from partners in crime to warlords trying to protect what little each of us had and our teachers were happy to support this, happy to protect that generational trauma they couldn't understand themselves. Things got more and more ugly.

Water indeed seeks its own level and it's the same with emotion, with thoughts, with spirituality, or the lack thereof. Sometimes others will impose their levels upon us. If our level is on a higher plane of feeling, of understanding, of knowing, of believing, those about us with lower levels will likely do everything in their power to lessen our levels. It was the same with our parents.

As they descended deeper and deeper into their lower natures, their lower selves, they took us with them. They had no choice but to do this. It seems to be a natural course in life whether one is seeking to lessen another's power or position or even raise it. It's that energy thing. It's that vibration thing.

When we spend so much time with lower energy with a place of higher energy being the starting point the depletion of our energy feels most destructive and in a bizarre way can be most instructive. Nourishment dries up as we spiral downward. This was how it was for me, how it seemed to be. I was a child with a blind faith and trust in a Power I couldn't see, touch, or feel but intuitively knew it was there. The circumstances thrust upon me began to crush this intuition into near nonexistence. Naturally I couldn't see it or even define what was happening as it happened.

Hurt people hurt people. They have to. It's a part of the

equation that is darkness. And broken people certainly break people or try to break people. As I look back, I can see how my emotions were pummeled. I can see how my connection to God was severed. I can even see how my physical body reacted to everything that happened after the split.

When I was in elementary school, I became very ill. As I look back and examine this part of my life and especially the fact that not one other student became ill, I can see that all that was happening outside of me was influencing me, weakening my immune system. I became so ill with bronchitis though I wasn't prone to breathing problems and haven't had them since. I remember being on the couch for weeks and not being able to think straight. I believe my body was experiencing a physical reaction to the outside circumstances. The internalization was wreaking havoc on my body.

The greatest eye-opener was the day I came to see how my mind was bent and how it adapted to the new surroundings. I have also come to understand that opposites are needed to define their opposite. All my experiences, as uncomfortable as they were and as difficult as they seemed to be, helped to define the depth of freedom once they were overcome.

With the split of my parents, and with the split within me, came a new way of thinking and it wasn't born out of Light. It was based in darkness, in resentments, in fears. I became delusional with a false narrative. I learned to use the delusion to navigate the stream of life.

Here is the treacherous part of it. As resentments bubbled to the surface they led to more resentments. My deteriorating mind set to trying to figure them out. When a resentment presented my mind would look for solutions within me, and at times within the family, but none would be found or had. By nature, this would lead to another resentment and still another and then another. I quickly had my own expansive tract of space that held these resentments. It was like a farm that needed constant tending to. I would use the resentments as needed. I protected them. I justified them. I fed them. I used their destructive energy to power my way through life, and most definitely to power my way through my family and its body of pain.

I met Peter, one of the many psychotherapists I'd visit and speak to about all of this, and he made an observation after he got to know "my story." The story that led to me visiting him. Peter was the one on my journey who taught me to listen to my feelings, intuition, and to cull my thoughts, for the light ones and the dark ones, all with the effort of trying to understand our place in the world.

My daughter was just about three when I went to him. As a new father the fear of failing as a parent came to the forefront of my consciousness. It was heavy as you might imagine. I owned a women's clothing store at the time and named it after my daughter. Madison. I wanted the logo to be distinctive yet simple. I wanted it to be "even and balanced" much like that was all I craved in life.

When I handed the printer the direction for the look of the logo, I scribbled the name on a piece of paper and told him that we have to make changes to the type to achieve the balance. I wanted all the letters to be lower case, didn't want them to scream at you. I wanted it to look soft. But the problem was the "d." The upswing on the letter stood above the top line of the letters the same as the dot on the "i." I didn't want this look, so we had to use a capital "D" to eliminate the upswing. The first three letters would be "mad," even in height, while the last three letters, "son," would also be even in height. Only the "i" would have the appearance of including something above the line of letters. The dot. When I handed the look to Peter, he saw the "i" first and read it that way, then went to left and read the word "mad." He finished the last word he saw. "son." He then read it at a faster pace. "I Mad Son." The state of my being below a fragile consciousness that I was always trying to evade was always trying to come to the surface to be seen and dealt with. This seemed like one of those instances.

We all have what some might call natural fears. To this day I have this fear of heights. I can't look over the side of a tall building from the roof. My physical body reacts to the fear of heights when I do it. Yet I can fly in a plane miles above the earth and feel no fear. This always reminds me that fear can be wildly misunderstood. They can harm us yet at times might offer some protection in a bizarre way.

Then there are these unnatural fears. Perhaps even more so wildly misunderstood. They're simply false and a response to circumstances about us. Mom and Dad's split, and subsequent divorce, set off fears in me that I would not come to terms with for decades. Fears that would run my life in ways I never understood while in the midst of them. They were born out of a lack of faith. Fear cannot be where faith is, it's impossible. I've come to understand that fear is the opposite of faith. The further I moved away from God the stronger the fears within me became. The stronger they became the more they attached themselves to the lower part of my nature. "Little Bobby" lived by them, needed them to ensure his survival. Fear is a thief; it takes from us. Fear is a liar, is cunning. It was the perfect match for my fast-changing constitution and the chameleon in me *needed* its destructive force.

The first fear, the deepest fear, the most destructive fear, the worst fear, the always present fear in me, was the fear of abandonment. It would become the power behind each decision I would make in life. The irony is that even after all these years and after all the sifting through realizations arrived at this fear still crops up. This one fear was the strongest magnet within my character, drawing to it everything needed to ensure it not only survived but that it would continue to gain in strength. Darkness is like that. Like God, it will provide what is needed to remain relevant or prevalent within us. Now there is some twisted irony. Almost a phenomenon, something that cannot be explained.

I see things in different ways most of the time. I think differently, even write differently. I have always attached my experiences to music or movies or better still can relate to lyrics and storylines in nearly everything. I still look for attachments all the time. My story always wants validation whether in a positive or negative manner. As I watch the movies out of the Alien franchise, I enjoy the scenes where there are what seem to be endless rows of those xenomorphic eggs. When I see them, I liken them to the endless supply of resentments and fears that were born out of the chaos that was my family. Each holding their own destructive force or intent to harm. As they hatch in the movie my mind triggers the thought "Here come the resentments and fears to destroy life." Alien. The problem most of my life was that I did whatever I could to protect these things as the Queen Mother did her eggs in the movie, even if it meant the destruction of you, your feelings, your thoughts, your property, and more. It was a vile and disgusting existence.

To ensure my survival my thinking led me to believe that if I thought, acted, and sounded like my parents then I would never be abandoned at deeper levels, that perhaps I would be fully accepted by them and others in my family. That perhaps they might turn the "parent button" on and assume their roles. It never happened. The opposite happened as I grew sicker and sicker with matching behaviors. They figuratively gave me a uniform to wear as a soldier in their war inscribed with the letters BS. Black sheep. Indeed, it was BS. Total bullshit.

As powerless as I was against the resentments and fears

Mom and Dad were equally powerless against their body of pain. They were equally powerless against persuasions in their families or their generational traumas that were freely handed to them, the same they freely handed to us. In other words, they never knew what they were doing and the effect it was having on me and my sister.

They didn't know like we didn't know like their parents didn't know like their parents before them didn't know. The good news I found is that this can all change with consciousness, with God-consciousness. And all I needed to do was arrive at the understanding that I did not have enough power within me to fight the darkness on my own. I needed God's help but that couldn't happen for quite some time because I held Him in contempt.

While waiting for Mom and Dad to assume the roles, as I discerned them to be, I was always waiting for God to do the same. I tried to force Mom and Dad to be Mom and Dad as I wished it to be and wanted to do the same with God. I believe there were times when I acted out hoping that God might show up to speak with me directly. I had some questions for Him and issues with Him that I wanted to discuss. In other words, I wanted to tell Him how things should be. I wanted to hand Him one of those family famous blistering letters.

I had the equation wrong. I knew the problem but lacked the proper method of solving it. I didn't know the steps to move from the problem to the solution. While trying to force Mom and Dad to be a Mom and Dad and trying to force God to do what I deemed to be just there was indeed a difference between the two. The more I asked Mom and Dad whether through telepathy, or by acting out, it simply wasn't going to happen. They weren't capable. I think because I never knew how to pray properly, how to speak with God properly, the result, the solution, remained out of reach for me. While I demanded, God didn't answer to my satisfaction.

My approach to God most times can be likened to that of a petulant child making unreasonable demands and the spirit in which I tried to pray was without an ounce of humility. It was wrapped in only thoughts of myself. It was selfish prayer which might *seem* to work on occasion but will always lack that key element of humility that adds depth to the power of a petition. The more I believed that God ignored me as my parents had, the more I resented Him, the more I felt He had abandoned me. This simply was not so. It was the greatest lie that emanated out my false narrative. It also became the strongest lie within the delusion. The fear of being abandoned by God terrified me and when I experienced this fear, I would seek escape from it with wild voracity.

I did what my parents did and ended up with the same result.

I have found that I cannot be whole as long as I'm fractured by resentment and fear, wallowing in a swamp of self-pity, or exercising my thoughts, heart, and soul by the delusion of lies I tell myself all in a futile effort of massaging my lower self, my ego, my effort to support "Little Bobby."

My inner critic was born out of the mayhem and chaos that is my family and he, that lower self, that ego, would cause me more harm than anyone else could. He would take me to the precipice of death and then realize he needed my body to get around so he would stop short of achieving his goal of getting me to jump off a cliff. My ego wanted me dead, but it needed my body to get around. He did succeed at near killing my faith though.

It would take me years before I came upon the fact that solving my own problems with the same power that created them is impossible, but I quickly learned that love in my family came with conditions. A whole lot of terms and conditions. But they were always hiding them and changing them and making it difficult for me to agree with them.

Fifteen

A Hard-Boiled Egg

I believe we all wear a mask at times. Perhaps it's a form of protection, a survival instinct, while moving within the stream of life. Some of us wear this mask unknowingly, and it just appears. A manifestation if you will. One day we are our authentic self and then the currents get stronger as we persist and then one day that abrasive moment comes along and hits us broadside. A new awareness is added to the depth of life we are navigating our way through.

The mask I attached to myself became personal to me; it was most definitely like the blanket I had as a young child. It became my security guard against forces outside of me but always added more power to the delusion I began to live at deeper levels as Mom and Dad did their thing. I loved my mask. I took care of my mask. I never wanted to take it off when I saw how effective it was as a tool. It became a part of the sails and rudders on my vessel as I learned to navigate the stream of life.

As I moved from day to day it became impossible to speak in a direct way to anyone about what was going on inside of me. I was loaded with fear and resentment which created layers and layers of confusion. Naturally. I didn't want anyone to know what I was feeling or thinking because I thought they might walk away from me, abandon me, if they found out I wasn't perfect. What I have come to know and believe is that there is perfection in imperfection, that we as spiritual beings, at our absolute core, having this human experience, are expected to be imperfect. It is natural although I didn't think it natural because it seemed to be painful. After experiencing the first reaction to my parents' split and the resultant pain, I didn't want to feel that anymore. I tried my best to evade it. The mask helped to deflect the pain of living life. It suspended me in time. Eventually the mask wouldn't relieve the pressure, and I would turn to other destructive methods to make me a better escape artist.

Though I carried the fears and the resentments against my mother and father with me there was a part of me that wanted them to get back together. This brought about behaviors that might not only get their attention but perhaps might get them to collaborate with one another thereby creating space for them to be together. It never worked. Sometimes I think it did the opposite. It deepened my mother's sense of failure and pushed my father away from me. My behavior was an offense against them.

In the six years after they split, before Nana passed away, I simply existed looking for bright spots. I paid close attention to Mom and Dad but also paid close attention to everything else about me. I tried to decipher messages. I tried to understand the adult conversations taking place around me in and out of my family. I tried to decipher different tools for living and I wasn't picking up on any in the family because of the clouds before me that the charged emotions created.

I watched television. Sitcoms and movies, cartoons and entertainment shows. To a greater degree each of these became my teacher. Each of these lent an alternative to what was being offered in my family. There was a stark difference between them and my family. Where it was easy to feel confusion in my family because of faulty communication it was easy to see clear communication in the scripts of what I was watching. Observing. Always the observer.

Each and every sitcom of the 70's added their twist to my character and allowed me to escape with little effort. I didn't have to *try* to escape while watching them, escaping simply became a natural consequence of watching them. But they created more layers of confusion. As controversial as some of these programs might have been they always ended with a plausible solution. The clear communication amid any chaos within the storyline was there. In truth it was refreshing.

In my family I believe you were expected to be a mind reader of sorts. You were supposed to guess what the other person was thinking or feeling because it was rarely shared and most times when it was shared the actions surrounding the feeling or thoughts didn't match. The lack of words attached to the feeling and thoughts turned me into an architect of confusion in my interactions with others.

I wanted you to know what I was feeling but couldn't tell you or express it. I wanted you to know what I was thinking, what was bringing about the feeling, but couldn't get past the fear that you might judge me which might lead to you abandoning me.

As my father moved on with his life and as his station visibly changed the three of us remained at the same station. Not much changed at all. While he moved on and bought a bigger home with his wife and her children we remained in the same smaller home. While he enjoyed the building of his life with physical trappings and the like most times we went without. While Mom told us to go make friends with people who had pools during the hot summer Dad installed a pool and added a huge deck to complement it. While Dad, his wife, and her children always seem to be wearing newer clothes we remained in the same. This messaging was harsh.

My father opened a business with his wife and enjoyed a different life than we did. This became the subject of one of the many arguments my mother had with him over the years. While I observed all of this, the message received was that we were undeserving, somehow less than. Not worthy enough to have more or enjoy more. While Dad lived his best life my mother was forced to collect welfare. She called it “being on the dole" when I was a kid. We used food stamps. There was something about this that created layers of shame in me a lot of times. I believe it was tied into all the fears and resentments; it was nourishment for them. I was the one who had to go to the bank to pick up the food stamps because Mom landed in the position of not wanting to leave the house.

Over time I would learn to feed my own resentments and fears. Of course, I didn't know I was doing this, but I wanted to ensure that they remained healthy and at the ready in the event I would need them. Shame, as well as guilt and remorse, became a multivitamin for them.

Mom withdrew more and more as I grew older. One day she was working at the restaurant with her friends and then one day she was not. One day she was outside of the house engaging with people in the neighborhood and then one day she was not. Every move my father made, or didn't make, became an all-out assault on her beaten down and now fragile senses. Eventually she would give up and retire to the couch. She would let herself go, completely.

As I look back it seems as though my father did just enough to massage his role as Dad, to bolster his delusion that he was a "Dad." You were limited in what you could purchase with food stamps. It had to be food, nothing frivolous. My mother asked my father if she could trade the food stamps for cash as he owned a market and he agreed. It wasn't an exchange between her and him. I would show up at his meat market with the food stamps wearing my layers of shame. I would sheepishly try to hand them to him without a word and would try to avoid eye contact. He would tell me to go to see Pat.

She was perched at the cash register behind the counter in the middle of the market and I would feel my shame increase 100-fold as I approached her. With my black sheepish look on my face, and black sheepish feeling deep within, I would clumsily hand her the food stamps, and she would hand me cash. On the rare occasion that I made eye contact with her she had that same "cat who ate the canary" grimace on her face that she had that Sunday morning at my father's apartment years before. It was backed by this contempt that seemed to emanate from her in waves of destructive energy. There was this weird feeling of malice and darkness that I always picked up from her. She had zero compassion, had zero empathy. Over the years I would find the courage to tell my father I didn't care for her, but it always fell on deaf ears.

The confusion I arrived at was this. While my mother and father were at war, and it seemed as though my father wanted nothing to do with us, it was the exchanges like this between him and Mom that kept the false hopes alive in me. The message received was that he wanted to help and perhaps could see in his wife which had become plain for me to see.

There were times in my life when it seemed like my father wanted to be a father. The more removed I became from these times, and the older I got, coupled with the benefit of hindsight, I see that it was my delusional thinking that sent this message to me. I was wrong. He always had motives.

When I was young it was arranged for me to work in the market on Saturdays. I loved being there. I loved working with the guys at the deli counter and at the back at the benches where the meats were cut. Their white aprons were covered with blood and drippings from the meats that were being broken down. The knives were as sharp as hell and worn thinly from use. Although I should not have been, I was allowed to use the slicing machines until someone complained that I was too young. I wanted to stand at the back counter breaking down the meat. I wanted to be and feel a part of.

I was allowed to get the orders ready for customers that were called in for pick up and on occasion I was allowed to stand at the back bench to process and break down different meats only after I cleaned up the blood-soaked sawdust on the floors of the coolers which were hidden away in the back of the building. You know I cleaned those as quickly as possible to get out in the front of the store. I wanted and needed this time with my father, wanted and needed this time with "the guys." The guys were amazing with me. They taught me and took an interest in me which was something that was seriously lacking.

I was already a bit salty at a young age and had some energy to fight back. The market was located on busy Park Avenue, which was the most direct way from one side of the city to the other. It was halfway between my home and Nana and Papa’s home. The traffic on Saturday was thick. One Easter holiday my father dressed me in a bunny outfit and tossed me out onto the edge of the parking lot. It was that pink bunny outfit like the one Ralph's aunt made for him in "A Christmas Story" and it brought to me the exact thing Ralphie felt in the movie. A sense of embarrassment. I was handed a pail of lollipops and told to throw them into the windows of the passing cars. I obliged, but it didn't last long.

My father came out and pulled me back into the store after he saw me flip someone off. Apparently, they said or did something to me that I didn't care for, and I reacted by giving them the bird. Of course, I don't recall it because I time travelled as the fluffy costume was zippered up, but he gladly told the story at Easter about the four-foot-tall pink Easter bunny flipping people off on Park Avenue.

The next "ending" at the meat market happened when Pat accused me of stealing. I was sent across the street to the gas station to get change for her. She handed me cash and a list to hand to the woman in the office there. When I returned, I handed it to her. Apparently, she thought the amount didn't match what I left with, and she accused me of stealing. It wasn't pretty. My father stood by her with this look of damnation in his eyes. That's all I remember because I time-travelled that day too. I would retaliate years later by stealing a gold chain from her after rationalizing that I had nothing to lose as she already held me in contempt. I reasoned that I might as well give her something plausible to support her condescension and initial accusation.

Needless to say, I would no longer be spending time with my father on Saturdays at the market. Pat truly succeeded in keeping wedges between my father and the three of us, and he gladly and blindly allowed it to happen. It began to snuff out the last bit of hope I had for a relationship with my father though miniscule vestiges of false hope would remain until the day he died.

The cement added to this situation was liberally applied by Mom. When she found out what happened she set out to remedy it the only way she knew how to. She retaliated. She even employed the help of one of her girlfriends to catalog all the deficiencies with my father. By the time she was done she had me thoroughly convinced that one of our neighbors saw my father walking into another neighbor's house with a bag of drugs. Think about how a twelve-year-old child is supposed to process that information. It simply is not possible. To make matters worse I had to call my father and tell him I wouldn't be working at the market anymore because "a neighbor saw him walking into the neighbor's house with drugs."

Though Dad did not do this he did in fact get arrested. They were trying to arrest him and charge him with illegal gambling and bookmaking but didn't have enough on him to make it stick. The irony is that they did pinch him with drugs. My wife once asked me "How did you feel when your father was arrested?" and my answer was "Not as bad as I felt when I was accused of stealing and then forced to carry out my mother's retaliation against him and his wife."

Here's how a curious mental twist began to take shape in my life. My mind responded while working from a place of delusion where nearly everything is permissible without prejudice. Naturally I was hurt by this incident, it felt like a blade cut me wide open. It also caused a reaction in my mind and changed my general approach in conscience. I went from trying to do the right thing with the goal of being accepted and not being totally tossed aside to a place of not caring anymore because I felt as though the effort to do the right thing was useless. In my mind it no longer mattered whether I told the truth or didn't. It no longer mattered whether I earned something or stole it. A peculiar mental twist was added to the layers of spiritual dysfunction I was living and living with. It was a part of that manifestation.

When I was growing up, we would spend a lot of time with our toes in the sand at the beach. Most times it was with Moo. She loved the ocean, the sand, even the seagulls. She always had a cooler packed with snacks and sandwiches and it included hardboiled eggs. They were already peeled and wrapped in foil. I loved to bathe them in salt and eat the outer white part before eating the yolk within.

My sister and I *became* the hardboiled eggs in my father's life. We started out as something in raw form ready to be turned into something else, molded. But it didn't turn out to be something healthy, it became sour and rotten. Over time my insides became as hard as the yolk within the hardboiled egg. And as the heat became relentless and was never turned off eventually my shell would crack under the pressure. I would come near bursting with fear and resentment and there was no way to prevent what would come to be in my life. It was a natural consequence born out of the circumstances.

Most times compassion was extended by some in the family, and then it ended. There were those in the family who took pity on us, but the day arrived when even that was withdrawn. This happened as I became an alcoholic and drug addict.

Sixteen

The Descent

I grew weary. I grew tired.

My *soul* felt worn and tired.

I felt as though I was living a life of unwarranted shame and each experience or interaction within my family seemed to exacerbate this. I was easily drawn to darkness; I was easily swayed as I descended into my own personal hell laced with layers of mixed messages and confusion. The realization that the puzzle before me was becoming impossible to solve was creeping in. I stopped caring about what people thought and cared about while caring only about what people thought about me. I began to live a mindfuck. Please excuse the language but that is what it was. My mind twisted tighter and tighter. I could no longer differentiate the true from the false. Realistically it was a level of insanity. I believed my own lies while the evidence in facts before me, and my senses, was trying to tell me something different.

This all happened and became a part of my nature not long after Mom and Dad split.

I was seven years old and in the second grade when I didn't want to do a handwriting assignment. I erased my friend

John's name from his paper and put my name on it. Clearly the writing styles were drastically different but in my young and twisted mind they were the same. When Miss DiMizio called me to the front of the class to address this. I protested and dug my heals in. Nope. It was mine. When that didn't work, I began to cry. This worked like a charm. (Many years later she and I would have a conversation about this moment in time and would laugh.)

It didn't take me long to figure out how to work people, how to be a con artist. I told her that my sister and I were out late the night before with my Dad and that I was tired. We were not out with my father, that lie was born out of the wish that we were. I was indeed tired just one short year after the split.

I was eight and in the third grade when we were encouraged to come up with an act for a talent show of sorts. I had this puppet that resembled a bird and put on some sort of skit with it. I don't recall exactly what it was but because it was a duck I did something to the song "Disco Duck" by Rick Dees. It drew a great applause from the teachers, parents, and students in attendance and I quickly learned that being an actor was a viable method of escape. I would become an actor in many ways, always looking for the best lines and roles that would massage my ego. That would allow me to feel a part of, allow me to feel accepted.

I was nine and in the fourth grade when I was assigned a book report. Of course, I had no idea how to do this and was deathly afraid to ask the teacher for directions. I didn't want anyone, especially someone in a position of authority, to think I wasn't perfect. I copied the short book nearly word for word onto my paper and turned it in. I got an "A" but more than that I learned that I could cheat and get away with it. I would take this far into the future as I tried to rely upon myself to navigate the stream of life.

My small elementary school was closing because of consolidating classes and changing times and we were not allowed to finish the elementary grades there. We were moved to another school, and I was separated from half of my class as they went to a different school. To some extent this ripped me apart, it touched on the whole fear of abandonment thing, but it soon subsided as I saw that I would have a new audience in my life. I began my role as the class clown, as the cutup. I began to fight with other students, especially if I didn't get my way or felt threatened by them.

I finished out the year and looked forward to beginning junior high school. I would go from a pond to a lake. I would have a bigger audience.

Then Nana died. And this changed everything.

When she left, she took a big part of me with her. Immediately there was a gaping hole inside of me and I wouldn't become whole for many years. Mom and Papa would feel the same way. The change in our energy was drastic.

I didn't know she was sick. I didn't know she was dying. She was the protector, and I believe she kept this from me to protect me to a certain degree. While she prepared for her death by rearranging all that needed to be taken care of, she was careful with her words. She chose them wisely.

The service for Nana was surreal for me. I could not make heads or tails of everything that was going on. Or of the coming and going of people and all the chatter that accompanied them. The fast pace of it all left my mind and heart spinning. One day my protector, my rock, my own personal God was there. Then the next she was not.

Mom didn't wake us up to get us ready for school the morning we found out. She had been at the hospital the night before with Papa to visit Nana. Mom left us alone at the house. By the time Mom got home we had already fallen asleep. I was on the couch in the morning when I asked her why we weren't going to school and she said in the gentlest way she could muster that Nana was gone, that she had died the night before. I fell apart and fell to tears. She later explained that when she and Papa had arrived at the hospital that the doctors were trying to revive her, but she wouldn't come back. The cancer had taken her, and her heart simply couldn't do it anymore. Her heart gave out. So did mine.

Deep within I wanted to go with Nana. I wanted to be free too. This was how I viewed death. A freeing of sorts.

A short time before this I came home from school, another one of the not a cloud in the sky sunny days, to find Mom and Nana sitting on the same couch I was sitting on the day Mom told us Nana was gone. They sat beside one another, which I thought was odd because they typically sat in different places in the living room. Nana seemed different. She knew she was dying though I did not. Mom knew she was dying too. I can see this clearly in hindsight.

There was this seriousness about Nana that registered deep within me but couldn't be defined at that exact moment. As though she had just finished giving Mom a list of detailed instructions, she then turned to me. In hindsight she was trying to tell me to be strong, to carry on the best that I could. To muster all the power that was within me to withstand the pressure of changing realities and to try to accept everything as it was. To try to draw the best in lessons from it all and to use them to the best of my ability. To lay aside the fear and muscle through the realities of life. To always put my best foot forward. To have faith. To have faith in God.

The words she chose weren't offered in the form of a command or as a directive. They weren't extended in a lecturing manner the way most parents choose to guide a child. They were offered in the same vain in which she always presented herself to me. They were offered with hope and wrapped with love.

"I hope you never smoke those marijuana cigarettes."

That was it. Nothing more, nothing less. She knew me intimately and fully recognized my character, especially the part of me that played the escape artist. I believe she knew that if I went down that road, I would pursue it to the gates of hell.

I didn't heed her warning or honor her passion and love behind it. As an escape artist I was always looking for something to be a better evader of reality. I smoked the “marijuana cigarettes" and a love affair was near instant which naturally led to other things.

While all of this was happening not one white flag was raised between Mom and Dad, their war continued. Their contempt for one another continued and continued to fall upon me and my sister. The battle raged on. It had to. That's the thing about conflict. Bad energy feeds it and most times it takes a Higher Power to intercede to bring it to an end.

During Nana's service during the evening calling hours, I stood in the line with Mom, Papa, and my sister. It was now the four of us. I watched as people, aunts, uncles, cousins, most of whom I did not know, filed through the room. Their loud voices became an assault on my senses and on occasion I would leave the room and seek silence at the other end of the funeral home. I also didn't want to accept the reality that Nana was gone.

When I returned to the parlor she was laid out in I didn't want to stand in the line. I wanted a reprieve from the constant flow of well wishes from strangers. I sat in the front row. I just sat there and looked at Nana lying in her casket. As I did, every single moment of time that I had spent with her seemed to merge into one. My heart and soul filled with the amazing love I held for her. My eyes filled with tears as the love seemed to leak out of me. I cried.

My uncle was there, and I remember being happy about this and I remember when my father came in, I was happy about this too. It was one of those rare occasions where he was the Dad instead of being just a father. It didn't matter to me if he was doing it out of obligation. I needed and wanted the love that Nana always gave me to be replaced with love from someone else. As I grew older, I wouldn't care who that came from.

My father came and sat down behind me and tried to console me. We were about ten feet from my mother as she was still standing in line. He didn't stay with me long. He didn't even stay at the service. He breezed in and out but his time there was just enough to cause a ripple in the stream.

In addition to the pain my mother felt because of all that happened, she was now experiencing the same exact type of loss I was. We both felt the same way about Nana. On an occasion after the services after the dust settled a bit, my Mom would turn on me. Perhaps it came from the generational pain, perhaps from her own pain center, perhaps it was simply an instance of lashing out. It was the same type of cement bag I was hit in the chest with at my father's apartment.

I sat in the front row at the service before my father arrived and he approached me. My mother saw it differently. She saw me approaching him. She saw it as a threat. Though she always wanted me to have a relationship with my father and wanted him to take an interest in his children she also wanted me to remain fiercely loyal to her cause, to her side, to her pain.

It always seemed as though Mom was happiest when I was alongside her resting in a place of absolute defeat. When all my friends in school were playing little league baseball I wanted to play as well. Naturally. The day we were filling out the necessary paperwork at our house she had me stand before her and simply asked one question. “You don’t really want to play baseball, do you?” It wasn’t a question; it was a pleading from her. She didn’t want to be bothered by any of it. I agreed that I really didn’t want to play baseball even though I really wanted to, really wanted one of “CW” hats that all my friends wore.

My soul was so exhausted when I reached for alcohol and drugs. They became a medication for me, they became the stimulant I was looking for, the energy, to go on living.

When Nana died, she left behind layer upon layer upon layer of profound lessons for me. Some of these lessons I'm still uncovering more than forty years later. She also left behind a huge bottle of Percocet's which made its way across the city from her house to our house and into the medicine cabinet in our bathroom.

I ate the Percocet seeking oblivion from the stream of life.

I would take being an escape artist and time traveler to new heights.

Seventeen

The Grand Architect

Following the funeral services and the way Mom became so enraged I spiraled deeper into an abyss of darkness. I grew accustomed to the Dad and Pat stuff. I learned how to compartmentalize things. The experiences I had became lessons in my life. I was taught how to not only navigate within the family but how to justify and categorize situations and problems and the feelings attached to them. When Mom came at me with an accusatory tone I didn't know where to put this. I didn't know what category it fit into and now Nana wasn't there as a center for me providing hope. I had a serious problem, and a problem always craves a solution. As I was the furthest from God and my God in human form just died, He certainly was not going to be the solution as I now held Him in contempt. I felt as though He had done all of this to me, not for me. I felt forced to blame him. I couldn't see the human element in all that I perceived to be tragedy.

A short time after the services Mom gave up to a greater degree. She was done. As she gave up, so did my father. His effort to try and play the part was hung up. We rarely saw him. We were alone. I want to attach the word "orphan" to the way I felt or to the new station I arrived at.

Nana had been supplementing our household for years and this allowed us to live without an interruption to utility services. It allowed us to eat. Now she was gone. Papa would pick up the reins, but he didn't know the extent to which Nana was helping us out and as Mom didn't have a close and healthy relationship with her Dad, Papa, and had her own catalog of fears surrounding him she had difficulty asking for help. She would ask for help only after it was too late, such as after the electricity was turned off.

I tried to balance the times when the electricity in our home was turned off for lack of payment as I watched Mom plead with the fellow who showed up to follow through with the order against the fact that my father, his wife, and her children were living in a manner that could be described as luxurious when compared to the way we were living hand to mouth.

As Mom spiraled downward, we as children tried to step up the best we could. We had been trying to live as adults in child bodies with child minds and child emotions since Dad left and now would do this at deeper levels as preteens and then as teenagers. We were forced to grow up. We took on paper routes to supplement the costs in our home and we learned to fend for ourselves.

Children begin to learn life skills from their parents, grandparents, family, and so many others at such an early age. I didn't have the full benefit of this. I did learn bits and pieces, but my vision was clouded by the emotions born out the chaos that was my Mom and Dad, and their soul contract with one another.

As we picked up the pieces the best we could we became parents to Mom. With this shift in titles, we assumed the responsibilities as well. The cooking, the cleaning, the laundry. I even began driving my mother's car to the store to get groceries with the food stamps at the age of thirteen.

On one occasion I was vacuuming the living room and Mom was sitting on the couch. The couch she would spend years on much like the character Darlene Cates in "What's Eating Gilbert Grape" sat on. As I moved about the living room the hose attached to the vacuum swung over the stereo cabinet when I turned. There were knick knacks that were sentimental to my mother arranged on top of this piece of furniture. I don't recall all of them but do recall the two rose-colored glasses with flowers etched into the glass. They were decorative stemmed glasses. They were Nana's glasses. I didn't know this but soon would. The hose connected with one of them and it fell over. It broke. Then Mom broke.

She launched from the couch and hit me with a punch I've never felt as hard before or since. It was the physical bag of cement matching the verbal cement bag Dad had hit me with long before at his apartment. It winded me and knocked me onto the floor. It was far more than this. It taught me how to lash out and would begin the deeper division between her and I. It was her physical reaction to the loss of Nana and a culmination of so much more.

I didn't understand the body of pain she was wrapped up in and where her reaction came from. I personalized this as I had personalized everything else in my life up to this point. How could I not? It was what was taught to me that was diametrically opposed to faith. To faith in God. To an understanding of God and what I am here for.

We tried as a family. Papa, Mom, sister and myself. We tried to carry on. Carry on with the holidays. Carry on with the chore of living. But there was something that wasn't there. Nana was gone but I felt something else missing. At the time, and while floating in what seemed to be a weird holding pattern in the stream of life, everything felt dead. It felt like Nana's death took everything worthwhile with it. There was an emptiness I could never put my finger on.

Papa would come across the city and have dinner with us on holidays. We would move the kitchen table, too big for the kitchen, into the living room, too big for that room, and have dinner together. Papa would sit at the head of the table and always thoroughly enjoyed what Mom prepared.

Though Papa wouldn't attend church services with us when we were younger, he indeed did have faith. As Nana always seemed to be the one to say Grace at the holiday table it now fell on Papa to do it. I don't think Mom had it in her to say grace. She was too angry, too hurt. Her division from God grew exponentially after Nana died.

Being a Mason Papa would begin grace by calling upon God and when he did, he called Him the "Grand Architect." This always intrigued me at deep levels. Of course, it was different than what I had been taught in church and in catechism but there was more to this fascination with it. The two words stuck to me, stuck to my thoughts and even my emotions. Mentally I asked myself what they meant. Grand being "impressive" and Architect being "one engaged in designs of large constructions." To this day these words that Papa attached to God have a deep and lasting and profound effect on me.

I couldn't fathom the depth of their meaning at a young age. My lack of faith or care to know was too small to want to know more. I had already been removed from the Honeysuckle Dream for so long that it seemed impossible to return to it. I was already trying to force my way through life with my humanness.

As much as I wanted a family, or the appearance of a family, it simply wasn't there to be had. It had already been fractured beyond repair. Moments at the dinner table where we would be united were short-lived. For me they weren't strong enough to hold me to any semblance of stability. My mind and heart became so far removed from the family. My desire to be free from them grew stronger and stronger. I wanted to be free of it all.

I was tired of living in the problem and grew uneasy. I would become easily annoyed and feel very little to no satisfaction anywhere in my life. I was broken and this was a problem and as every problem indeed craves a solution I began seeking a solution. I groomed myself to evade reality, I became an escape artist. I groomed myself to be a time traveler, to block out the compliment of senses experienced by circumstances. All of this seemed to work as a defense and as survival methods for me, but the day came when I realized they weren't numbing the consciousness that I was trying to make unconscious.

I didn't know that I could have turned to The Grand Architect at any time to seek refuge. I was wholly trusting and relying on all that was human, all that was not God, as I grew more and more resentful towards Him.

I didn't have any understanding of soul contracts, perhaps the agreements we entered before we arrived here. The experiences we agree to have before we are born. I have come to believe that every experience was uniquely designed for me. But not only for me but for those around me. Their experiences had to be the way they were and will be the way they need to be by design. All to learn from them. But to learn what?

One thing. How to trust and rely on God. On The Grand Architect. But not only on Him but also to trust and rely on His Design. Before I began my journey back home to God I would break away from my family as best I could and travel some colorful roads. Again, all of that by design, sometimes a painful design. All of it bringing levels of pain and misunderstanding, not only to me, but to my family. I would take my pain, and all their pain, and all the generational pain, and begin to retaliate. I wouldn't see it as it was happening, but the day would come, a reckoning, where all would become crystal clear to me. Where my faith would be fully restored in me.

First, I needed to have the greatest battle of my life. I had to use my finite power against God's Infinite Power. I had to try to battle His Design. I needed to feel my failure in power as a human while trying to contest His Power.

My soul contract was about to get interesting, and where the contracts others had always affected me, mine was about to affect all of them. And when this happened, they didn't care for it as much as I never cared for the effects by them. It became a very twisted synergy.

When I began using drugs and drinking, I simply didn't care anymore. I was young, twelve years old, and at this age didn't want to be here anymore. I really didn't want to live, didn’t want to feel. The fears had worn me down and took any will to live that I had. Fear was greedy and it seemed to want to take my life. This was indeed the problem, and I wanted a solution. I came up with two. The first was the natural consequence of not wanting to feel it anymore, death. And the second, a medication to numb me. I chose the latter first.

Eighteen

Comfortably Numb

My use and abuse of alcohol and drugs lasted less than six years. It began in the typical peer pressure way. My friends wanted me to get high with them, so I smoked a joint. I wish I could tell you it was an instant love affair, but it wasn't. It didn't take me instantly. I didn't become a drunk or an addict from the start. That would take some time. About two years.

I can share these two points though. I had the power of choice in the beginning. I could determine what I was going to drink and use, who I would do it with, where I would do it, when I was going to do it, and how much I would do. And then there was the effect.

The effect is what I loved about it. As an escape artist this new element brought into my life added serious value to escaping reality and the feelings associated with it. It quickly became a medication of sorts, a resource I badly needed. I had these problems that craved a solution and here before me was something that seemed to be just that. In time I would even be able to use all of this to time travel. I would eventually move from gray outs to black outs.

Was I predisposed to becoming an alcoholic or an addict? I

believe it was a part of the design in life God chose for me to experience. I also believe it was a part of the design in life God chose for those closest to me so they might bear witness. I wasn't an alcoholic or addict from day one. I was certainly a thrill seeker, and these substances made thrill seeking more lively, more colorful. The drinking and drugging seemed to bring me back to life in many respects. In the beginning when I was drinking and using drugs I felt as though all that was holding me back washed away. I didn't get in trouble with it in the beginning. I also didn't *need* to do it. That would come later. But I *wanted* to do it.

Eventually I came to know that the body and mind of an alcoholic and addict are simply different than the body and mind of the person who is not. Science can't explain why this is so, yet it is. Something that can't be explained is a phenomenon. To some extent when I began there was a sense of phenomena to it all. I couldn't explain to myself how these substances seemed to work so wonderfully at keeping reality and its attendant feelings at bay. I didn't care about the phenomena part of it all because what I experienced was phenomenal.

My soul was exhausted when I happened upon alcohol and drugs. They became a welcome reprieve for me. Though my mind and body weren't quite changed yet into being a full-blown alcoholic and drug addict, I can share that I couldn't wait to get high again after the first time I did. I couldn't wait to use substances to escape reality again. I now know this isn't enough to be an alcoholic or addict. This was still simply a method, a vehicle, at this point to evade reality. I enjoyed the ease and comfort this new solution brought to me.

By the time I lost the power of choice, the power to choose whether I would drink or get high, it was too late. I didn't see it coming and when I finally did, I couldn't stop on my own limited power. Before I crossed the line of exercising power over it all to not having power there were indeed instances where it was having an effect on me, doing some damage, but the effects weren't strong enough to warrant a decision to walk away or exercise any will to stop. Why would I? The *medication* was still working.

As time went on and after crossing the line into being an alcoholic and addict, becoming bodily and mentally different, the medicinal effect began to wear off. The alcohol and drugs weren't working anymore. And as they worked less and less, I chased the effect more and more. Each waking moment became an effort to recapture the experience I had the first time. Working from a delusional place when I began the descent into alcohol and drugs, I erroneously thought I could get back to that moment. My mind became more and more fractured, more and more confused. My sense of powerlessness in the face of what I used to have power over left me bewildered.

Alcohol and drugs, once the solution to a wanting problem, now became a problem in itself. As I journeyed, everyone in my sphere was sucked into the vortex of confusion and pain associated with it. That's the thing about the use and abuse of alcohol and drugs, everyone gets to play along against their own will even if they don't use the substances.

I began with a joint which quickly became a gateway to other things. I moved through all the different classes of alcohol except for wine. Never cared for it. I moved through the different classes of drugs as well but stopped short of crack and shooting up. I still believe to this day that if I had gone there, I might be dead. But I suppose that wasn't to be a part of God's plan. I became a pig drinker and would eat anything in your medicine cabinet all to continue to evade reality and now I was doing it to satisfy the physical cravings and mental obsession that developed in me over time.

When I wanted to stop and found I could not I was truly

screwed. Naturally. But there was more to this being screwed here. In the time I was drinking and drugging I estranged myself from anything that resembled the remnants of my family. They grew thoroughly disgusted with me and rightly so. They were experiencing the same powerlessness as I and couldn't help me in the least. But the one who never gave up on me was Mom.

She left that couch, so to speak, to battle for her son. She threw every ounce of energy she could muster, and all the love she had in her for me, at the problem. She didn't give up and wouldn't give up until her son got clean and sober. She was brilliant as she waged this war on me and for me.

Amid the use and abuse of alcohol and drugs I most times, unknowingly and with an oblivious vision, destroyed everything around me. Most of all, the relationships in the family. Where they had already been fractured, I took hammers to them and proceeded to break them down into the smallest bits.

The moment came when my mother would scream the same two words at me that she screamed at my father. "Get out!" I ran. At fourteen, two years after I began with the alcohol and drugs, I was already exhibiting signs of alcoholism and addiction. My father and Pat took me in. They didn't know that I was already a potential alcoholic and addict but would soon come to see it. In just two short years Pat would scream the same two words. "Get out!" I began to hear these words often, verbally, and of course in my mind. I returned to Mom's house and would get sober two years later.

Where there was once hope created by this medication it was now gone as I reached the end. While the idea of wanting to check out was suspended for a bit it now returned with a harsh voracity. It was all I could think about. I wanted to die.

Sometimes this is indeed the most effective position to land in within our life experience. It brings with it not only pain and suffering but something else. A desire to be whole. To be free. To be willing to move from one place to another. It also brings with it a shift in vision and what is seen, what hasn't been seen. I went from resenting the time and energy Mom was putting into trying to help me to break free to wanting to accept the help from her.

With a phone call I placed after another weekend of debauchery I was told that there was a bed available for me at a rehab and I agreed to take it, agreed to accept help. I had arrived at a place of admitting defeat, a place of realizing that my power to solve this problem simply wasn't enough to effect a change in my course. I simply couldn't steer my vessel in the stream anymore and didn't want it to take on any more water. As much as I wanted to die there was something deep inside me that did not. It was the little bit of faith trying to get to the surface after being buried by years of resentments and fear. It was that spark of Divinity installed within me that I arrived here with. It was the Honeysuckle Dream.

There is far more to this story about which an entire book can be written and indeed one that I did write. The point of sharing on this matter is simply to pass on this. My power as a human will always have a finite nature to it. My understanding of this was reached by this experience. My understanding that God has all Power began at this time in my life. It began when I got clean and sober. It began as I returned to that vast space of reality that contained all the fears and resentments that could no longer be medicated by substance or thrill-seeking experiences such as sex, gambling, smoking, etc.

I went to rehab for thirty days two weeks before I was supposed to graduate high school. I called my father before going as if this might convince him that I was not defective and perhaps worthy of love. All he could muster to say was

"Okay."

During treatment I was told I had to find God.

I had to begin anew my return to the Honeysuckle Dream.

Nineteen

I'll Take "His Side" For A Thousand Alex

The war that raged on between my mother and father came with some rules, some terms and conditions. As Mom and Dad were so attached to their own bodies of pain the rules weren't always clearly communicated. At times they were. I began to refer to this as the "triangle." Though there were four of us in the small family unit, mother-father-son-daughter, it always seemed as if there could only be three who were speaking with one another at a time and the odd one out was held in the highest of contempt. This held true as rules of engagement in the family for most of my life except for a couple of years. The two years I lived with my father and his wife and her three children. Rick found the triangle analogy and theory to be interesting when I shared it with him in later years as I aged into adulthood.

After Nana passed, and as I sought oblivion from reality in a thrill-seeking manner, it was rare that I spoke with Dad. The rules shifted after the funeral as Mom sank deeper and taking her side took on depths to match her descent into depression. I quickly began to take on new characteristics as my use and abuse of alcohol and drugs increased. My dependency on them was growing rapidly. I was becoming as powerless over them as much as I was powerless over everything around me. The more I tried to exercise some control over everything, and failed, the more irritable I became. The angrier I became with my mother. With my father.

The more that I was expected to wear the uniform on her side of the battlefield the more belligerent I became. I simply didn't want to wear it anymore. I didn't want to live like this anymore. Something inside of me was telling me that the never cooling kettle of resentments and fears, now mixed with a visible desire to just give up on her part, wasn't healthy. I was a teenager fueled by alcohol and drugs and I wanted to break free. I wanted more.

I think every Mom screams "Get out!" at their children at least once in their life and it typically means that they don't have the resources to deal with you at that moment. When she screamed it at my father he listened, and he got out. I was taught what these words meant at a young age and when she screamed them at me, I did the same. I called my father and went to live with him. He once told me that he was always waiting for the phone call and knew one day it would come. He thought it would happen when I was sixteen. He took the call when I was fourteen. When I went to live with him, I was already on the edge of slipping into alcoholism and addiction. He had no idea what he was getting into, but he was happy to have me desert my mother's side of the battlefield, happy to hand me a new uniform, and happy to have me join his side. I was so angry at Mom that I gladly accepted the uniform and position along with his unspoken terms and conditions.

My father didn't want me.

He wanted revenge. He wanted to retaliate. He wanted to win the war.

Fear, especially the fear of abandonment, pushes us to do things that oppose faith while embracing and making colorful attributes a part of our constitution. Hope, especially false hope, seems to justify the fear. It validates the necessity of fear in the most twisted ways. It gave mine a false reason and justification. As long as the fears could be seen as healthy then I wouldn't need to turn away from them. They have this darkness about them that is indeed cunning. They have their own life, always seeking to survive by any means possible. "Little Bobby" was driven by and lived by fear.

This fear and many others were suspended for a short time as I moved away from Mom and closer to Dad. His attention, and the attention from his wife and her three daughters, brought me hope. It was a false hope, and false hope has little in a lasting effect. While I felt like I was on vacation from Mom I was simply prolonging the inevitable with a geographical cure. I thought that if I changed the people, places, and things in my life that I would be happier. It didn't work because I took the problem with me. The problem was me. The problem was my lack of God-consciousness. Of course I didn't know this. How could I?

My mother fought to keep me from my father, to get me back. Although I was already with him, we all ended up in the courthouse with the attorneys, and finally the judge. I refused to go back to her, and my father couldn't be happier. As we sat at the conference table, Mom, Papa, Dad, lawyers, judge, and myself, I felt a twisted satisfaction that I was now holding some kind of sway over my parents. As happy as my Dad was to have won this battle my mother was equally distraught. Papa looked on with a level of acceptance, this was always his way. It was determined that I could make the decision at fourteen and the message sent and received to me was that I could now do whatever I wanted. In a sick way this added to my already sickening depth of spiritual sickness that was the undercurrent of my alcoholism. It bolstered my justification for all that I was doing. It sent the message that I was in control.

The honeymoon period of living in a new place with new people with new things ended quickly. Reality would soon return and any relief I felt with the move became a new level of angst. This dread pushed me to smoke more pot and do more dope. It wasn't easy to drink while living with Dad and Pat, so drugs became the go to for me. I began to regret what I had done to Mom and felt like a traitor. I missed Mom and Papa and my sister. I wanted to go home but didn't have the courage to say it. I would have to cause an explosion to make that happen.

In a rare conversation with Mom, she shared how Papa was cutting the lawn now as I was no longer there and that he was stung by a bee. He had an allergic reaction to the sting and had to be treated. This created so much guilt and shame in me. It prevented me from reaching out to ask if I could come home.

Fear is a thief and causes us to easily give up that which is the healthiest for us, most especially what little faith we have while living by the fears. It steals so much more. It stole my drive and caused me to constantly settle for less. Fears were driving a better part of the currents in the stream of life for me. This is what happened after Nana died. As Mom was increasingly giving up at deeper levels, I did the same.

I was always a great student and always got straight A's. I was expected to take college prep classes throughout my junior and high school years and expected to go to college. I did excel but as I moved into the future after Nana died, I didn't have the energy for it, didn't have the energy to be successful. I know the need to be a people pleaser played a greater part in my success for years as it is related to grades. I know the fear that I might be turned out or tossed aside played a part in wanting to remain of value to my family. I didn't want them to look upon me with disapproval and then make the decision to abandon me further as if there were depths to abandonment. My desire to be a great student and succeed was easily tossed aside as I placed more and more trust on the alcohol and drugs and began to accept defeat.

When I moved into my father's house I was enrolled in a new school system. When I met with the guidance counselor to pick my classes she didn't have my transcripts yet, she didn't know the courses I had taken over the past two years. She didn't know where to place me, so she asked me what classes I wanted to take. Though I hadn't passed the previous classes with the usual A's I did know the subject matter. I was simply too stoned to test well in them.

I decided to retake the classes I had already done. My course was set to take trigonometry or calculus at the end of my high school years, but I gave up the opportunity. My course was set to be in full conversational French by the end of high school, but I simply didn't care. The reality is that I was looking for the easier and softer way now. This became a better part of my nature as my dependence on alcohol and drugs continued to take on more pitiful proportions. Instead of moving into geometry I decided to retake Algebra I again. Not only that, but I also chose Algebra I, Part One. I began French class with the introduction level although I had already taken it for two years. I settled for less. All of this, and so many other instances of settling for less, layered more and more guilt, shame, and a deepening sense of remorse in me. Self-hatred and self-loathing became a better part of my fabric.

Not only was I feeling remorseful about abandoning my mother and sister, but I also now felt remorseful about settling for less. Although Nana wasn't here anymore, I could *feel* her disappointment in me as I felt her looking down on me from above. I sought to escape these feelings in the only way I knew how. Oblivion, and I acted up. I became that belligerent and insufferable teenager.

At about this time my father lost his business and had to go to work for someone else. He took on three jobs and was rarely home. I felt as though I was in a prison locked up with a warden named Pat who was equally as miserable as my father with the turn of events. I became afraid that in the cutting of costs to manage the new circumstances that I would be a line item to be eliminated by the cuts. Fear had this way of working me into a state and influencing my mind and its false narrative. It's "story."

I don't remember the reason for the call but remember what happened. There was a reason for my father to speak with my mother and it naturally turned into an argument. With this came the screaming that my mother always landed at, and you could hear her plainly through the phone. I remember the look on the faces of my father and Pat and two of my stepsisters as this happened. It was coupled with laughter. It felt like this satisfaction was arrived at by them with their condescension and it felt dirty to me. I remember feeling this pit in my stomach as it happened. It was mixed with the fear that if I didn't participate in it, I wouldn't be a part of the family. I managed to laugh with them, but my heart was wretched at the thought that my mother was in so much pain and was being ridiculed. I didn't want to be on my father's side anymore but couldn't say it. I felt as though I had no place to go. I certainly didn't think Mom would take me back.

When I went to live with them there wasn't a bedroom for me in their home. One was built downstairs in the raised ranch and a piece of the integral two car garage was used to accommodate this. While I was grateful for the space that seemed to be created with the same care my father created the elf with, I was kept separate from the family upstairs. Although I felt like a cellar dweller the space created for me seemed to feel like the unfolding of the bed that was in the spare bedroom at Dad's apartment years before.

At the time this phone conversation took place with my Mom I had been allowed to sleep upstairs in the bedroom my stepsister had. She was away at college after her high school graduation, and I felt as though I graduated to accommodations upstairs. I didn't want to lose what I felt was a promotion. I always participated in the assaults and affronts of those I didn't want to fall out of grace with.

I rarely spoke with my mother while living with my father, never spoke with my sister or Papa. I never felt as alone as I did at this time. I could always see other people with their circumstances in the stream of life rowing their canoes or drifting in their floats from where I was but now it seemed as though I was adrift in darkness with little to no contact with anyone. I wanted to go home. This place was not my home. There was very little love there. I gave up caring and began to rebel.

As easy as the classes were in school, I began to fail them. As Pat demanded more and more of me, I refused to listen or take directions. As Dad seemed to withdraw, I withdrew. As cold and dark as their house became, I became darker and colder.

I sat in the driveway one day smoking a cigarette and when Pat told me to put the cigarette out, I refused. I began to rebel and the more I fought the more she pushed back. I clearly had a lot going on, but therapy was never spoken of or looked at as a remedy. Instead, Pat enrolled me in karate. I had little interest in karate. She signed me up to take guitar lessons, but I had difficulty playing the guitar. I'm left-handed and they tried to force me to play right-handed. Of course, this added to the list of things I failed at.

When I was encouraged to take an interest in things she had this way of dismantling the encouragement or sabotaging it. I loved it when my father and I set up an aquarium in my bedroom. I had my own personal pets, and I was encouraged to take care of the them, to keep the tank clean and healthy for them. Pat came home one day as I stood before the kitchen sink with a pile of elements from the tank aside me. I was cleaning them; I was following their direction. I don't know why or what the reasoning was, but she wasn't happy about this. Naturally I was verbally shamed and made to feel defective for cleaning my tank but there was something more.

I gave up a bit more every day. The alcohol and drug abuse brought this about but, in many ways, it was the environment, and messages always sent literally and figuratively that were bringing about the will to just give up.

As much as they didn't know who was moving in with them in the way of my character, my beliefs, my ideas, my attitudes, and my emotions I did not know of theirs. Growing up watching sitcoms that seemed to always hold to family dynamics and problems experienced *along* with solutions achieved I became lofty in my thinking that all families matched these story lines. All families, except for Mom, my sister, and me. I watched the other whole families in the neighborhood that I grew up in and assumed that each home was a productive sitcom matching those on television. This was a narrative that I came up with as a form of sick nourishment for the fears and resentments I carried around with me.

I also believed that my father had moved from our sick horror story to his own sitcom that was normal when he traded us in for a new wife and children. With this twisted belief system, I wrongly thought that I was going to be a new cast member in their sitcom. Indeed, I was a new cast member but what I didn't know was that their sitcom was a horror story of its own accord.

I felt used most of the time. I always had an amazing work ethic, always loved working and accomplishing something.

Papa instilled this in me but when I lived there it was different. When I was told to chop all the wood that was delivered there was zero pleasure in it. I felt like a hired hand where the only payment was ridicule and the checks issued, the love, were worthless.

Dad and Pat went away for a couple of nights and used Pat's mother's car to travel. When they returned and walked through the door there was no greeting from them. Instead, I was told to go wash the bugs off the front of the car. I felt like an employee walking around on eggshells afraid of being fired. Being a people pleaser became a requirement in their home.

One day as my father and I drove through the city I grew up in I cannot recall where we were coming from or where we were going but I do remember him sharing something with me. He told me that I had saved his marriage. That he and Pat were almost at the point of getting a divorce and because I came into their lives the discussion was suspended, and the decision was made to stay together. I felt a dismal failure.

All I ever wanted was two things in my life. I wanted a whole family. I wanted a Dad. When he spoke these words, I felt as though the chance of my mother and father getting back together would never be, a false hope was crushed even harder. With these words I came to see that the brilliant and successful sitcom I thought they were living simply was not. I became confused as these truths crashed upon me.

Twenty

"What Is Fist Punch?" Alex

My sister and I were Irish twins. Actually, we missed the mark by two days, we are a year and two days apart from one another in age. My stepsisters are older than I am. One a year older, one is two years older, and I think the oldest may be three or four years older.

I was fourteen when I moved in with them and I felt like a transplant. As my consciousness was numb, I didn't have the capacity to feel as though I was imposing myself on them but the youngest would express her displeasure about it at times. Comments and an energy that seem to hit the mark as they were flung across the room in conversation or by body language.

I was moved from a place of "have not's" to "have's" and certainly didn't know how this worked, this difference in class. I moved from lower-middle class to upper-middle class in the blink of an eye and wasn't accustomed to living like that. I had only witnessed it in all of them from afar while growing up. No one in my family spoke of money, its persuasion, or its management. It was like a taboo subject.

I was taught to be a taker. I was taught to take whatever I

could. Not only that, but I was also taught not to share. It wasn't a classroom setting that spoke to these lessons, it was the stream of life, and all that happened in its currents, that brought these unspoken lessons to me.

When I held a possession, I held it closely as I was afraid it might be taken from me. When I was offered something, I accepted without hesitation. I once expressed to my father that I needed a bike. He told me that I could have one of my stepsister's bikes. I gladly accepted this offer and then he told me I had to go get it. They abandoned it at someone's house when they bought their new home and moved to another city. Somewhere deep inside it felt as though this was going to be a cruel trick, as if it wouldn't be there when I showed up to retrieve it. I didn't want something of Pat and her daughters, I wanted something without these attachments. I wanted something exclusively between my father and me.

This whole interaction and moment in time churned up the sediment on the floor of the stream and reminded me of the yearly reminder from Mom that this Christmas was "going to be a light Christmas" as well as reminding me of the effort put forth by Nana and Papa to be and act as parents that extended into providing for my sister and me. I remembered the sweet moment in time when they gave us brand-new ten-speed bikes for Christmas. What I recall the most was the love and energy behind them with the efforts and the way in which they always extended their care and love. This was seriously lacking with Dad and Pat and the glimpses of it were so few and far in between. Hell, I never even had a key to their house growing up.

When I ate, I did so as though it might be my last meal. This is what doing without does to some and what it did to me. One afternoon I was in the kitchen cooking something to eat and remember feeling a bit of ease and comfort that there was something to eat. I sat at the kitchen table and as I ate Pat came home with my youngest stepsister. It became weird very quickly. Pat was upset that I was eating and using the kitchen. She rarely cooked so I know it had very little to do with perhaps ruining my appetite. It was the typical contemptuous extension of judgement she always handed to my sister and me.

My youngest stepsister, the high-school cheerleader with the long blond hair, looked at me with a contorted and grimaced face mimicking the look her mom perfected and said in an incredulous way "Look at how he eats Mom, he's a heathen!" I wanted to be close to her as we were closest in age yet most times, she was a cactus. I always kissed her ass, but she always spoke to me from a hilltop of superiority as though she was trying to keep me in my place. That of the lowly servant.

Years later Dad and Pat made the decision to move to Arizona and sold their house. They bought a mobile home and drove across the country with their pets. Though I was a young adult I didn't want him to go. I wanted him to stay here. I visited them for the last time at their home before they left to see the camper they would be travelling in. Perhaps my intent for the visit was to plead with him once again not to abandon me.

Dad had this "Big B." It was made of tin or aluminum. It was about five feet tall. It was part of the sign that was atop the meat market "Bo Peep" he bought years before. It was at the curb when I visited and asked him if I could have it. I recall loading the "Big B" into my car when I left and feeling this would probably be the only thing I'd ever have from him. "Little Bobby" kept the "Big B" for years until one day "Mad Bob" tossed it aside, the same way he did the elf with the purple socks.

Our last time together before they left to drive across the country was at my aunt's house where some of the family was gathered. I recall Moo being there along with my aunt. Dad and Pat were there with my youngest stepsister. I don't recall my other stepsisters or cousins being there. But I do recall the last harsh impression left by my stepsister.

My father gave me a ring that day. It was a ring his father made. It was gold and it had a blue synthetic stone set in it. The ring is still with me and sits in a drawer in my kitchen. I won't wear it. It has a weird energy to it. One day I asked my son if he wanted it, and he outright refused to take it. He said there is nothing good or nourishing in it.

As I sat on a swing in the lower level of my aunt's house in the three-season room with my stepsister, she gushed over the fact that my father had given me the ring. Now I'm not sure if it was amazement that he was moved to do so or some sort of extension of how she looked at me years before when I lived with them, but I can tell you that the comments were offered with this condescension that she seemed to pick up from her mother. She implored me to take great care of it with this drippiness that would have soaked a sponge as though it were the most valuable thing in the world. I don't think she understood that what I craved the most was a relationship with my father. I don't think she understood that this token, this ring, was indeed just that. A souvenir. A parting gift as the game show came to an end. I wanted to puke and couldn't wait to leave there. When I left, I had tears streaming down my face.

Dad and Pat left for Arizona and I wanted them to take all the resentments and fears that I had buried deep within along with them. They couldn't do this for me. The best they could do was to extend an invitation to visit them with an offer to pay the plane fare. I flew out from Rhode Island two years later at a time when I was already feeling that my first marriage wasn't going to make it. I was looking for an escape. I was still looking for love and acceptance.

It was the one and only time that I felt welcomed into their lives. When I arrived one of my stepsisters was there with her friend. She was visiting as well. Everyone seemed to be in a lighter place than we were in years before when we lived with one another. Perhaps it was the benefit of age, but I suspect it was the result of that geographical cure that seems to change our mindset for a bit of time.

The stepsister who stayed with us during this time was indeed my favorite. She and I were alike, and she always encouraged me to go with the wild spirit that we both seemed to share. She could be mischievous and a bit of a trickster but there was never any malice in her. She always worked from a place of care and concern. She remained close to Dad and Pat well into adulthood and looked after them. She always seemed to extend that same effort with me. She had compassion and possessed an unspoken empathy and understanding. Perhaps it was what she came to understand as Pat and her father divorced when she was young.

Our time in Arizona was near spiritual but that experience or feeling derived from it wouldn't last. It was near spiritual only because of the area they lived in, Sedona, and of course the heightened senses that is the natural effect of being in a new place. While my body had grown older there were many parts of my constitution that did not. My feelings. My mind. My emotions. My spirit.

When I left for Arizona, I left my wife and daughter behind. They did not make the trip with me but I took my old JVC camcorder with me so I might capture some of the trip for them. My daughter would never see or understand it as she was less than two years old, but I thought that perhaps it might help my wife understand all that I kept hidden deep within and might even help our already fractured relationship. I was wrong about this. My father took me all about while I was there and what I captured on video became a powerful lesson for me when I reviewed them.

All my life there have been these incremental periods of growth, individually and collectively, within my relationship with my father. I can see how natural this is. When I was a child, we grew together emotionally and mentally even if in the smallest strides, and then he left. We stopped growing. I stopped maturing in the relationship. When we were brought together whether with one of his visitations or holiday celebrations at a family member's home we always picked up where we left off.

We experienced these small growth spurts during these times and because our time together was more and more limited the growth came to a standstill. If I was six years old when he left our home, it is likely I would have the maturity of say an eight-year-old by the time I went to live with them at the age of fourteen. Perhaps I grew emotionally over the two years I lived with them and reached the maturity of a ten- to twelve-year-old. As I reflect on all of it there is this feeling that by the time I reached the visit to Arizona as a married adult with a child I instantly regressed to the maturity of an adolescent.

When I arrived back home to the East Coast and watched the videos with my wife, I became sick to my stomach. What I witnessed was an adolescent version of myself though I was an adult. I believe I was twenty-four at the time yet the version of myself that I watched was the fourteen-year-old people pleaser that answered the words "Get out" from my stepmother. I fell into a bout of uncontrollable tears and sobbing. I reached out to a therapist the very next day.

The video brought to the forefront of my mind all the past instances I experienced that mirrored this effect. I remember one Christmas when I visited Dad and Pat's home. I was an adult when this visit took place, as I arrived with gifts. I sat next to my compassionate stepsister, and she asked me what I got for my father as we all opened gifts. I immediately felt like this little child. It was this instant regression back to the time where the maturity of the relationship Dad and I had been left off at. I bought him the game "Connect Four." The deeper essence of this was the need for a Dad and longing for a relationship in this manner. The need to mature.

On the list of things I would have liked to have done in my life the greatest thing might have been given the chance or courage to speak directly to all of this while it was happening. I thought I was going to play a part in the sitcom. The productive sitcom I wholly believed my father was living in after he left us. But the reality is that it didn't hold the solutions to the problems a sitcom typically addresses and deals with. I found this was indeed the case in Dad and Pat's home. There was little in communication, and you had to not only walk on eggshells but had to guess what everyone else was feeling or thinking.

I was not close to my older stepsister, but she was there to guide me when needed. She was accepting and extended care to me. Perhaps some pity. She did make it a point to spend time with me on occasion. As I look back, I'm confident that my stepsisters had their own bag of "stuff" as it's related to the divorce of their parents, their father and Pat.

Being the constant observer of people, their ways, their words, their feelings, and their energy, I have grown this ability to decipher and translate all this very easily. It's easy for me to read energy and I arrive at a fair assessment most of the time. She and I shared the commonality of being the oldest child. She is the older of my stepsisters and I am older than my sister. Although being a people pleaser is a common trait in the child of divorced parents, I believe the older one is more susceptible to this shortcoming. I saw this in her, I felt this in her.

My mother was not the only one held up to ridicule by Dad

and Pat. They held my stepsister's father up to ridicule as well. I witnessed this and came to understand this to some extent with my older stepsister as she interacted with Dad and Pat. I watched her participate in it the same way I felt forced to participate in it. It felt as though if we didn't, we would be cast aside or abandoned entirely.

The effort to dominate or control another or outcomes in the stream of life typically looks like one of two ways. They're either passive-aggressive or aggressive. I came to see that all that I experienced in my family was passive-aggressive, mostly due to a serious lack of communication where everyone was expected to be a mind reader. My stepsister's father seemed to be the opposite. Though he may have seemed aggressive he always made it crystal clear what his position was. You didn't have to guess. I really did like the fellow.

As I watched the interactions between everyone in Dad and Pat's house there were moments when I recognized that they were holding this man up to ridicule. I heard the words, could feel the energy that surrounded it. My stepsister would participate and even had this physical participation that defined his aggressive, communicative manner. She would clench her hand into a fist and pound it into her other hand that was open to receive it. There was a word she said as she did this though I cannot recall it what it was. It added to the physical effect.

She went away to college, lived at college, and when she finished her courses, she came back home. She married a short time later and quickly moved out of state. I fully suspect she couldn't wait to get away.

The narrative in the letter that was a heat-seeking missile of a letter that Pat sent to my mother years before I would move in with them was rich with put-downs and insults against my mother. It ridiculed her to no end and criticized every element of her effort at being a mother including the statement that my mother had been poisoning our minds against her and my father since the divorce.

Pat wasn't that far off the mark with her aim. She did hit the target, and the damage caused reverberated for years afterwards. The irony is that I saw how Pat had done the same thing with her children when I lived with them. Passive aggressive or just plain aggressive, controlling others and attempting to hold their hearts and minds hostage will always be an ugly affair.

With the absolute clarity that is hindsight I can see that while we all had a part to play in the mayhem, seen and unseen, we, all the children, had very little in the way of communicating with one another. We weren't shown how to verbalize, and didn't know how to speak to the heart of what we were experiencing as we were experiencing it. The irony is that though I do not speak with my sister or stepsisters we have the most in common with one another when you peel back the layers of denial attached to everything.

While living with Dad and Pat I grew more and more dependent on alcohol and drugs. As my father spent more and more time away from the house working, as I refused to play the part that Pat expected me to play, as I gave up more and more on my schoolwork, as I began to lie and steal more and more, as I became more and more belligerent with the "Cheers" attitude it became clear that my time with them was coming to an end. I was happy to see this happen and really didn't care where I lived. It isn't easy living in a place without love.

When Pat was forced into the position of screaming "Get out" I truly welcomed it. I called Mom. As mothers will do, she came to my rescue and picked me up past midnight a short time after my father came home from work to find that his wife had arrived at a decision to toss me out. I left with only the clothes on my back the same way my father left our house years before.

Twenty-One

Others

It has taken me so, so many years to find purpose. To find the purpose of my life experiences. To find the purpose of living. The purpose that best suits me. This has been the journey of a lifetime. That right there has been the best and most important chance or experience that I will ever have. Finding purpose. Finding the purpose of it *all*.

Though the journey, the time spent in the stream of life, can feel brutal at times I have come to see that each moment, every experience, each and every nuance, has been divinely designed for me. I believe it is for you as well. All that happened before this moment had one aim and it was to get me where I am now.

The resentments born out of experiences were necessary. The fears as equally necessary. They were needed for one specific reason. They were a toll to get me home to God by ultimately exposing my failure in managing my own life. This is hard to fully explain with words unless one has a similar experience to support the words. It is equally hard to explain what God is. I believe that understanding must come from personal experience. At least it had to for me.

I always believed in God. I was taught to believe in God but the experiences I had at the human level, and at the hands of others, most times born out of ignorance, screwed with the teaching and my chance to believe.

I always believed in God but felt he didn't believe in me. Perhaps I had a fear of God much like I had many unfounded fears of my parents, of my family. The knowledge of my family was the same as the knowledge I had of God. It was topical. In my family you rarely discussed how you were feeling, what you were thinking. We simply weren't taught how to do this; we were taught the opposite. We were taught how to hide. Hide the feelings. Hide the guilt. Hide the shame. Hide the remorse. I was taught how to cast judgment and aspersions. I took these teachings and unknowingly applied it to my relationship with God. I have come to know that I cannot hide a thing from God. That He is Omnipotent. All Knowing. This knowledge was paid for, and I paid dearly for it. I would have to reach nearly full destruction before I was willing enough to learn this.

I came to intimately know my family with time, with experience. I became them. I became that which I grew to hate. I became my mother and father. I did things while on each of their sides that created layers and layers of shame and regret. This always pushed me to the place of wanting to escape. And the ultimate escape from reality is death. I wished for this every day. I carried this longing to leave here near my entire life. In some way it was a longing to return to the Ultimate Parent. God.

Years after I got clean and sober and started to sift through the ashes that were pieces of my life a psychotherapist asked me one question. "How did you get out of the family?" I couldn't answer the question because at some level I still felt a part of the body of pain, that generational trauma. I still felt the need to protect the mechanisms in place that made up the inner workings of the family and the relationships within it. Eventually this incessant need would leave me. But it didn't happen by my own accord. I needed serious help with it.

As I grew to realize and concede my powerlessness over alcohol and drugs all that I had been trying to escape with the alcohol and drugs came to the forefront of my mind and heart. The medication wasn't there to keep the realities at bay, and I had to confront them. How long did this take? Years. Many years. Countless resources and money, but the greatest cost was time. I had to be broken down while I was broken down. I came to know that every breakdown comes with a breakthrough. And that I need to look for it.

I also had to have another experience. Although my trust and reliance on things human was strong, was perhaps even a sick dependency, I had to come to see that it never really worked. A look at my life, especially as it related to my family, gave me the clear vision that as humans there will always be a necessary element missing from our limited power to fully recover from some things. There was no way I could recover from the depth of resentment and fear through the aid of others. As humans we all have these resentments and fears and perhaps this is why it is difficult for us to bring about a full recovery from them in one another. We are limited by the extent to which we carry them. Our "stories" might bring relief but most times the relief is not lasting, not fully effective. At times our stories can act like the cheerleader inspiring others to try something different, but we have to reach the point of fully wanting something different while reaching for a solution that really works. One that is the most effective.

I have found God to be the most effective.

While I believed in Him and didn't think He believed in me I simply didn't know Him. I had an idea of Him, passed on to me by my family though He was rarely spoken of after Nana passed away. I didn't *know* Him. I needed to know Him to understand the depth of power He could and would yield in my life. To not only allow Him to remove the darkness of resentments and fears from me but restore me to soundness of mind, to pull me out of the delusions I long lived by. I had to return to the Honeysuckle Dream but didn't know how to. I didn't know how to have an experience with God that would not only deepen my relationship with Him and restore my once childlike faith in Him but would change the course of my life and those closest to me.

When I got clean and sober, my new life, and lifestyle, came with a host of friends. Many of which I still have in my life today all these years later. We had a few things in common. We were living without the benefit of alcohol and drugs to evade reality and to a greater extent knew the depth of powerlessness we had over living the depravity that came with the use and abuse of alcohol and drugs. The thing about living a life of depravity, doing those things you swore you would never do, living an unprincipled life, is that it all catches up to you and takes you down like a tidal wave. It also puts you in the best position to be lifted. Lifted by God.

It brings about a willingness to turn from the old and turn to the new. To reach for something entirely different. Perhaps this is the most powerful part of our story. The sharing of it brings to others the hope needed to change their course thereby allowing them to share their story bringing about yet someone else's change in course. This is what I drew from this host of friends. We had a collective journey and varied experiences not only with life but with God.

As I started my journey home to God, my return to innocence, my return to the Honeysuckle Dream, I had small educational variety experiences. These were aha moments brought about by the peeling back of layers and layers of persuasions that had been passed on to me by my family.

Each layer peeled brought with it the pain I had tried to evade for so many years. Most times I didn't want to look at these things, didn't want to re-feel them but it was necessary. I had no choice. There were times when I would take the wrong fork in the road on the journey home seeking refuge, seeking an escape. Without the benefit of alcohol and drugs I turned to other things. I soon came to see that they didn't work, and I would return to the path set beside the stream.

It would take a failed marriage and failed businesses before I was ready to meet the terms and conditions that God set before me. It would take years and years, clean and sober, moving forward with the need to try to control everything around me, including people, before I would see my absolute failure on all fronts. It would take the arrival of my first child before I would begin the heavy work necessary to recover from the fears. It would take a new marriage and my stepdaughter's arrival in my life to open my eyes to the fact that love does not have to be conditional. Ultimately it would be the birth of my son that would bring about within me a deep desire to flip the script and leave the generational pain of my family behind me. None of this would happen without God.

None of this would reach a full accomplishment until I came to not only know God through an experience, an awakening, but also come to wholly trust and rely on Him for all matters in my life. It would be the most difficult yet rewarding journey in my lifetime, the journey held the greatest of moments in the stream of life.

Twenty-Two

Not The Brady Bunch

Our stories, our lives, can either be loved or hated by ourselves, or by others. Our stories are powerful. They have the power to heal. They can inspire *us* to heal and can inspire *others* to heal by lending a sense of strength and hope.

Our stories can also cause serious harm and destruction and out of our stories we can take harm to others in a reactionary manner. This is what I have been sharing thus far. The damage experienced at the hands of others who in fact knew not what they were doing. That's the thing about living a life without a conscience brought about by a disconnect from God, a disconnect from faith. Brought about by a darkness that comes to life and insidiously dwells within us. Again, unknowingly most times.

I have spent a great deal of time running away from my story. A great deal of time hating my story. All of this was inspired by a deep sense of self-hatred and self-loathing I never fully understood until I sifted through all the ashes. I spent years in the ashes moving about while looking at them seeking understanding. While holding them and watching them disintegrate in my hands as they fell to the ground to create a different form. There has always been an underlying productive alchemy in the tragedy.

I have always been able to see my story, review my story, and examine my story in bits and pieces. This writing has shown me that indeed a story can be transcended, can be overcome, can be looked at in a *whole* manner rather than reaching into parts that have been compartmentalized for so long. Are there still parts that I hate? Indeed, there are parts that still hurt, but not so much hate. I don't think we fully heal from certain parts of our stories. The scar tissue remains. At times these scars become irritable. They itch our soul. I think what we learn, what we *must* learn to do, is to let go. That was never easy for me. It was never easy for Mom, for Dad, or for my sister. A greater part of my extended family as well.

As I go deeper into my story it does become a bit painful when looked at in its entirety. As the scars are rubbed, the irritants return to me. As I go deeper into telling my story there is a part of me screaming "Please stop! Please stop typing! We cannot do this in sittings like this and at this pace." There is also a part of me that doesn't want to share the story. That would be the fear part. There are also vestiges of regret that I suppose I'll always feel, and the next part of the story contains these. It contains many of these regrets. I have learned that repeating circumstances are lessons that I refused to learn which wholly explain why it seemed as though I was living my own Groundhog Day for so long. If I don't tell this story, I will continue to carry the regret with me, perhaps even the guilt and shame of my own existence. Shedding light on something lessens its darkness. Exposing darkness to the Light weakens its power.

Perhaps you have the impression that it was all bad. That there was no love from Mom and Dad, and this is largely true but to a small degree there was love. It was conditional and came with terms and conditions I didn't understand, and it was confusing. As Nana called me the sensitive one, I can see she was referencing my emotional arrangement. I always felt things at such a deep level. So much so that it cast a haze upon any chance of thinking clearly. The bad always overshadowed the good and the good did not have a chance to grow or become a part of my center.

For years my stream of life was a tragedy, and I always lived in the shadow of this tragedy. Where I thought each one of you were living in a productive sitcom, I believed I was cast in a dramatic horror movie where the two genres couldn't be crossed over. This vision changed as I grew older and especially as I moved back to my mother's home as a teenager when Pat screamed "Get out."

When my sister and I were young, I think at six and seven, we were walking on the ice at the local pond. Angel's Pond. Naturally we were unsupervised and not a soul was around. The pond was tucked in a valley behind a row of houses at the end of our street. It was lined with trees on the far side. It was absolutely freezing out, but we didn't care. We were those orphans who wandered wherever we wanted to go. We didn't know the nature of ice, which parts were thin, as we made our way to the other end of the pond. We were walking right into the outlet where the ice was the thinnest. I was walking behind my sister. She made it to the edge and onto the shore. I did not. The ice crumbled under my feet, and I dropped. I went into the water and my feet landed on the mushy bottom. I was in the water up to my chest.

I didn't panic. I wasn't taken under the ice. My instincts told me to just keep moving forward. To walk with the ground that I connected with. I began the hard walk, and I made my way to the shore as my sister had. I laughed as the relief washed over me. I remember thinking "Holy crap that was close!" Years later while in the swamp of my emotional and mental pain the scene from one of The Omen movies where the man was carried in the currents under the ice to his death would come to mind. I would lapse into wondering what it would have been like if this had happened to me. I wanted to be free of the pain that badly. I wanted to be free of my existence that much.

I trudged home and by the time I got there it felt like I was walking in braces. My pants were frozen solid. I had to lay down and shimmy out of them. I stood them up tall in the middle of my bedroom. "I survived" is the thought that crossed my mind as I looked at them and my beat red legs. I never told anyone in the family what happened, and my sister and I never spoke of it. I don’t think she was aware it was happening.

This is where I am in this story. Though the previous chapters have brought with them relief they have also left me a tad twisted in thoughts and feelings. Our stories can do that when examined as a whole instead of just in bits and pieces. I find myself in resentment, re-feeling that which hasn't been felt in quite some time, and a part of me wants to abandon this writing. See how that works? It makes sense when this trait becomes a part of your nature, when this lesson is the greatest one taught in the family. Indeed, I became everything that I hated about my parents, everything I held them in contempt for. When I was in elementary school there was a book about everything we needed to know we learned in kindergarten. I never read it but the title kind of stuck somewhere in one of the compartments within my mind. I can tell you that everything I needed to know about survival I learned from my mother and father. I also grew into a place where survival instincts were wrapped in selfishness. I didn't have the capacity to think of or include others.

Though my older instincts are telling me to stop this writing, to go back to the full and rewarding life I live now; to walk away from this, I will keep trudging through as I did when my feet hit the pond floor. I will continue to stand as tall as my frozen jeans did.

I left what I thought was a tragedy, Mom's house, and took on a new role in a new sitcom that I thought included a solution, Dad's house, then I went back to the "tragedy." I didn't even know that in addition to now being an alcoholic and addicted to drugs I was addicted to chaos. I became addicted to the body of pain that was my family. I was playing my part and glad to be a supporter of their generational pain. I was glad to take the reins when they handed them to me and at times, I didn't want to relinquish them. I didn’t want to let go of the pain, the chaos.

I moved away from my stepmother and three stepsisters who had a bond that I could never have or could ever enjoy. I simply couldn't connect with them at a real level because I resented them. Resentment really is the ultimate blocker. I moved back in with my mother and sister after almost two years of silence between us. I had, in essence, abandoned them, and when I returned, I felt like I was imposing. My mother and sister had become best friends while I had become spiritually sick at deeper levels.

I didn't know what I was moving into, and they didn't know what was moving in. I had learned to walk on proverbial eggshells at my father's house and I took this lesson with me to my mother's house. When I arrived there my sister was different. She was diffident. She resented me. She still does to this day.

The depth of depravity I began to live, the lack of conscience and immense depth of selfishness, increased drastically when I began drinking and using drugs. The deeper I got into it the less I cared, the less I cared about others. My sister included. Deep in my heart I cared for her. Deep in my heart I still do. But as my desire to escape the deeper currents in the stream increased, I was willing to toss aside relationships. I suppose all that happened between her and I had a causation, a starting point, being the family dynamics, but there was something more there. There always has been. We became competitors looking for scraps from our parents. Looking for validation.

Mom once called us "partners in crime" but indeed we became adversaries and as such set out to hurt, wound, or destroy one another in any way that we could. Our relationship became one of constant retaliation for harm done to one another. The real harm, and the imagined harm born out of delusion, set in motion by the body of pain we experienced with our parents. My own self-hatred and self-loathing bred into all the relationships that I had with others and none more so than the relationship I had with my sister. We no longer speak with one another though we share the same in the way of many personal experiences and share the same characters in our stories. And there is the ultimate tragedy within the tragedy. The fact that our relationship was indeed destroyed by a family's body of pain and at times with destructive forces brought on by our own parents, inspired by them. The irony is that my sister and I have more in common than we ever realized.

My drinking and use of drugs grew and in proportion so did my reactions to and in the stream of life. I became explosive and at times violent. I lashed out. I lashed out verbally and by the time I got sober and moved out of my mother's house there were holes in the walls of my bedroom. Though I never physically hit my sister I often hit her with words. To a great extent we can hurt others with our words more so than with our fists. I would do this long into adulthood, and she would return the favor. It added to the need to destroy one another.

As I look back, I believe we were both looking for our place in this world. Perhaps even our purpose. We wanted to find where we could be relevant, and no place was more coveted than being accepted within our family. We wanted a role that was clearly defined but they kept changing the rules without communicating them to us. As I tried to find or define my role, I grew even more selfish.

My sister accepted me when I moved back home but I think there was a bit of a reservation as I was imposing on them and her relationship with Mom, and as I had abandoned them two years before. I also think she was looking for a reason to abandon me. I don't know what the scene was, whether it was a game or exercise of some sort, but there was this one instance that seemed to solidify the division between us years before when we were younger.

The question was posed as to whether I would be willing to donate a kidney to my sister if the need arose. Without hesitation I said "No." The selfish part of me answered, the one who wanted to survive answered the question. It was "Little Bobby" who answered. Of course, I would donate a kidney to my sister if she needed it but she didn't know this. She took this answer to heart. She immediately fell into a state of anger, she was understandably hurt, and no amount of convincing on my part could change her feelings or move her back to a place of trusting or believing her brother. This solidified the distance between us. We became even more fractured. While my mother and father used each of us in their own war and gladly taught us how to be at war with others, we turned on each other. It was now game on. It turned into decades of exhaustive one upping each other. It was disgusting and we had no shame with the depth at which we would go after one another. It was painful. Though far removed from one another now, the memories can still foster pain today.

We became adversaries much like our own mother and father. We took on their chemistry and took their plans for battle and tried carrying them out to the best of our ability with one goal. To destroy each other. This was to preserve whatever scraps were left on the table. Scraps in relationships and even resources in the family.

The self-hatred and self-loathing Mom had, and the extreme lack of conscience that Dad had, found a way of breeding into our relationship. That's the thing about spiritual sickness. It's like alcoholism. With the alcoholic every person within their sphere is affected in some way. We can't see this while it's happening and by the time we become fully aware of the damage caused by alcoholism the damage is rich. It knows no bounds.

Spiritually sick people pass on the same. They pass on their sickness, their darkness, without conscience, without awareness, of what they're doing, and this brings about a sickness within others. It all feeds into one another and new depths of spiritual depravity are experienced individually and collectively. Water seeks its own level in the stream of life. A sick person will make another sick person sicker, and that person will return their sickness in kind thereby trying to make the other even sicker. Together they will travel without knowing this but deep inside they may suspect that something is wrong. That it doesn't have to be this way. That there is something different. Perhaps they move to a place of remembering their own Honeysuckle Dream and reach a decision to make some sort of effort to get back to it. To get back to God.

Two sick people do not make the one well, whole. It is impossible. Simply impossible. However, one sick person and one well person can make the collective well. The adversary, one without faith, cannot become well if they hold onto the past, if they do not let go. The well person cannot continue to fully deepen their faith while tied to their past, tied to their resentments and fears. Tied to the sick person. Faith cannot flourish where resentment and fear, spiritual sickness, lives. Indeed, the well person might inspire the sick person to decide to let go but it is in the hands of the sick person to do the painful work of letting go. To stop leaving claw marks on everything.

I was indeed inspired by those people who recovered their faith by letting go of their resentments and fears. I came to see what they came to see and have had the privilege of working with others to see them break free. I came to see the abject futility of living a life of spiritual dysfunction and disconnect from God.

Our actions, our demonstration, will always speak louder than words and in this we find the essence of our story. Where are we working from? A place of hurt and division? Or a place of patience, love, tolerance, and kindness? When spiritually sick I had to work from a place of hate and division with a desire to maliciously hurt others. It was mind-boggling and simply ugly. It was dark. But as I became more and more spiritually fit, as my realization that I had failed completely, as I regained my faith and sought to deepen my faith, there was no longer a place within me for hate and division, for resentments and fears. They can't exist with any lasting effect.

Perhaps the ultimate goal of our existence is to find the strongest point in our faith with a continued effort to increase it thereby bringing about not only the power to withstand those extreme currents in the stream but also to withstand temptation. The temptation to play God. Isn't this the true essence of what resentment is? Our unrealized effort of trying to hold sway over another or a situation, to control, that leads to a failed endeavor at or intention of playing God. I believe resentments against ourselves, resentments towards others, ironically, are resentments toward God. They are an offense to God. They are a destructive force and have the power to not only kill faith or keep it in the dark but also the power to kill relationships. To take what was once sweet and turn it sour. They hold the power to kill our Honeysuckle Dream.

Twenty-Three

Who Is Responsible?

I walked into adulthood, an expected rite of passage when one reaches eighteen years, with all the terms and conditions from my family wrapped around me. I didn't want them anymore, but they were ingrained in me, they were a part of my constitution. "Little Bobby" dragged them behind him as he did that blanket that was cut into pieces when he was a small guy. As much as I detested it, I carried my childhood with me as well. What other choice did I have? I tried to hide it the best I could, tried to evade it the best I could, but it was impossible. I moved into adulthood with the madness that was my upbringing and became "Mad Bob." I graduated to a new level of madness and unconsciousness.

All that I had experienced became this mixture that persistently haunted me. It relentlessly lent its persuasion upon me and to a very little extent can do the same today. These experiences would ironically become the tissue out of which I would undergo the art of transformation. I wanted to return to the Honeysuckle Dream but didn't know how to.

As these elements of persuasion were added and embedded in me over time they brought about reactions from me. They brought varied efforts to cope with them. They held battles within to ensure their survival. Of course, there was an ignorance on my part about all of it. With time these elements began to bubble up from deep within. They resembled an old school coffee percolator that sits atop a stove. It begins to heat up, gets angry, but it's still a weak brew. With the applied pressure of heat, experiences, the brew takes on a new look, it gets darker. My nature did the same. Eventually the brew is done. In my case it was beyond done, bitter. It reaches its boiling point, and something needs to be done with it. It needs to be taken off from the heat or allowed to just sit there and dry up. I didn't know that I didn't know but the day came that I had to learn how to know. Or burn out.

I tried to cope and shift away from the reality of Mom and Dad, and their war, by chasing the feelings away with alcohol and drugs and it worked for a bit. When I got clean and sober all that I had tried to medicate within came back to me but on a grander scale. It hurt more than it did before I started with the alcohol and drugs. I had simply prolonged the facing of pain.

I came out of a thirty day stay at a posh rehab where I was dried out and weaned off all the drugs that I had been taking without any care or concern. In the end of the alcohol and drug abuse my goal was to check out, to leave this world. This became my "go to" as far as a solution. I felt these pulls before I began drinking and drugging, the wanting to die, but was too young to really entertain them in a cogent way.

Being clean and sober brought a sense of renewal to me for a bit. I felt refreshed and reborn physically and was genuinely happy to be free of the madness that came with the physical and mental sickness of it all. I believe my family did too. The thing about the use and abuse of alcohol and drugs, alcoholism and addiction, is that you can point a finger at something, a substance, and lay blame for situations and circumstances upon it. The real cause though is most times entirely ignored, blissfully ignored.

At the heart of all that was killing me before the madness of alcohol and drugs began was my lack of faith, my disconnect from God. Faith is perhaps the most valuable muscle that we have and perhaps the one that is most easily ignored, totally neglected at times. From the day I walked away from the Honeysuckle Dream my muscle of faith began deteriorating and the more and more I trusted in things human, including myself, the more and more the muscle suffered and fell into atrophy.

I came home from treatment and walked right back into the reality of my role in the family with all its attendant pain and suffering, including the pain and suffering I caused to Mom, Papa, and my sister. I believe it was difficult for them to forgive me. Even though one can point a finger at the substances to place blame, thereby trying to relieve the pain caused, the reality of the real cause is soon revealed. My character spoke volumes to those about me that indeed the problem wasn't the substances, those things outside of me, it was my character, governed by those things held deep within me. The resentments and fears. The alcohol and drugs were merely a symptom.

When I started drinking and drugging, I stopped growing. My emotional and social maturity came to a standstill. I simply stayed where I was. It's a weird thing that happens. It happened in my relationship with my father so many times over the years. Though I was eighteen when I came out of treatment the person that arrived back at Mom's house was in essence twelve years old. My stunted growth overshadowed the bliss that her son got clean and sober.

I dragged my childhood into my adulthood, but not only that, I was in essence a child trying to be and act like the adult. Of course, my family wholly expected me to be an adult. I expected myself to be an adult. It didn't go too well. In many respects Mom dragged her childhood into adulthood and didn't mature in many areas. She remained this little girl and her reactions in the stream of life to others and natural happenings about her showed this. I would do the same for many years as an adult. I would swing from "Little Bobby" to "Mad Bob" back to "Little Bobby."

We all carry our childhood with us but some of us hide it better than others while others seem to learn from it and transcend it better than others. I learned to do both. It took longer for me. A lot longer.

Without the benefit of medication, alcohol and drugs, I had no choice but to live in the hell of a constant review of my life. This always brought about anger from within, those resentments, and touched off the fears. I would be in a state of trying to adjust the sails and rudders as I navigated the stream of life as I grew older trying to understand everything. Everything about the past and everything about the now. What I couldn't do and wouldn't do for a great many years was take full responsibility for my part in any of it. It was far easier to keep pointing the finger at Mom and Dad as the cause.

While in high school with the madness deep within me, while experiencing a lack of faith that was detrimental, and using alcohol and drugs, I became violent. One night I locked myself in my bedroom to escape the reality about me after an argument with Mom and she had no choice but to call my father. She needed help. He answered this one time and came to the house. It was the visit I spoke of earlier, the "next time he would be inside our home" reference to being back in the house.

Though I grew to hate him there was still this false hope in me that was powered by the delusion that he might play the role of Dad one day. There was also a deep sense of fear about and inside of me. The fear of not getting what I wanted. I'll go to this in a bit.

Dad showed up and demanded that I open my bedroom door. It was barricaded with whatever furniture I had in my room. I refused to open the door, and he became enraged at me. He threw the door open with the weight of his body and came at me. I fell onto my bed as he landed on top of me with a clenched fist. I don't remember his words; I remember the fist. I remember the trembling in it. I remember the white knuckles. I remember the energy of his anger and pain. I remember his powerlessness as a human being over another human being. I remember his effort to exercise some control over another and a situation.

Then it stopped. He didn't punch me. He didn't do what his father had done to him. He stopped in his tracks. I'll never know why as it was never spoken of again. I never asked him why he did it or why he didn't do it. He never told me why he did it or why he didn't do it. It just stopped when I screamed and began crying. I tried to communicate my pain realized out of the madness that was my family at this very moment. I was always trying to do this. The pain was as constant as my never-ending reflections.

An appointment was made to see a psychiatrist at the local hospital that specialized in the treatment of adolescents. It was a hospital associated with the same hospital my mother sought treatment at following the loss of my brother. When I told one of my schoolmates about this appointment, he made the comment "So you're a fruit cup."

I met Linda Bell and began to tell her my story. She listened without judgment and wanted Mom and Dad to sit in on one of the sessions. They agreed and the three of us sat in a small sterilized-looking room with her as she began sharing her assessment of where I was at and what needed to be done. I was already using alcohol and drugs as a medication to cope, something she didn't know. Thankfully she made no suggestion that I be placed on prescribed medications. The day would come well after this time when I would seek treatment by medication.

Her assessment was harsh for my mother and father. She placed all that I was experiencing and all my reactions to what I was experiencing squarely in their lap, more so in my father's lap. She tried to hold them accountable. My mother softened a bit and took it to heart. She began to open to me about her struggles and pain. My father did the opposite. What little was left between us in conversation or communication abruptly ended. When we were together, alone or in the company of others, we were empty shells to one another.

Weekly appointments were set up for me to continue seeing Linda, to continue my treatment. My father would be the one to take me to the appointments. My mother was not a part of this and threw the responsibility on him. These were some of the most painful moments that he and I spent with one another.

They took place after his wife told me to get out and there were layers and layers of unspoken words between us. We never ever discussed life or what happened. The rides to and from the appointments were done in silence. I wanted to scream and yell, to tell him exactly what I was thinking, to express what I was feeling. I really believe that he wanted to do the same, but his own body of pain forbade him from doing so. As he drove me home from the appointments, I could feel his energy and his confusion. I could feel his inability to communicate. I could feel his pain as he struggled with his own balance of trying to cope with reality. I could see and feel his effort to remain unconscious.

My parents and family wanted me to behave and to live by a set of principles superior to theirs, superior to those they were living by. Their expectations were that I would practice self-discipline and be better at it than they were. It was impossible for me to do it. I was truly limited by what was before me, by what my teachers, my family, were not only telling me in words but by what they were showing me by action. My father was clearly showing me how to be a Dad and it wasn't hitting the mark, it was all over the place. There was a part of me deep within that made the promise that if ever I had the opportunity to be a father I would be doing it differently. I would try everything in my power to stop the generational pain and generational trauma.

The desire of wanting to flip the script was born out of the chaos that was my relationship with my father. Out of the ashes that was this relationship came the willingness to learn to be different no matter the cost even if this cost meant letting relationships die, letting them fall be the wayside. There has always been great fear in this for me.

I have always placed a dependence on relationships, especially with my mother and father as sick as these relationships were, and even with my sister to some extent. There was a fear of letting them go, a fear about taking the realization and fact that they weren't healthy and doing something about them. These relationships were covered with those "claw marks."

Though the most dominating fear that truly guided my life, all the thoughts, emotions, and attitudes I carried with me was the fear of abandonment there seem to be just two fears. When fear is reduced to its lowest form of understanding I see the two of them clearly. The fear of not getting what I want, and the fear of losing what I already have.

As sick as I was, I became accustomed to being parented in the manner that Mom and Dad passed on and in some sick way as I craved and wanted more, I was happy to live on the scraps. I did this because I was afraid of losing even this. This was coupled with the constant fear of not getting what I wanted, which was more in the way of parenting.

Though these two fears are always at the base of all fears. The others that arise out of them are equally destructive. They were a force that created reactions in me that I never understood. The sicker I became with these fears, always exacerbated by resentment, the more I set out to relieve myself of them and this always hurt me. In many ways it hurts those about me. There were times when I set out and intentionally hurt others as I was hurt. The more hurt I felt the more I set out to create pain around me. I tried to bring others to my level. I got caught up in the hurt people hurt people and as I was broken, I tried to break those about me.

Even though I could return to my friend and tell him that the shrink told me I was not the fruit cup, that it was my parents, I was in truth not without blame or responsibility. I had to take full responsibility for myself, and my actions born out of the chaos as I grew older. I had to learn to let go.

Twenty-Four

Spiritual Thirst

There are three parts that make up my being. My body, my mind, and my spirit. When one of them is suffering the other two are naturally affected. The other two will always suffer as a consequence. My body and mind began to decay as my spirit suffered from its disconnect from God and my lack of faith. Of course, there was this part of me that always wanted to check out and never thought I would make it past the age of fifty. Even at the highest and best moments in my life there was always the desire to check out. I simply didn't want to be here.

A few years back I contracted Covid and became ill. I wasn't hospitalized yet I spent ten days on the couch in a fog. It felt like that time long ago when I had bronchitis. Eventually I recovered but the effects were pretty mind-blowing. I sought help from my primary doctor in finding a remedy and he sent me to a specialist, an endocrinologist. She was nothing short of brilliant with me. Being a scientist and wanting to learn her interest in my case was inspiring to me. She also has this way about her. She has this ability to tell you the straight and hard truth with a bedside manner loaded with compassion. She basically told me that my body was in terrible shape and that I needed to do something about it.

To remedy this, I began working with a trainer at his gym and began to see results. For the guy who spent most of his life without an interest in self-care or a desire to live I'm now at the gym nearly every day taking care of the vessel that God gave me. The vessel that houses the light God gave me. I have truly come to believe in the absolute synergy that takes place between body, mind and spirit.

One day my wife and I stopped at the juice bar attached to the gym and I ran into a fellow event professional while there. She was working out and I hadn't seen her in quite some time. As we exchanged pleasantries and tried to catch up with one another I shared that I spend time at the gym daily and pointed to our trainer expressing that he was so instrumental in bringing me back to life. She commented "You've been brought back to life so many times." It was a profound statement to me. It was truthful.

I shared with her that I was writing again, writing this book, and she was happy to hear that there was going to be a follow up to the first book. She expressed that she was at the gym to repair the damage that having three children caused to her body. I told her it wasn't damaged; it was their gift to her.

We all see things through a lens that is focused by the depths of our experiences. Our vision is either clouded with resentments and fear, the insane need to be in control, or by faith, a simple trust and reliance on Something Bigger than us. My experience has shown me that there is no middle of the road here. I'm either trying to play God, ruled by fear and resentment, or I'm obeying God, trusting and relying on Him and His Plan. I believe we all leave the Honeysuckle Dream and at that exact moment our spiritual thirst begins. We then spend so long looking outside of ourselves seeking to quench this thirst. We spend so long looking in the wrong places.

I've found that the depth of my past, the good and the bad, became the height of my future and all I needed to do was make a decision to seek God. While I wallowed in depression and tried to oppress my thoughts and feelings it would be the opposite, the expression of these, that would make room for God to be let in. I had to take responsibility; I had to do the work of uncovering that piece of Light installed within me. I've come to see that I never needed to *add* anything to my life, that I already had everything I needed deep within. What I really needed to do was subtract a lot from my life, I had to *remove* some stuff.

This required a willingness, a willingness to want something different. This willingness would be inspired by what became a series of bottoms in my life. It was inspired by a great many highs in my life. As I moved into adulthood and tried to move away from the destructive forces of the generational pain, I spent a great deal of time searching for a solution. Many hours sitting on couches before therapists. Many hours spent speaking with those who had similar experiences. Many hours spent reading self-help books while seeking different philosophies and persuasions that might work. All this only created temporary relief. Although the relief was not lasting it did eventually bring me the understanding that there was a part of me that needed to die. Needed to be let go of.

I simply had to put all of this to rest. I had to let it all go and I had to fully accept the entirety that was my life. I had to let go of the expectations and the false narrative, the delusions. I had to let go of what I was brought to believe in that was born out of the false narrative. I had so many of these ideas that were cemented within me, at my core, and they needed to be broken up and sifted through. They needed to be examined in a way that might bring about an ability to return to God. The question was, has always been, how? How do I do this?

For many years I thought that if I did the opposite of what my parents did, I would succeed where they had failed but this didn't work for me. As I walked into my first marriage that I had so much hope for I truly believed that I could be a better husband. Better than my father was to my mother, better than he was to Pat. I thought that if I did the opposite of what had been done to me by my parents as a child with my own children then I would be a success as a parent. I was wrong. So very wrong.

I brought my childhood, my security blanket, with me. It was all doomed to fail as I tried to live by and in the shadow of so many resentments and fears. For years I tried to play God and as my friend Big Ed once told me I looked like a fool when I was trying to wear His shirt. He told me God's shirt would never fit me. It was simply too big for me.

I was introduced to a variety of twelve steps programs by the treatment facility and by different therapists over the years and tried to make use of what they offered but could never quite get the full gist of what was there in the way of a solution. The premise with them and with many other persuasions and philosophies is that if we are to be truly free, we must not only accept the reality of life but need to let go absolutely. To move from a place of self-reliance and reliance on others, a form of human aid, to a place of trusting and relying on God, the opposite of human aid. My difficulty in this has always been in relinquishing control and the way I held onto the control was by never facing and being rid of the resentments and fears. How do you let go of that which has become your absolute center in life? Your misaligned purpose?

For many this is a monumental feat. Mine would come at the hands of some harsh realizations in failure. After years of trying to be the *opposite* I arrived at a place where I saw and felt this solution was indeed a failure. Acting "as if" didn't work. I arrived at a place where the only solution to my problems would be God's Grace and my willingness to accept it.

Twenty-Five

Finding Our Purpose

Would you believe me if I told you that every one of us has a defined purpose? That each moment and nuance experienced and felt while engaged in the stream of life was divinely designed for you? Would you believe me if I told you that each moment's arrival at its next arrival included messages within that leads to our discovery of our individual purpose? That even these layers of experiences and messages add to the overall message for all of us as a whole? Would you believe me if I told you that indeed you have a destiny to reach while here outside of the role of just surviving, that we are all capable of so much more than this? That we are all capable of thriving?

If you're in the position that I was in when I entered adulthood, a position I held onto for dear life because I was afraid to let go of it and afraid of God, for a great many years while an adult, at least until I was near forty-five, I'd truly understand if you said that everything in that previous paragraph was impossible. I once truly believed it amounted to a lofty dream.

I believe that when I turned away from the Honeysuckle

Dream, turned my back on my still infantile faith, turned my back on God, the search for my purpose began. The search for my role while alive and breathing began. Though I spent a great part of my life wanting to check out, to leave, to die, there was still something in me that would not give up. Real hope seemed to make its way to the surface at the times I entertained wrapping my vehicle around the telephone pole I picked out; around the telephone pole I would often visit. Real hope, a fundamental and infantile idea of God, of Something More, always came to the forefront of my being as I dry-fired a pistol up the side of my head or into the roof of my mouth practicing my exit from this world. I suppose you could say it wasn't my time yet. That there was a purpose for my life. That indeed there was a reason for me to back away from that cliff and to keep trying to surmount the nastiness of self-hatred and self-loathing within.

We all have a story. We'd hardly be human if we didn't because in fact this is a part of the human experience. It is simply the way it is. For years I truly believed that my story was unique, no one else felt the way I did, no one else wanted out as badly as I did. No one was as lost or as confused as I was. Being the type who had not only a sensitive arrangement about me but the inability to see past myself with the selfishness and self-centeredness created by a separation from God and my early life experiences I simply couldn't see other people's stories. I was afraid to look at them because I didn't have the resources of strength to see or deal with more than my own.

I did find my purpose and I'll share that it hasn't a thing to do with me. Not in the least. The life I live today is absolutely brilliant and the freedom from the bondages of the past are amazing. As a result of the freedoms, I'm allowed to share my story freely, without fear, in the hope that just one person might experience their own awakening and movement home toward God.

When I was a young kid at the age of twelve, I had the dilemma of still being a virgin. Hell, I didn't know this was a problem or that I had this problem. I wasn't aware of the problem until this young teenage girl who moved into my neighborhood pointed it out. She said she could solve this problem, and I agreed to let her.

Fantastic right? I got the bit of my whip worked up in another way and I was off. Here's the thing that happened. As I felt tossed aside and was already looking for a place to fit in, I was also seeking to be found. I was looking for my purpose. Naturally I was seeking love as what I had at home seemed to be anything but that. From the very first time I equated sex with love. I equated love with sex. I couldn't wait to do it again as it was in fact like a drug for me. It transported me away from reality and allowed me to pull my canoe out of the stream for a bit and rest ashore. It was a fabulous summer of learning for me. When it came to an end it hurt like a son of a bitch. It was that abandonment thing all over again.

And so, this equating sex as love and love as sex went on for quite a few years, even into my first marriage. It arrived again later in life when it took me into a relationship with a woman twice my age. I think I was looking for Mommy at this point, or a wild escape while clean and sober. It made an appearance as I experienced sexual abuse at the hands of a man. It even arrived one day as I became an abuser. I took it with me into every relationship whether I was the aggressor or the victim. The baser instinct in my life was as misaligned as my heart and mind were.

I learned to seek escape in relationships. Mom always said she was more attracted to my father's family and the idea of having a large family than she was to my father. In many ways I did the same thing. My first wife's family was a large family, she had four siblings, and her mother and father were still together. We started seeing one another in high school. We were two inexperienced teenagers. I was looking to escape my family, and she seemed to be accepting of hers. I wanted to be a part of her family where acceptance seemed to be a component. I wanted this safety and stability. We came from different ends of the economic spectrum, and I also wanted the element of economic security in my life. I reasoned that she came from the place of "haves" and I from the place of "have nots." I wanted the opposite of what I had grown up with.

Eventually we married and my goal was to *not* be like my father with the hope that she wouldn't be like my mother. Our daughter was born in the afternoon on yet another one those not a cloud in the sky sunny days and I remember walking downstairs after holding her and walking past the families while announcing that she was here, and that she and her mother were both fine. My stride never faltered; I kept walking.

I walked out of the hospital doors and looked up into the heavens. I was clean and sober, and my head was as clear as it could be at this moment. The storm within was quiet on this day and I felt hope for the future. With this hope I gazed into the sun and petitioned God. I literally begged him to "please let me do a better job than was done with me." Perhaps it was part of the answering of this prayer that allowed me to tell you my story now with the hope that together we get to move to a place of higher consciousness and faith. We never know the how and when of a prayer's answer. I have come to know that a petition offered without selfishness and with humility is always answered.

The marriage lasted a couple of years after nearly ten years of tumultuous times together that matched the worst storms in my life. With the place I was in and with the level of damage within me coupled with the depth of self-hatred and loathing, there was never any hope for success in this relationship. It never had a chance like I felt I never had a chance while growing up. No chance at all. Self-hatred and loathing not only fueled my lack of conscience, it blocked my ability to care for others.

My daughter was born when I was a few years clean and sober. I had been clumsily trying to find God and a purpose for living but kept falling short. As I looked into her eyes, I knew I had to find Him and find Him fast otherwise I was going to pass on the damage. I didn't want to pass on the generational trauma and didn't want to be put in the position of abandoning my own child through ignorance. To say my first born changed my life is an absolute understatement. It changed the course of my life. I called a therapist a short time after she was born.

My first epiphany after Madison was born arrived in the form of a few questions I would ask myself but really wanted to direct at Dad. "How can you walk away from a child that is yours? How can you toss them aside as though they are worthless?"

My second epiphany seemed to confirm what I had lost so many years before. That God is real. That the moment I experienced before the honeysuckle was not a part of the delusions I lived and that it could be experienced as an adult.

I have searched my entire life for where I was supposed to fit in and for my purpose, but that search has always been on a human level, a three-dimensional level. It wasn't until I experienced the innocence of my daughter's arrival that I began to search for and experience the Fourth Dimension, the spiritual side of life. It is in this dimension, the layer of life not seen and often easily ignored or dismissed, that I was not only found but where I found my purpose. This is where my tour has not only been the most magical and mysterious.

It has been miraculous.

Twenty-Six

Not Fade Away

I have tried nearly my entire life to evade realities and feelings that hurt me. None more so than those that emanated out of my family and most especially the fear of abandonment. As they would arise so did the nightmare attached to them. A nightmare is defined as a terrifying dream in which the dreamer experiences feelings of helplessness, extreme anxiety, sorrow, etc. This was exactly what I lived daily, and it moved me to living the most colorful defects in character while experiencing a constant weakening of any moral fibers that were instilled in me.

While you might think that everything in my life was bad, and that all my experiences were bad, they were not. There were many sweet moments loaded with pieces of healthy direction by family members in my life when, at times, they were able to lay aside their generational trauma. The reality is that these healthy elements weren't strong enough to overcome or overshadow the constant nightmare that is the inevitable result of living in a constant state of resentment and fear.

As I grew older, I tried with every ounce of my will to

move away from the nightmare. I tried to lessen its effect on me so I might be, or even feel, better. So I might be able to live fully without the constant drag of the nightmare. In hindsight I came to see that my approach was all wrong. I always thought that I had some kind of power over the nightmare, but I didn't. My power simply wasn't enough. Exposing the nuances and implications that held sway over me through therapy helped but only to a certain degree. I needed to embrace the nightmare, not run away from it.

As therapies brought a bit of understanding to the fears and the feelings that I experienced over and over and over it never really lessened them. I would try to remove myself from the family, I would go dark at times for long periods. This seemed to help a bit too, but it was another mechanism, method, of evasion. I was still trying to run away. This nightmare was rooted deep within me, and it wasn't having anything to do with my efforts to evict it. There were moments when I felt as though I had triumphed over the fears, felt as though I had the upper hand, but they too were short lived. It felt like the nightmare faded in strength at times, as though I lost it and its effects as I tried to navigate the newer realities in my life while growing older and into adulthood.

The fact of the matter is that the nightmare remained, still remains today, and it also became an evader of sorts. It would hide within me to ensure *its* survival. And when it needed to feel relevant or exercise its persuasion on me it came out of hiding and began to rule me and my character. It never seems to end.

Of course, the benefit of time weakens things in our lives. Helps them fade away and lose their power, but the fear of abandonment is always present in some form. It was always the *reminders* all around me that would reactivate it. And when these presented themselves in my life I would fall back.

I would fall back to being "Little Bobby." The little one who never healed. I would then approach life from that angle and most times disaster would follow.

The times that I withdrew from the family were spent trying to throw things away. Just as I snapped the elf in half and tossed it across the room, I would throw away any reminder. If I looked upon something that pulled me back to the nightmare or brought the nightmare to the forefront of reality, I quickly tossed it away. I don't have one picture of myself as a child. The last one that I held onto for many years was torn in half and tossed away like the elf was.

When Mom moved out of Blaine Street and into Papa's house across the city a great many things landed in his basement from our house. When there was a fire in Papa's house, and they were forced to leave for a bit so it could be repaired the contractor had a large roll-off dumpster brought to the house to accommodate the debris from the demolition work. I remember going into the basement on another one of those not a cloud in the sky sunny days and seeing the furniture. I wanted to puke; this was my physical reaction to seeing the furniture from my childhood home. The drawers still held many of the items that were there 20 years before when my father left us.

With the instant return of the nightmare, I grew angry. I felt this familiar energy from within that typically brought some kind of violence with it. I opened the bulkhead, and the sun smashed through the darkness and musty smell of the basement. I picked up the first piece of furniture and tossed it into the dumpster after looking at the contents of the drawers. The many pictures of what once was that I always hoped would return. As I reviewed these, I grew angrier, and I continued to toss everything into the dumpster watching it smash into pieces. I cleared the basement and filled the dumpster with any reminder of the past as if this was enough to end the madness. It was a physical effort to change the stream of life. It didn't work. I couldn’t even think of asking my mother or sister if they were okay with me tossing it all away.

It took me time, but I've come to see that violence is a physical reaction to not getting my way or getting what I want. A form of control, most times over others or circumstances. It is indeed a form of playing God. I’ve also come to see that most of the pain I experience in my body can be directly related to my spiritual or mental status.

The reality was sinking in that my father was gone and was never going to return to any type of consciousness, and this disgusted me. As the reality that I was now a father sank in I landed at a new place. With the *hope* that the fears and nightmares would fully fade away I began to see that I might be a better father and husband. I took on the "I'll show you, I'll do better" attitude. And I threw every ounce of my self-will at it.

I would do anything in my power to not be like my father.

Beg, borrow, or steal I would be better.

I did beg. I did borrow. And indeed, I did steal.

I had it all wrong though. I was trying to force something, a baser instinct of the lower self, instead of allowing it to happen as intended, a place of trusting in the higher self. I became a control freak trying to hold sway over people, places, and things. I kept trying to fill the God shirt.

When Mom's first grandchild, my daughter, was born Mom was reborn with her. She came back to life somewhat. She seemed to be placed in a different position. It was like the dream she had of having a big family might still have a chance of being through her own children. She had a wonderful bond with each of my three children, but she experienced the same drag of fear and resentment and to a great extent still dragged her nightmare along with her. She now had a new role as I had a new role. I had the privilege of being a Dad and she had the privilege of being called "Nana."

As much as each of us tried to evade the realities of our past and tried to embrace these new roles by letting the past simply fade away it was impossible. It wouldn't fade away.

I would try to navigate adulthood, and now fatherhood, from a child's perspective as this is where my level of maturity was. As I journeyed through the stream of life there were constant reminders that brought to the forefront of my sight the fears and resentments I lived, and used, as a power to muscle through life.

I still carried the false hope that Dad might show up one day to express his regret, to express how wrong he was. I tried at any given moment to hold him to account. As I played the role of father and as my daughter got older, I actually became more enraged. I remained the mad son. Time was not sunsetting the resentment and fear; the nightmare was having the opposite effect on me.

On one occasion I drove out to The Cape with my daughter and thought to pick up a box of Rice Krispies and some marshmallows. I had the idea that perhaps my father would engage and make Rice Krispy Treats with his granddaughter. He wasn't incredulous but he surely had very little interest in being a part of my plan. He laughed at it.

I truly believed that with the birth of his first grandchild, not one of his stepdaughter's children, he would have this amazing epiphany and would come running to see her. I thought he might soften and want to embrace the new role with the same passion Mom and I had taken ours on with. It never happened though it did create yet another false hope within me.

This seemed to crush me, and I still felt as though I couldn't tell anyone my secrets because I thought they might take their love away, but the reality was that I didn't need to tell anyone my secrets. You could see them in my eyes. You could feel them in my energy. I began to carry this sense of defeat with me in a heavier manner.

Papa liked to go out to dinner on a Friday night and the invitation to join him was always open to anyone who wanted to join. There were many nights when it was just he and Mom and on occasion I would pop in and sit with them for a while. One night I stopped at "The Post" and sat down. I didn't want to eat; I just came to say hello and to visit with them. I had developed this inability to sit still for long periods as if the monsters from the nightmare might catch up to me if I didn't keep moving.

Mom could tell something was amiss with me; she could always see straight into me and through me. When she asked, I told her I was fine. She wasn't buying it and pressed me. I didn't want to share it. I knew Papa wasn't having anything to do with it and I knew as he was one Manhattan into dinner his reaction would be far different than hers.

I gave in and expressed my continued disappointment with my father as his son while now being a father myself. Papa's response to this was a mind blower for me and held instruction within it. He very rarely shared memories of his childhood with us. When he did share any of them, they were the uplifting moments. At this moment, he had reached the point in his life, the age in his life, the maturity in his life, the understanding in his life, where all that he had experienced with the generational trauma seemed to have faded away. Though the memories were there he had acquired a great understanding of what would take me another thirty years to see and understand. Mom and I were not there yet. We couldn't fathom living without the fears and resentments yet, without the nightmare. He was in the place of total acceptance.

"Yeah well at least you didn't have to rip your drunken

father off of your sisters like I had to."

Mom and I sat there speechless. Though the restaurant was a swirl of activity and loud noise you could hear a pin drop at our table and at that moment time stood still. Absolutely still. I could feel it. I wanted to hear more about this, but Papa wasn't giving it up. He put it back into one of his own compartments. Perhaps he shared it to stop the direction of the conversation, this I will never know, but it showed me that we all carry something from the previous generation that is freely handed to us. It is our responsibility to see and understand it and perhaps make the effort to stop it. To try something different.

As much as these words brought with them some pain and sent the lesson that I must choose my words carefully it also brought the lesson that there is a time and place to speak of reality and then there is a time and place where I mustn't speak of reality. I also learned one other awakening from the nightmare with my visit.

My personal responsibility of flipping the script and making the effort to stop the generational trauma appeared when my daughter was born. I didn't know this at the time. It would be revealed as I grew into being a Dad and Husband, as I experienced more in life and travelled further along the stream.

Years later, as Papa was nearing the end of his life, he and I were sitting together in the living room at my sister's house. We were watching the news. Our country was at war, and we were listening to the latest happenings. Any mention of war touched Papa deeply as he proudly served in the Pacific Theater during World War II.

As I looked over at him, he had a tear rolling down his cheek. I asked him what was wrong. I thought maybe he was in pain from the cancer or was having difficulty breathing. It wasn't this at all.

He said he didn't think he was leaving this place in better shape than when he got here. This was a profound statement born out of what I rightly imagine was his own personal review. I protested this statement and told him he was so damn wrong. That indeed his place here and his demonstration in my life changed me and made me a better person. That my Mom, sister, and I, and by extension our children, would have been truly lost without him.

Perhaps some of us can have a monumental effect on others but most times we are that pebble that is dropped into the water. We create ripples that emanate outward from us and touch the lives of others. We do change the nature of the stream, and most times haven't the benefit of knowing how. A few words. Maybe a few actions. Whatever it is, it is felt and seen and has an effect not only on us but on others as well.

I believe our gift to God is to allow the fears and resentments, the nightmare, to fade away after coming to an understanding of them and an understanding of how destructive they are, especially to our connection to Him. Our gift to God is to not only find our purpose but to carry it out in a constant manner. Perhaps the nightmare doesn't fully fade away and remains to simply remind us of how far we have come, thereby inspiring us to go even farther. Inspiring us to move away from a life propelled by self-will to a life lived by God's will, by God's Grace.

Twenty-Seven

I Am You; I Am Not You

As I entered adulthood there were two other things that I took with me. The drive to never repeat what had happened to me. I failed at this one. The other being the remnants of that childhood faith mixed with a bit of hope. This kept me alive, kept me moving forward. Would you believe that from the time I moved into my first apartment as a young adult it would take me north of twenty-five years to learn how to let go of the fear of abandonment? Even then the coming to understanding of how spirituality can work remained elusive for a bit.

Over the years I was shown pieces of Light that kept the faith and hope in me alive. The hope that I might get free from the madness that began with my separation from God. I did everything in my limited power to transcend the pain and suffering and there was the rub. When one is suffering the malaise of spiritual disease and has drifted into a false reality with a narrative that keeps them from seeing the truth of what really happened, the cause, then this same person falsely believes that they have the power to repair the severed connection to God. This was the solution I chased for years to no avail. The self-propelled and self-willed effort to fix myself with the hope that I could change it all. The past, the present, and the future. I was so wrong.

In truth there was this insidious thing inside of me, call it ego, the lower self, whatever makes sense and works for you of course. What I found was that this *thing* exercised a sway and impression upon me that fed into the opposite of faith, the opposite of trust in God, the opposite of hope. Instead of a real faith in God I had a fractured faith in myself born out of chaos. Instead of trusting in God I trusted wholly in myself because in a deep way I held God in contempt for the station I had been brought up in. Instead of a real hope born out of faith and trust I became powered by false hopes, they were attached to and empowered by the delusion.

I attempted to separate myself from the family, and at times, specific members of my family, so often over the years. I believed the problem would be solved in this way. I attempted to separate myself from my past each time a memory or resentment made an appearance or made itself known as well. But when I thought I had succeeded and reached my new destination I found that I had brought myself, and my luggage, my baggage, with me. There was no escape from any of it. There were only brief moments of relief.

I continued to fail at realizing my dream of being a different person for a great many years. I spoke of wanting a different life, of wanting a different life for my children, and made an agreement with myself that I would do anything to achieve this end. Beg, borrow, or steal I knew I had to make it happen, had to break this cycle of generational trauma. I added more drama instead. Living a life of delusion allows one to live without principles or conscience, most times it requires it. The result of this indeed added to the tragedy in the play I was trying to direct.

I fought with my family as a whole and with certain family members for years always with the goal of getting them to take responsibility for their ways while trying to evade my own responsibility. I tried to live a principled life by living in an opposite way and the failure of this effort led to even deeper confusions, more questions, deeper resentments, an increase in fears, and of course self-loathing. I tried to put a mask on it all and continued to compartmentalize the ever-growing catalog of perceived injustices.

My life became this long hallway with rooms to the left and to the right. At the end of this hall was another door, the last door. This one was rimmed with a Light at its edges that seemed to want to burst through and wash down the hall. Behind the doors on either side of the hall were periods of my life that held memories hostage. Memories riddled with resentments and fears. Most of the doors were locked. Some of them had yellow tape across them reading "Do Not Enter." Some were chained up while still others had trip wires with grenades attached to them. I was the only one who held the keys to these doors, the only one who could open them and let the Light in.

I remained lost in this hallway until I exhausted every ounce of energy within me. I tended to this place, guarded this place, at all times, with the fear that you might see what I was hiding. In other words, I tended to the mask I wore with the greatest care. You weren't getting in; I wouldn't let you in. I was afraid to let you in, to let you know me, because you might leave. You might abandon me. Always the fear of abandonment at the forefront of the other fears that closely followed it.

I relived my parents' nightmare in my first marriage. I entered it with all the hope one has with new beginnings. Hope for the perfect relationship where I played the role of husband in the most ideal way. I couldn't do it. Hope for a perfect relationship with a child where I played the role of father in the most ideal way. I couldn't do it. I didn't have the resources within me. I tried though. I had the ideal in my mind but didn't have the experience or even the experiences of others to draw upon. Nor did I have the power.

My family always had those terms and conditions but never shared them, you had to guess what they were and hope you got it right. I remember thinking I never ever wanted to lay these conditions on my children. I also didn't want them to see or feel love with conditions attached to it. One night as I was trying to convince my three-year-old daughter to go to sleep. I told her "If you go to sleep I will ..."

There it was. A condition. My attempt at conditioning another to do as I pleased. I would take this element of my nature to the extreme. I remember what my ex-wife said to me in the most sarcastic and spiteful way after she heard me say it. *"You said you would never put conditions on our daughter."* She was right. And with this failure I felt the failure, the powerlessness over the mayhem inside of me against the desire to be better. The desire to be the perfect husband and father. The fact of the matter is that it is indeed impossible to be perfect in our roles. The perfection lies within the imperfection and the perfection is seeing the imperfection and learning from it, taking responsibility for it.

My first marriage ended as quickly as it began. As I went through the separation and battle for the custody of my daughter Mom was always there. She sat on the sidelines watching. Not only watching but now reliving her own divorce and it cut her like a knife. I think she wanted the same as I. I think she held within her the same as I. She wanted to see a perfect marriage. She also had the mustard seed-sized piece of hope that things could be different. The divorce seemed to crush that hope.

Mom relived the pain and suffering of her life over and

over but never more so than through my first marriage and to some extent through my second. Mom found it impossible to let the past go, as I did, for many years. She was constantly bringing up the past, reminding me of it, while I was trying to shut the door to it. This always threw me off. My divorce was in truth doing the same to her. It was bringing all that she tried to evade and placing it before her. There were times when her reactions matched those that she had had so many years before. She took sides with my ex and held me in the same contempt she held my father in, and this cut me like a knife. The last thing I ever wanted was to be compared to my father, to be held in the same light.

The reality is that I am my mother. I am my father. I am my family. There seems to be this code embedded within me that carries all the details of our pasts. I suppose the trick in life is to break this code. Maybe by breaking it we do get to flip that script. My life has always been the balance of trying to break free, trying to uphold a code I knew very little about with an obligation to protect family secrets, and the need to not make waves in the family while creating the wildest tidal wave possible while screaming "Something is wrong here!"

As I continued, trying to navigate the stream of life, I made incremental progress at uncovering and exposing the delusions and had some more of those aha moments along the way. I also made some promises to myself, some of which I would never be able to follow through with as they didn't come close to matching God's plan. The self-willed promises versus the God-willed promises.

Following the failure of my first marriage I remember walking on the beach with my daughter. As we held hands, I felt that this was all I needed in life. I made the promise to myself that I would never marry again. I had my daughter during the week while she spent weekends with her mother. I could be the responsible Dad during the week and live anyway I wanted to on the weekends. I'm not sure of this but I think that when I promised myself to never marry again, I heard laughter in the heavens. Perhaps it was Nana who was devising a plan to send me the one who would teach me the essence of unconditional love or perhaps it was even God who scoffed and thought "Silly child."

I navigated life and the stream as best as I could always striving to be a better person, a better man, a better Dad. I also tried as best I could to recover my connection to God. The renewed search for Him began when I got clean and sober, and I *intuitively* knew that this was the answer to all my problems. The search was hindered by the belief that I had to look outside of myself. I didn't know that the search had to take place within. I didn't know that I had to walk down that hall and open the doors. I didn't know that I had to sift through the resentments and fears, the blocks, and come to a full understanding of my failure. My failure in power and the dilemma that it always presented. A dilemma that began and came to be when I left the Honeysuckle Dream.

My second wife, Mia, appeared in my life shortly before I separated from my first wife. Ironically my first wife introduced me to her. She was in fact married and had a daughter. As couples we spent time together as did our daughters. We were all close. Although I became separated from my wife, I held the belief that we would get back together. It was a false hope and an effort to evade my senses, and the truth, of what was before me. Delusional thoughts guided by the false narrative that it was impossible for me to fail to have a successful marriage. As I expressed my false hope and delusion it would be Mia who told me the hard truth about the relationship. I thought I knew everything about it and upon hearing the truth that my wife was seeing someone else I knew my first marriage was over. The delusion had been smashed. Years later I would have to do the same thing with every other delusion about life that I held. They would have to be smashed by the truth.

A short time later Mia separated from her husband and when she told me this was going to happen, I implored her to try to work it out. I knew the effects my parents' divorce had on me and was already afraid of the effects my divorce was going to have on my daughter. I didn't want her daughter to experience the same. No words could stop their divorce from happening. As I grew away from my wife and she grew away from her husband we grew closer and closer as friends.

Mia was the first person who ever showed genuine care for me in the way of seeing my defectiveness in character and even the defectiveness in my thinking without judging it. At times I have arrived at the thought that she saw me as "a project that might be repaired." The day she shared those truths about what she knew about my marriage to smash my delusions she shared so much more with me. She showed me that love is real. Caring for others is real. That love and care can be extended in an unselfish manner and wholly without condition or motive. There was absolutely nothing in it for her to be gained by taking the chance to try to guide me and awaken me.

Our relationship was born out of the essence of one soul caring for another without any reason other than to be helpful. Helpful without any conditions. This moment in my life ran contrary to all the others that preceded it. Sure, there were fleeting moments in my family when this happened, but they were overshadowed by the mayhem and chaos. They held no real value or lasting effect on me. This one did.

From the very beginning she always inspired me to want to be a better man but more importantly had the energy and will to support this. She had faith in me that I could transcend the madness within and more importantly she had a faith far bigger than that of a mustard seed. And the greatest thing about faith is that it indeed can move mountains. Or another person to a new station in their life. It can bring about a change in vision and inspire the hope deep within that is a natural part of faith.

We were friends before anything else and though we didn't know it at the time this was born out of faith. Faith in God and faith in one another. Mia ripped my mask off and tossed it aside. Although I would try to pick it up over and over again, she would continue to tear it off and kick it away. She also stood before me many times without any words and simply held the keys to all the doors that lined the hallway making up all the periods in my life. I didn't know she had found the keys but was glad to have someone willing enough to stand beside me while I journeyed back in time to smash delusions brought on by spiritual illness while unlocking the doors.

This began the period that became the beginning of the death of my ego. A new beginning that marked another ending. And as the ego dies the soul awakens. The soul can be repaired and prepared for greater things and experiences. The dark night of the soul is necessary, and enlightening.

Twenty-Eight

Your Life Is Not Yours

The hydrangea plant and flower are one of my favorites and as a floral designer they are a basic staple in my work. I use hundreds of them each week. It has always fascinated me how their color is determined. We have them planted all around our yard and from time to time I move them as they get bigger or to make room for new plantings. What gave pink flowers while planted in one area now produces blue or lavender flowers in another area. The color is determined by the nature of the soil the hydrangea is planted in. The levels of acidity and alkalinity create this miracle. The same holds true for us.

The family soil we are planted in will determine what is produced. My family's soil was not rich with nutrients, it held a vast broadcast of toxins. These toxins became the tissue of my life out of which I tried to not only break free but also tried to work against in an opposite direction. It is often said that "a leopard never changes its spots" and perhaps the essence of the message sent when someone references this adage is correct. But it is correct to only an extent. While family trauma and drama become encoded upon, and within us, it does not mean that it cannot be changed. Yes, the spots remain, as scars, but they can be changed in character so that our nature changes. We simply need new soil.

I needed new soil. I needed to be ripped from the soil that is my family's generational trauma and needed to be planted elsewhere, both literally and figuratively. I needed to come to the understanding that my life is not my life. I needed to understand that the easiest way to change course in the stream of life was to turn back and attempt a return to the Honeysuckle Dream. I had to return to God and come to understand what my role is while I'm here. I needed to come to an understanding that would not only help me to know deeply that my time here is extremely limited, it is rented, but to also understand that the easiest way to live through this period of my existence, this life, was to let go of all that became bondages holding me prisoner against my will, against the part of me that is indeed truly connected to God.

I could see the truth of my life before me but didn't know how to embrace it. It always screwed with my senses and the truth seemed to evade me. I intuitively knew this for a great many years while trying to stay afloat in the stream of life but the question that always presented itself was "How?" How does one change its spots if you will?

I suppose time is of value here as it helps to bring us deeper and deeper understandings. The value of experiences cannot be discounted either. It was both the understandings and experiences that helped prepare the ground for me, the new soil that I might be planted in if I were willing to do the hard work of tilling the resentments and fears and the resultant persuasions they had on my spots.

As I navigated my divorce I felt the failure. The fear of failing became as destructive as the fear of abandonment. Sometimes I think it took the place of the latter as I grew older. I didn't want to fail as a husband, but I did. I didn't want to fail as a father but there was a chance I might. I didn't want to fail at keeping my mask on, but this was a failure that was needed to transcend the fear of success. It has always floored me that we can have two fears that run in opposition to each other, and that they can empower each other leaving us in the middle of their tug of war. Fear is just so damn messy.

As I began to experience the fear of failure at the end of my marriage the feeling of not wanting to be here returned yet again. I was trying with all my might to keep up an appearance that I had everything together as a young adult and father by trying to keep my mask tight to my face, but it was becoming more and more difficult. The pain grew as I grew older, it was not fading away. It was building to a crescendo.

In a fit of anger and rage, and in a effort to evade the pain of my existence and current circumstances, I jumped into my old VW Scirocco late one night with one desire, with one thought. I wanted to flip it over while cruising at a high speed. I wanted the pain to end and thought that if I could transfer the emotional and mental pain to physical pain, I might find some relief. If by chance I didn't survive that would be a plus. Realistically I was not of sound mind at this moment. That's the thing about resentment and fear, they alter our sanity, especially when they emanate from traumas that are not fully understood.

As I rounded a turn and shot down the four-lane road that passed by the house I was renting a police officer began chasing me down. I was turning the wheel to the left and right rocking the little firecracker of a car while flying in it at a high speed. When he put his lights on a thought crowded into the madness of my mind and brought me to a stop. Though I did not have the will to live at this moment I knew and felt my daughter needed me. This thought ended as the thought of pulling over and stopping arrived.

I unfolded myself from inside the black car and stood beside it with my hands up as the officer approached. I held my hands up in the air as I didn't want him to draw his gun. I was dressed in a long black wool dress coat, sweatpants, and worn work boots. My appearance matched the disordered arrangement of my mind, and the officer told me to stand still, not to move. As he got closer, he recognized that something was wrong and asked, "What the hell is wrong with you?" I asked him to put me in the back of his cruiser and told him that I had a momentary lapse of reason. I sat in the back of that car for what seemed to be two hours with the heat blasting and with my hands tied behind my back with the bracelets on.

While I am wearing a mask, I only want you to see a particular part of me while hiding what I don't want you to see. It was a wild series of events like this one that would act as a crowbar trying to pry the mask off and each time the attempt was made there was some progress though I didn't see this as it was happening.

There has always been a synchronicity and synergy between each and every event in my life and mixed within was the synchronicity and synergy of the thoughts and feelings attached to the events. Whether the thoughts or feelings led to the event or created the event or were the result of the event made no difference. They were all interwoven and for good reason. Carefully designed with one aim. To bring about consciousness. To bring about God-consciousness.

There have never been any definitive endings in my life. Though there appeared to be changes that seemed like endings, people, places, and things removed from my life, there were always thoughts and feelings derived from them that became a part of me. No real endings, just fade aways.

Each experience has brought with it a push to regain consciousness and has been the force behind getting me back to the Honeysuckle Dream.

Mom thought my divorce was the same as hers and that I felt and believed as she did, but it wasn't so. We may all have similarities, but we all think differently. This is wholly based on our personal experiences and the lessons attached to them. The new level of consciousness born out of the lessons.

Though I felt failure as I moved forward from my divorce as my mother did with hers and though there were some eerie similarities between them there were indeed layers upon layers of differences between them. Mom's approach to hers was different than mine as she wasn't working from the same code as I was. The one embedded in by her childhood was different. While it appears we might all take the same approach and make the same execution after a decision is made, the fact is we do not. Though there are similarities in the show of life, the people, places and things, what is behind them in synchronicity and synergy is truly different. This is so because we are all at different places in our understanding of, and level of, consciousness. I'm not trying to speak from a spiritual mountaintop, I'm simply trying to speak to facts I came upon born out of my experiences.

I grew into being a father. Not having the benefit of having one before me while a child I didn't know how to play this role. I was working with small bits and pieces. I had to learn through on the job training so to speak. I had boatloads of help from those closest to me. Trying to be a "Dad" began a new level of consciousness within. I quickly moved from "I'll show you" to "I can do this." The motives within me shifted as I watched my daughter growing before me. I fully recognized that I could be present, could be different, and quickly saw the perfection of imperfection. I learned fast that what we can do is be the absolute best with what we have and work with what we have. Though it might feel deficient deeper understandings can be achieved and our efforts can always match their depth.

Mia and I married, and we became a family of four. Our daughters had this incredible bond, a bond that was there from the start, long before we married. Over the years our friends have mentioned on many occasions how they admired what we did with our marriage and how we made it all work. We both truly understand that all of this was by divine design and that we simply played our roles to the best of our abilities. We had our daughters with us all through the week and they were with our exes on weekends.

We built a wonderful life and navigated the stream before us filled with endless hope. I held the hope that our children might have something better than what we had. We took our collective life experiences and passed them on to our girls. We passed on what was given to us but did it in a way that hopefully didn't create the same trauma that was within us. We tried to put our slant on all of it.

As the four of us grew together I withdrew from my family, and this was caused by a few things. At the forefront was the idea that I didn't want my girls to experience the same corruption I had. I wanted to protect them. This is natural, a natural response as a parent. But there was more.

Being a parent can in fact be the easiest role to play and embrace if one is free from the bondages of the past that are tethered by resentment and fear. I tried with all my might to lay these resentments and fears aside as the currents grew stronger in the stream of life because of the busyness brought about by the kids, work, etc. I wanted to be done with all the past, wanted to leave it where it was. In the past. It was indeed impossible for me to do this. More time would be needed as well as the smashing of delusions that were created by all of it.

The past couldn't be left behind by Mom either. My new marriage touched off her resentments and fears associated with my father's marriage to Pat. In many ways she would hold me in the same contempt she held my father in, and by extension would do the same to Mia. These instances would be tempered by her desire to play her new role as "Nana." These times became the most eye opening for all of us, our children included. It felt like the lessons to be learned were increasing in their depth and at times there was something inside of me that still wanted to evade reality.

My family never seemed to get the message that I wanted out, wanted out of the trauma and drama, that I was just done with it all. That I *had* to be done with all of it. But like the character of Michael Corleone expressed "just when I thought I was out, they pull me back in" escape became impossible until I severed all the ties. This took me years and years to work up to.

If I thought that my daughter Madison was the spearhead in creating a renewed effort to wanting to solve all the riddles of my family so I might be free and perhaps end the vicious cycle it was now matched by my wife's daughter Demetria. She indeed would be a matching spearhead when she entered my life. From the very first day we met when she was a toddler, long before Mia and I were married, we had this connection similar to the one I had with my daughter. From the very beginning I treated her as if she were my own.

She opened my eyes to so many things about not only the role of being a father but also the "stepparent" relationship. As we grew as a family and my love for her deepened, I continued to be reminded of the relationship I had with my father's wife. Or the lack thereof. Loving my wife's daughter came naturally to me, I didn't have to force it. This was a blessing. Even if there were a space between her and I where love needed to be learned and earned this effort would have come naturally just because of loving her mother. She was indeed an extension of her Mom, she was a part of her Mom, and I wanted to love every single part of her Mom, including her. As I said, it was natural and in place before we married. It wasn't natural for my stepmother to be a Mom to my sister and me. This always confused me. How can a parent not want to be a parent, not want to be a better parent?

It was a case of water seeking its own level when it came to Pat. She and my father were perfect for one another and in this respect my mother's need to relate my marriage to theirs was spot on. Mia and I might have had different experiences in life and in our childhoods, but we also shared the same desire to have and be better. To have all that we ever desired and more importantly to be better than what we witnessed and lived. Here is where *our* water level has always remained consistent with one another's level.

Mia and I made every effort at smashing delusions as we became aware of them, but my Mom could not. She was in constant conflict with herself, constantly trying to bring the similarities between my father and I into the spotlight. She constantly tried to liken our marriage to that of my father and his wife and this created division. It stoked her resentments and fears while bringing about a new level of consciousness within her as Mia and I would fight back against her efforts to cast her aspersions upon us.

The cycles and circles in families can run round and round at fast speeds and when one removes themself or tries to remove themself those who remain in the circle will try with all their might to get you to return to it. My sister was constantly trying to do this with us as my mother had moments when she left the circle. As distasteful as my Mom thought her past was, as difficult as her own life experiences were, and as much as she didn't have the ability to let it all go, she did have this amazing awareness about herself and what all of it did, and was doing, to her. She also possessed something that would help to guide me as I navigated the renewal of life through marriage and fatherhood. The ability to admit when she was wrong. So wrong about so many things. She also had the ability to offer sound guidance when she was in this space, this frame of mind. She also battled the need to protect the family secrets while respecting the insanity within the circle as she tried to break free from her past and the drag it had on her.

The arrival of her grandson would change the entire script attached to the role she had played nearly her entire life. As it would mine. Our soil was about to be changed and none more so than mine.

Twenty-Nine

Turning Points

Years ago, a fabulous spot-on book came upon the world's stage closely followed by its movie. It was *The Secret.* While it was simple in messaging and made perfect and absolute sense it presented difficulties for me. The fact of the matter is that it is common sense boiled down to its lowest denominator. I have always tried to live by its tenants. The simple idea of intent and the resultant manifestation. Indeed, the things or circumstances in our lives are the direct result of our thoughts or ideas as are the actions we take. Our decisions are born out of the thoughts or ideas we entertain. My difficulty with this came on two fronts.

The first difficulty was of course my lack of patience. I wanted the things I wanted, not always material, as soon as I thought of them. I wanted the Universe to answer on my schedule. I always wanted to hold sway over the Universe. It became easy for me to see this as one variable that made any intent or manifestation of it impossible. It was relatively easy for me to remove this block.

The second difficulty was far more challenging to overcome. The second block was in truth the closed channel between God and me. This channel has two ends. Of course there is the Big Guy who has His Will. I believe a piece of this was installed in me at birth. It's the piece I was sent here with. It's that intuition deep down inside that serves as a compass and barometer. Call it what you will but I have come to see that it is in essence a piece of Light that God gave me. Then there is me.

My Light got buried. As I left the Honeysuckle Dream and a cloudless sky the storms began raging. Raging outside of me and then within. The resentments and fears arrived and grew as a snowball does when it is rolled on the ground in the snow. As these grew, they began to block the channel. Eventually the power and energy from and of God became dim. They were nearly snuffed out. They couldn't work properly. This is where my will began to exercise itself in my life. What I found was that my will was always running in opposition to God's will.

I began to try to hold sway over everything as God does and it was a failure. Always a failure. As I tried to hold persuasion over things I also had intents, dreams, goals. They were wrapped in the selfish motives that emanate from resentments and fears. The opposite of working with The Power. I always tried to manifest particular things in my life and sometimes it worked. When it worked, I began to believe that I had the same power as God. The ego, lower self, is cunning like this. It romances you and lulls you into thinking you're fine when, and while, you are cut off from the Power that is deep within. Conversely, when it didn't work, I took it upon myself to make it work and this requires some colorful principles that I believe also run in opposition to God's will.

Mia saw all of this in me and didn't understand it. She didn't know how deeply these fears were embedded in me and how I had no choice but to work with what I had in them. As I attempted to control everyone and everything about me, she would have nothing to do with it. She had fears, we all do, but she was arranged in a way where she could fully recognize them and transcend them easily. In other words, she had faith. Faith that what was to be, would be. I didn't have that. I had the insane, self-indulgent idea that was always battling the ideas of God.

This all began to change with two things. The first was the fact that I was getting older, and life's experiences were changing me. This is natural. It was the tally of failures in life experiences because of living like this that began to open my eyes.

The second was the arrival of our son Hans. As I walked the beach so long ago vowing I would never marry again and heard that laughter I also had the thought that I needn't have any more children. There was a fear within me that if I had a son I might be exactly like my father and my divorce seemed to bolster this fear. Not only did I hear God and Nana's laughter with this thought that day, but I believe there was a chorus of laughter in the background that accompanied it.

When our son arrived, he brought with him many new awareness's. My eyes were pried open even more to the reality of the fears and resentments that I had been living. His arrival quickened my journey of finding out how to be free of them so I might be a better father and husband.

Mom was brought back to life in many ways when Hans was born. She was truly excited about the arrival of another grandchild and entered a dream state. She had been decimated years before as her third child was taken from her, and the divorce that followed, but now her stream opened to a clearing of celebration and this profound love. The water was as flat as a pancake, and she was simply floating. She felt as though the baby boy she lost so many years before was now here for her to play the parenting role too. It was a sort of redemption wrapped with forgiveness.

Mia and I had this unspoken agreement between us that our children would not have what we had or didn't have when we were kids. We wanted more for them. And not just the material part of it. We wanted them to have more in the way of love. In the way of being parented. In the way of being shown. In the way of being free from the insanity that is generational trauma. Don't we all as parents come upon this way of thinking to some extent as our children arrive here?

Mom had difficulty with this as she had fixed ideas born out of her own experience. I had fixed ideas born out of my own experiences and so did my wife. Mom's inability to let go of the past coupled with my desire to throw my past away created an alloy with my wife's ability to let the past go that brought about many battles. Where Mia had the ability to let go, trust God, Mom and I did not. Our intents were born out of our lower selves, the places that held the most pain.

As I held my son and was a bit older, and a bit more aware of the resentments and fears, I wanted more. I wanted more for not only him. I wanted more for all my children and my wife. I wanted to give them the absolute best life that I could, but I would have to battle my way free from the lower self and get myself back to God. I would have to begin living a clean life by a set of higher principles instead of the colorful ones I had been living for so long.

The arrival of our son created a turning point the same as the arrival of my daughters did. They opened my eyes to possibilities. The possibility that I might be able to flip the script. Each experience I had after turning away from the Honeysuckle Dream was a turning point. Some of them were so small that they passed me unnoticed while leaving an impression that would become a part of another turning point's impression and still yet others were so profound that they demanded immediate attention.

I intended to be a father like no other father in this world. I intended to be a husband like no other husband in the world. I put my mask on even tighter and set to work to make this happen. I never asked God for help, I solely trusted and relied on myself to make it happen and it would all crash. My version of The Secret was not like the version that would come out years after I came to this resolve though I erroneously believed it was.

Thirty

Planting - Watering - Fertilizing - Sowing

The dark things, dark thoughts, and dark feelings that are ignored grow in strength and power. Neglect has a way of producing decay. Darkness indeed does the same. Unconsciousness does the same. Delusion does the same. And this darkness festers. It permeates every part of our life.

If I thought living with the fear of abandonment, and all the other fears that are closely wrapped up in it along with their distant cousins was difficult growing up it became more difficult as an adult as I assumed more roles such as friend or employee, and especially that of a Dad. The difference was that I was becoming fully aware of the fears now. The effort to evade them landed at a place of futility. The need, and desire, to break free of them arrived as the consciousness of them hurt as badly as they had passively for so long.

As an adult and as my life naturally expanded, the cast of characters in my sitcom took on more and more depth. The characters came in and the characters left. This brought on even more awareness of the fears. The causes and reasons for them which eluded me for so long were now being exposed. This began with my divorce, continued with the arrival of my first daughter, and sped up with my second marriage and arrival of my second daughter.

It was the arrival of my son that placed the consciousness of *all* my existence and my exact nature squarely in my lap for examination. I had no choice but to see what couldn't be seen and no choice but to feel what couldn't be felt for near my entire life up to this point.

My family taught me by their own demonstration that people are expendable, especially when their script, their way, runs in opposition to theirs, when the truth is exposed. I indeed did the same with them and for so many reasons. I eventually stopped speaking with my father as the well ran dry and I finally saw the uselessness in it. I wanted more out of life, wanted a life filled with nourishment. With my children at my feet and at my side I was growing the ability to listen and look for the messages whether they were positive in nature or negative in nature. My ability to *see* was deepening.

As I had two "Dads" in Papa and Rick growing up I drew all that I could from them, especially their lessons related to parenting, that were passed on to me. Papa would remain the rock in my life until the day he died. Although he always expressed how much he missed Nana and how much he would have liked to have gone with her he lived for quite a few years after she passed. Sometimes I think his soul contract required him to stay here until my Mom, my sister, and I were in better places.

Rick came and went from my life. At times we simply drifted apart and still others I shut the door on him. He always played the "hero" in the family, trying to repair the damage, trying to mend the bonds that were broken. Mending something that can't be repaired comes with its own awareness and eventually he made the declarative statement to me that he "was done being the hero in the family." While playing the role of hero he always tried to place my father and I in the same room. He tried to keep the generational trauma alive. He didn't know that his own brother never respected him much like my father never respected anyone else in the family.

Though the role of hero in the family has its myriads of lines and sub roles it most definitely includes making judgments without end. The difference is that there is typically some form of love associated with the judgements when playing this role. As the role of hero was denounced by him, he seemed to enjoy the freedom from it but kept the element of arbiter. His judgments cut me like a knife at times and I would walk away, and attempt to shut the door, on numerous occasions. His last communication to me via a video message sent through the only area I neglectfully left open was a three-minute effort by video to get those last verbal punches in as he announced his cancer diagnosis and his decision to forgo any kind of treatment.

The value in distancing ourselves from others or situations is that it always brings with it clarity and this clarity brings understanding. It brings us greater consciousness. It was like this for me with Rick, and even my sister.

Though I had failed in many ways as a child and as a young adult, the failure included the necessary element of wanting to learn from it. It also brought the vital desire to repair the damage. Of course this is always dictated by consciousness. The deeper the consciousness the greater the desire to transcend and let go.

I always endured the continuous finger pointing from my family members and retaliated in kind. Most notably the aspersions from my sister and Rick. While they were always looking outside of themselves at others I grew in the opposite direction as I grew older. I began to look inward. I had a desire to get back to the Honeysuckle Dream and something inside of me told me that I needed to do the hard work of sifting through the ashes. I had to lapse into deep reflection while trying to maintain appearances and play the role in my family to the best of my ability. This lasted for years and seemed like an eternity.

I suppose one of the greater gifts of transcending fear is the eventual arrival at the belief that each one of us carries with us many similarities in our human experience. It is, was, impossible to speak to these in my family. Even when I tried or when my demonstration sent the message that there was internal strife or growth taking place it always got personalized by someone in the family. The principle of live and let live seemed to be lost on everyone in my family.

One day as Rick and I walked the beach during one of those periods in my life when I was trying to uncover and examine the darker parts of my journey and my nature, trying to bring them to the Light, I was in one of the most reflective times I experienced as an adult. As I walked my eyes gazed downward at the sand. It matched my spirit, I was down. I was at the point of reaching defeat. My shoulders were slumped. I have come to see that my body reacts to not only the cast of characters in my life or the script of the sitcom but to the internal struggles that come along. My downward gaze was one of reflection while seeking awareness's.

Rick's gaze was upwards and reaching for the sky. An upward gaze is either the result of being oblivious or accepting. In his case I'm leaning toward oblivious as the place of full acceptance of those about us and their journey through life and way about them leave very little room for condescension, unchecked judgment, or criticism. He always offered the critiques without invitation or reservation long after giving up the role of hero.

The arrival at this conclusion came in a conversation later in the weekend when he felt no resistance at all in exposing his air of moral and spiritual superiority by mentioning that my gaze was downward and his was upward. No question as to why. Simply the blanket of misunderstanding cast upon me that became the new backbone of our relationship.

Before Mia and I married, one of my cousins who is fully aware of the family dynamics, asked Mia a question. "Are you sure you want to marry into this? This family?" My wife could have run but she didn't, and as she began to witness the insanity and depth of generational trauma she wouldn't come out and say that she should have run but she will remind me of this conversation. In essence, she would say she should have run. But she did not. She believed. She had faith and believed in more, and believed in me, even in the face of the odds stacked against me, her, us, and our children.

We plant, we water, we fertilize, we harvest.

Indeed, this is what can be done, must be done, with that mustard seed of faith. My wife had this seed, and it grew. Mine remained tiny for so long but as we decide what to pass on to our children in what was given to us, we can also pass on this seed of faith. Mia passed her faith on to me and from it grew hope that I might gain freedom from the pain, from whatever trauma lurked beneath the surface. Beneath my mask.

She planted a seed in me by resisting the onslaught and constant assault by my family, by putting her foot down and letting them know that the family dynamics would not work with her and were not welcome. She watered the seed within me each time she resisted the trauma as it tried to make its way in. She fertilized it by protecting our children and refusing to allow them to be a part of the trauma. And as they grew into adulthood, we witnessed the harvest. We were able to see that things can be different than what was given to us. The age-old family scripts can be shredded and a new one written. It takes serious moxie to do it though.

As our children grew not only in age but in their experiences, I was allowed to see things from an entirely different perspective. I could see through their eyes. As they lived their experiences, I had the opportunity to relive all of mine which empowered me to want to break free more and more. As they succeeded, I remembered my successes at their age. As they failed, I remembered my failures at their age. My mother did the same as their grandmother, but her reactions were a bit different. She couldn't let go of the family script she held.

These times were difficult for all of us as my wife and I stood firm in what we were doing and wanted to do with our children. Fighting for your child is never easy but I quickly learned that this part of my role as Dad is pleasurable, satisfying. It also constantly reminded me of what I didn't have. I was also becoming aware that everything I was saying and doing was not going unnoticed by my children. They were watching and looking up to me as I had always done with my parents.

As much as Mom wanted a bigger family when she married my father and wanted to be a part of that family, she indeed was different from them in one amazing and admirable respect. She had the ability to admit when she was wrong. Something that would allude me for a long time. Each difficulty that we had with Mom landed at a conversation between us. Something that never took place on my father's side of the family for a heap of reasons. Unlike so many in our family we grew into this, and it deepened our relationship right up until the end of her life. In many ways I believe it continues to deepen our relationship even though she isn't alive today.

As I always wanted more for my children, wanted them to not only have a "Dad" but to also have a better set of principles instilled in them, I did whatever I had to do to make this happen. I now had to struggle to keep my mask affixed to my face while at the same time continuing the effort of taking it off. It was a catch-22. I wanted them to have the same principles that Papa tried to instill in me. The same ones that delusions born out of fear would not allow me to practice.

As our children grew older my family members would come in and out of their lives, our lives, as if there were this revolving door that never seemed to stop going round and round. This one came in and as another arrived, they left. As another paid a visit still that one left. At times there was a welcome mat in place and at other times there was a sign that said "Go away" which was most times ignored. This went on for years as did the discovery of just how decrepit and destructive the fear of abandonment truly is.

As the door made continuous revolutions, so did the revolutions that I came upon in thinking and awareness. As I grew more and more aware I grew more and more weary of the generational trauma. I knew I had to be free and that it was killing me and killing any chance I might have to feel peace and quiet, ease and comfort.

Unfortunately, the storm hadn't reached its apex yet. I would have to lose the familial relationships that brought nothing but pain. I would have to experience the loss of Papa. I would have to experience the loss of Mom. I would have to experience the loss of Dad. And I would have to experience the near loss of my marriage to Mia. I would have to experience the loss of material things. I would have to come close to losing my life by my own hand.

Ironically it would be the loss of self that would truly set me free.

Thirty-One

The Confounded Bridge

As I spent the obligatory thirty days in the rehab at eighteen, two weeks before I was due to graduate from high school, we had open visitation there each Sunday for friends and family. Mom never came as she was thoroughly exhausted from the battle she took up in the last two years of my drinking and drugging while trying to get me clean and sober. Who could blame her?

I went into the rehab and as I came off the drugs and my body dried out from the alcohol the reality of my senses, and the deepest reason I began to drink in earnest for, came back to the forefront of my being. That already weary fear of abandonment. I wanted help but not only with alcohol and drug abuse. I wanted help in resolving this fear. I wanted to be free of it. I wanted my Dad to man up as they say and take responsibility for it.

I worked it out with the psychologist on staff to set up a time for my father to visit. I wanted the good doctor to fix all of this for me. When my father arrived, I was in the small auditorium they used for lectures and different teachings. My design for repairing this was to have the doctor take care of it without me being there. My hope was that my father would experience this incredible shift in his awareness. Neither one of these things happened.

I was called out of the lecture and brought into the office where the doctor fully expected me to confront my father. The reality is that though I was eighteen at the time I really wasn't. My level of emotional and mental maturity matched that of the time period of when he left my mother, sister, and I. And there was no way "Little Bobby" was going to make waves and take the chance of causing such a ripple in the stream that might capsize the false hope that I might one day have a Dad in my father.

Rick was here on this day and as the visitation grew to a close the three of us sat at a table in the cafeteria. It felt eerily familiar to me. It felt like the time I visited my mother when she was in the mental hospital but without that hope. It felt sterile. It felt unfruitful. If silence can be deafening this was far more offensive. Barely any words were spoken between the three of us, but Rick tried. He was still playing the role of hero at this time, so he had no choice but to try.

Rick took a pinch of salt from the saltshaker and threw it over his shoulder, perhaps believing that this might somehow wipe away the bad luck, the circumstances, that we experienced. Both individually and collectively. He then shared that "it takes thirty days to break a habit." I believe he was speaking to the habit I grew into as it relates to alcohol and drugs but maybe there was something more to it. Maybe he was referencing the generational trauma that seemed to be sitting in the empty chair at the table with us with its menacing grimace and its overbearing shadow it was maliciously casting upon us.

I spent countless hours and exhausting amounts of energy trying to eradicate the fear of abandonment and as I look back it was so much more than a habit. It was ingrained in me at such depths that it took on this cleverness in always trying to be evaded as I, in similar fashion, tried to evade reality. It was going to take far more than thirty days to be rid of this. It was not a habit. It was a living creature, as all fears are, and I was its host. I know that sounds a bit bizarre and you might feel it far-fetched but when you look at the issue of fear and all its attendant suffering experienced it does make perfect sense.

As fear feeds on its host, it taps into the lower self in cunning ways. It uses our ego to its advantage while lulling us into believing that we have control all the while dictating what will be and what will be felt. It was nasty and corrosive for me.

The arrangement of the ego, the lower self, is cunning. While one might think they are having success at reducing their ego or killing their ego it uses this feeling or belief to remain alive thereby ensuring it will never lose its dominion over the host. My lunacy resulting from a delusional place of thought was the belief that I might gain the upper hand over all of this. By my own limited power. It would take years to get across this bridge of thought to land at the other side on the shore where faith would reveal that within my admission of powerlessness over this cunning thing I could be led back home to the Honeysuckle Dream, back home to God.

I haven't any clue how the belief I would not live past fifty years was arrived at. Perhaps it was that long-held desire of simply not wanting to be here, not wanting to be alive, that brought me to this conclusion. This belief led me to think and do, not think and not do, many things. Holding an end date seemed to create a deadline of sorts.

I mentioned that I recently began getting my teeth repaired five years after my dreamt about expiration date. I didn't think I would need my teeth after fifty, so I neglected them as I had a great many things throughout my life. Fear does this to you. It's a thief. It indeed feeds delusion and creates dangerous fixed ideas that adversely affect us.

As I work with a dentist, a periodontist, and an orthodontist and as they work as a team to remedy the problem, they expressed that it would take time to achieve the solution I desire. The same has been true with the fear of abandonment and all the other fears that are the result of that fear. It has taken time to work away from it, to cross the bridge.

Mom held, and passed on, one of the strongest lessons for me. She went from a person who was riddled with pain, largely in this state for most of her life, to a person who felt hope. I noticed this shift in her. This change. This amazing thing happened as my wife and I grew together and as our children grew older. My three children opened *our* eyes. We were open enough to be able to see through their eyes past the generational trauma that we both carried. My wife and I had this silent vow with one another that we would try to stop the trauma and drama, and my mother saw this. She had awakenings as a result.

As the spirit of being able to admit when I was wrong came about, or was forced, she found it as well. This sent the clear message that we can indeed change at any moment if we have the willingness to admit when we are *not* right. That we are wrong. This allows us to see things differently. This allows us to open our minds and perhaps let something different in. Something that might bring nourishment to us. Something that might be of use in combating our ego, our lower self.

The spirit of being able to admit one's mistakes and spirit of being able to take full responsibility for them opens the door for faith to be recognized, for God to be recognized. Isn't an admission of being wrong an admission of powerlessness and not only that, isn't it in fact an admission at some level that we need a power stronger than us, stronger than human power? Isn't it an admission that we need God's Power and help in overcoming obstacles, especially the often-misunderstood obstacle of the ego, the lower self? Isn't it one of the strongest turning points we will experience?

When I landed at this station the fog that had been closing in on the bridge and obstructing my view of it began to dissipate. This was yet another beginning of letting go of fear in an absolute way and like all good things it would take some time to get there. I would have to face the problem head on and would have to meet God on His terms instead of the terms I always tried to set between us.

The journey would be amazing, in fact exhilarating, but it was going to hurt. The lasting gain has come too far outweigh any momentary pain. The result has been freedom.

Thirty-Two

Abandoning The Fear of Abandonment

The walk across the bridge is not a casual one. It requires serious effort. It is not a flat crossing from delusion to reality, from selfishness inspired by resentments and fears to a God-consciousness brought about by the blistering truth of our failures. The bridge is arched, and the process of crossing requires courage as strong as the bridge itself being held by its Center. As strong as God.

My journey across the bridge lasted years and it seemed an eternity while in the midst of it. It felt like I might never gain freedom from all that was binding me to fear, from all that was keeping me from returning to a place of innocence, to the Honeysuckle Dream.

I continued to act as the adult with my mask affixed to my face the best I could while trying to be a good Husband and Dad and though I fell short many times I never stopped trying, never stopped trying to set right any wrongs as I became aware of them. I was constantly open to learning and my wife and children inspired me to never give up. Was it perfect? No. Indeed as I look back, it has been a messy journey. Not only painful for me but for those closest to me.

In many ways I failed as my mother and father had failed.

There are numerous things that I have said and done to my parents, my sister and her family, and most especially to my own children that I not only regret but have the willingness to repair to the best of my ability with not only words but with my actions, my demonstration. I now understand that every instance and happening in my life and the lives of those about me, even you, has been designed with one goal. To get me home to God and more importantly keep me at home with God.

I estimate it took twenty-five plus years to be free of the fear of abandonment since first seeing it and recognizing it for what it is. In that time, I engaged in relationships and have even abandoned them. Ironic huh?

I built businesses and lost businesses.

I bought homes and lost homes.

I bought vehicles and have lost vehicles.

I took jobs and have left jobs.

I became a thief and was even generous at times.

I have made a lot of money and have lost a lot of money.

I have had the best of things in life and have gone without.

I have tried and I have failed.

The failures have been the tissue out of which I would find the ability to not only sit in the pile of ashes and rubble about me. I would find the ability to sift through it all and fully examine the nature of fear that was brought on by that first resentment. While I had many successes throughout the laborious journey, the failures did hold the greatest lessons. That, and loss. I had to experience losses before I could begin to lose fear. I had to experience the loss of my reliance on things human before I could fully trust and rely on God. This began with the loss of Papa.

We were fortunate enough to have him in our lives for so long. He remained here better than twenty years after Nana passed away and when he died, he took with him whatever hope I had remaining in me, whatever faith I had left. After he passed away, I fell into a sort of oblivion and didn't share it with anyone. When I look back it feels like I took every lesson he taught me in mechanics and applied them to adhering the mask to my face. I tried to manage to the best of my ability, but the fact of the matter was that this Rock in my life was now gone.

Though I was married and surrounded by my children I felt alone, at a loss for what to do, and how to do it. My principles for living drifted even further away from all of those he tried to teach me. A liar, a cheat, and a thief are what I became. All the while trying to hide this from those about me. I wasn't that good at hiding it though. Those closest to me could see it and at times tried to act as my conscience.

My sister tried and I pushed her away once I got what I selfishly wanted. I pushed Rick further away and our relationship only survived because his husband and my wife were so close. The two of them held the commonality of being married to the same mayhem of generational trauma that Rick and I carried and shared with one another.

Though I tried to manage well I saw my failure in transcending my fears in deeper ways. I would try to battle them with things outside of myself. Under the malaise of spiritual sickness and delusion I would make decisions with little to no thought. I expanded our business, and this ultimately became my undoing. The weight under the pressure of financial obligations and the inability to bring the business to match these with the recession we were in nearly destroyed us.

It destroyed me in so many other ways. The outside remedies I always sought were being removed or were bringing more pain to the problem. The problem being that constant inability to let go, the inability to trust God, the inability to understand the reasoning for all things whether perceived as being good or bad, the inability to meet challenges as they were presented to me.

I was clean and sober for many years yet sought other things to relieve the pain of my intolerable existence and now I was at the end. There was nothing else before me to create the relief I needed. I grew paranoid and extremely self-conscious. Every fear became as electrifying and held the same doom as a raw nerve exposed in a broken tooth.

At the suggestion of one of my dearest friends I sought treatment from my doctor and explained all the symptoms I was experiencing. When I finished my personal assessment with him, he simply said that I had an anxiety disorder and was depressed. All I could offer to him was "You think?" I was so damned tired.

He prescribed for me and began treating these symptoms. Of course, the false hope created immediate relief and eventually the medications he treated me with gave me some more relief, but the problem was that he was treating the symptoms. He wasn't treating the cause of the place I found myself in when I went to him.

In the beginning it all seemed to be working but it was simply a band-aid that numbed my consciousness. It even numbed whatever conscience I had left as a part of my character. With each level of doom I experienced the doctor would increase the dosages or add another medication to what was already in place. Eventually I was taking a cocktail of meds and when I reached the breaking point and felt ruled by pill bottles that should have had "Fukitol" typed on their labels I threw my hands up.

I returned to the doctor, and he told me he misdiagnosed me. He arranged for me to visit a clinic to get tested for attention deficit disorder and when I went through the battery of tests, I passed them all with flying colors. This brought me to another round of different medications and ultimately they failed, as again they were treating the symptoms.

That's the curious thing about spiritual disease. The symptoms closely mimic the diagnoses that most doctors easily attach a label to. The last time I visited the ADD clinic and met with the RNP who barely looked up from her iPad each time I entered her office she did not expect my assessment of the position I felt I was in. Each time I previously visited her she would ask me how the meds were working. I would explain that they weren't while also reminding her that I was clean and sober. She never listened.

Without looking up or making eye contact with me she would ask me what medication I would like to try next. Every four weeks or so I would give her the name of the next medication on the list, and she would give me the script. I wholeheartedly believe that if I asked for oxy's and valium with a chaser of Dilaudid she would have asked what dosage would work for me. It was so bizarre.

The last visit with her would be the first time she had made eye contact with me. When she asked how the medications were working, and I explained that they weren't, she asked me what I would like to try next. I told her that I was all set with the medications and only came to wish her a goodbye. She asked me what I was going to do. I told her "I'm gonna beg God for help."

I began carrying a pistol with me and when I opened the garage door, I looked beneath it to make sure no one was there waiting to pounce on me. I would take the bullets out of the magazine and dry fire the gun onto the roof of my mouth and up the side of my head practicing my exit from this world. Paranoia became the new norm for me.

My daughters had fled our home long before I reached this point, but my wife and son were still there. They were hostages to my pain, my generational trauma, my inability to let go of fear, the same as I was. Their ability to hold tight and to remain with me became instructive. They became a better part of the hope that I could move away from the fear of abandonment. Their ability to stay, to not abandon me, sent the message that it is possible to move away from abandoning people and things about me that seem difficult to a place of facing them head on. This may sound confusing; indeed, it was for me. But a light began to come on inside of me. It was a spark of hope.

In the face of total destruction would come the necessary elements to create the fertile ground to move me to a different soil, to new nourishment. I combat rolled out of bed onto my knees one morning with big splashy tears in my eyes and petitioned God as I had never done before. I always prayed to some extent but never offered one like this. This one was wrapped with humility, the opposite of the drive of ego I was under for so long. This one was wrapped with contrition and free of the arrogance born out of selfishness. This prayer was offered with all my heart. And this prayer would be answered in a way that was indeed miraculous.

Though I wanted out. Though I didn't want to be alive anymore. I didn't have the courage to follow through with taking my own life. I couldn't pull the trigger or muster the spirit to wrap my truck around the telephone pole. So I asked God to help me.

"God please come get me. I want to come home!" That was it. That was all I needed to ask with feeling, intent, willingness, and humility behind it. I now know that prayers coupled with these elements are always answered and answered quickly.

He spoke loud enough for me to hear Him over the sound of the noise created by my speeding truck a moment before smashing it into the telephone pole as I held the gun in my hand. I had asked God to come get me two days before I heard Him say “Stop. I am not done with you yet.”

God came and got me.

Thirty-Three

Searching For God

When you want something bad enough, in my case help from God, and it's backed by not only a willingness to put in the effort to attain it but an extraordinary sense of humility that is born out of a sense of failure it comes to you easily. I was at the end and needed help. I wanted God's help because I landed on the side of the stream where powerlessness held court.

I had lived a life powered by the fear of abandonment and all the other fears that seemed to feed its destructive nature. Most times I was oblivious to this as I tried to manage it all. I always tried to play God and hold some kind of sway over the fears. It simply didn't work. My life became a pile of rubble because of my failed effort to manage it.

I could no longer control my emotions or thoughts. My personal relationships were a mess, and people grew weary of me. I developed, and held, a fear of people. I felt absolutely useless and was having difficulty in my business and its affairs. Financial instability was killing me. Misery and depression became the baseline of my existence, causing me to collapse into a state of paranoia. As much as I had always tried to help those about me over the years, I couldn't even do this anymore. I couldn't even help myself.

Was I abandoned by God? Does He abandon us? I truly thought He did.

I was wrong. So very wrong.

He was always there waiting for me to turn around. To turn my life around. To begin my journey back to the Honeysuckle Dream with earnestness. To return to Him.

All I needed to do was ask. When I asked him to come and get me, He obliged. I just never imagined I would be brought home to Him in the manner He did.

My petition to God was not only heard it was acted upon by Him. He set a course before me and quickly arranged and rearranged my life in a way that was truly miraculous. If I had been on that Magical Mystery Tour, it was now going to become the Miraculous Mystery Tour. All the characters in my sitcom were about to change, roles would be shifted, and everything that did not suit all the necessary changes to see the elimination of fear and resentment was about to be removed from my life. These miracles still take place in my life today and I imagine these shifts will continue until I leave here.

While we might think God has abandoned us and that it is His sole responsibility to seek us I have found that it is not. It is my responsibility to seek Him. When I am in this position, in this mindset, He will perform the *miracle* needed in my life as He indeed has done. There can be no other word attached to what has happened to me. Miracle.

I was sick, spiritually sick, with deep resentment and fears that could not be moved or removed by my finite power, or by another human's power. I was firmly wedged in a place of darkness protecting all the locked doors in that long hallway, feeling absolute powerlessness. Then I was freed from all of it. I'll use the word saved here. I was able to open the doors, especially the one at the end of the hallway rimmed with Light and allow Him to do His work. Allow Him to remove the contents behind each door, behind each compartment. And as the Light bathed the darkness the darkness lost its power.

As a result of my heartfelt prayer, I was introduced to a few fellows who were once in the same position I found myself in. They had been restored to health. Restored to their faith deep within and were learning how to exercise this muscle. The greatest exercise in strengthening the muscle of faith is by helping those who find themselves in the same position they were in. Helping them to get free. This is what these fellows did with me.

When I petitioned God to "Please come get me. I want to come home" I wanted Him to come pick me up with a limousine and hand me a bouquet of flowers. I wanted Him to show up and sing *my* praises for *my* valiant effort at making it through the life I lived. It didn't work like that. He sent a group of men who carried a roadmap that they used to get free from the resentments and fears. Though my life was different than theirs in many respects the destructive nature of resentment and fear were indeed the same for each of us. Though our stories may be different they are indeed the same in many respects. They used their personal stories to bring about, and outline, my work necessary to gain freedom.

Some of the greatest lessons learned while I was growing up, while I was in the rapids in the stream of life, were learned through those about me and their character. Their life experience, and thoughts and feelings associated with them, had a bearing on me in a deep way. The same happened with these men. They opened my eyes to the reality of my situation and helped me smash all the delusions I had created and was living by.

We all have a role to play in the sitcom that is our life and perhaps we are all teachers to and for one another. Perhaps guiding one to faith is not only the most powerful lesson we can teach but is the most powerful role we get to play while we are here. The departure from the Honeysuckle Dream into the delusions created by self-propulsion and then the return to that infantile faith that needs to be picked back up and nourished. That is exactly the gist of the journey that I needed to fully understand. I needed to go back and pick up my mustard seed, my faith, and plant it. It would require work on my part, but the terms weren't difficult as I was continually asking God for help in the same way I petitioned Him when I combat rolled out of bed that morning with the tears falling from my eyes.

The principles of self-examination and the roadmaps to follow them have been around since man arrived at the first resentment and fear. The difficulty is not only trying to figure out what to do with what is found in the examination or even how to discard it. The difficulty is our lack of power in the human will to achieve the needed separation from what we find and then come to terms with. Many of us can't see that we need God's Power to achieve the break. I came to see this under the weight of the futility I was living.

I had to do a review to uncover all the deficiencies in my life as they related to the fears and the resentments. As they related to all the relationships in and out of my family. As they related to my heart and emotions. As they related to my mind and its thoughts. As it related to my spirituality, the core of my being.

I examined each fear I could recognize and more importantly how I tried to manage them, how I tried to rely upon my limited power to live with them, to muscle though them. This exposed my abject failure in doing so. I had to examine my part, my role in the sitcom, my side of the street, and see the lack of value in it. This exposed the depth of selfishness I had lived since leaving the Honeysuckle Dream and further brought to Light the layers of delusion that were not only created but were lived by me near my entire life from a little child, "Little Bobby," to an adult, "Mad Bob." I came to see the depth at which I was a self-seeking individual always looking to support the relevance of the lower self, the ego. I had to see how I took each resentment and the negative energy from it and turned it into a constant stream of retaliation towards others. I had to catalog a list of harms that I had done to others while in this state and feel the guilt, shame, and remorse of it.

This was all done in a judicious manner. It had to be. I just wanted to be free and wanted all that was killing me deep within to be put to rest. As I watched it wither away while being fully exposed to the Light my mustard seed of faith began to grow. The balance on the scale shifted. The men about me who unselfishly took on the role of guides planted different seeds. They watered them and at times would fertilize them. God provided the harvest, the miracle if you will.

When I combat rolled onto my knees and petitioned God I had, in essence, decided to let go of the insanity that was my spiritual sickness. The intense examination brought me to a new station. While arriving at the full view of my failure to bring about any change in my life, my own personal powerlessness, I had to make a deeper decision. I became willing to have God remove me from the soil laced and loaded with toxins and replant me in a different soil. I was willing to let go of self-reliance, the ego, and embrace faith in Him at deeper levels. I became wholly willing to just let it all die. The resentments and fears. I became wholly willing to have them replaced. I became open to the idea of being reborn to a new life.

I've worn eyeglasses since just before Mom and Dad split

and over the years my script has changed. I've constantly needed new ones. As I grew from a child into a teenager and then into an adult the same thing happened with the vision of my family and myself. What I have been able to see has had this way of falling out of a proper focus but in the moments clear focus returned it offered a sense of hope that became a part of my fabric. The experience that I had as a result of these men arriving in my life with a roadmap, as a result of God's Power and doing, have brought every little thing into a lasting focus. My lenses and vision are different. They are more powerful, and their focus rarely needs adjusting.

The experience I had was indeed a God-experience. It was a spiritual experience, and I didn't realize how spiritually thirsty I was until it was fully quenched. It was a spiritual experience that still lingers today and continues to grow exponentially. I did not make this happen. God made this happen. What I always tried to use was some sort of twisted magic, an illusion, to solve all my problems. What God used was none other than a miracle. There really is no other word I can use to describe what happened to me, and my family. It is miraculous.

I have come to see that all the good that was there, and even the bad parts, were a by-product of God-consciousness. They were indeed the tissue out of which God-consciousness must be achieved, must be reacquired. All of it was necessary. We might think that God placed us here and then perhaps to some extent has abandoned us and maybe He has. But perhaps it is also a test of sorts. A test of the human will and a test of our faith. A test that gauges our true understanding of the difference between God's infinite will and our finite will. Perhaps the ultimate goal while here is to pass this test and take the lessons learned from our own experience, our own story, and pass it on to those who would accept the teachings with willingness and humility.

Thirty-Four

The Deepening

Discovering spiritual principles is simple. In fact, we are exposed to them all the time. I think a great many of us don't see them though. We are blocked or easily dismiss them because it is far easier to rest in the satisfaction and mayhem of resentment and fear, those almost unnatural though necessary irritants we encounter in the stream of life.

While the discovery of spiritual principles is simple, living by them is another story. Here is where difficulty arises. For many it is not easy living a spiritual life. It goes against all that we are handed in the way of generational trauma, in the never-ending spinning of the circle, cycle, that is our families, and even against what society lays at our feet.

The move from mayhem and chaos, from delusion and unhealthy persuasions, from trauma and drama to peace and quiet, to comfort and contentment, to love and tolerance, can be quite dramatic. It does take time and is a reconstruction of sorts. As my world came crumbling down and I began to move in the opposite direction powered by a new energy I know is God there was no way I could go back to the life I was living before the awakening I experienced. I had to fully leave it behind me.

As I was growing into this new skin, after shedding the old skin, Mom had taken some great strides at pulling herself out of her own trauma and drama. She even remarried after Papa died. Her spirits were buoyed for a time, and she had some awakenings that were the natural consequence of getting older.

She made every effort she could to come to terms with her past and all that she experienced in it. She came to her own place of reconciliation. With her past, with herself, and with me. Even with my wife. We were able to have the long and deep conversations where we spent hours trying to sift through the ashes to better understand all the nuances of what we each experienced, individually and collectively. We were both able to take full responsibility for the colorful parts we played and the damage we had done to one another.

Perhaps it isn't only our responsibility to reacquire our God-consciousness that is ripped away from us while here but to carry a message, our story, before us as we continue to *deepen* our God-consciousness. Perhaps in carrying our story and message of this amazing triumph we are to right any wrongs that we are responsible for as a result of living in spiritual dysfunction. Mom began doing this with me before I could do it with her. I had the fortune of being able to bring all that I discovered back to her to begin the process on my side of the street. It lasted until she died.

Mom and I had the same problem. We had the same problem that so many have, most times unknowingly. We had that disconnect from God at the hands of a resentment and it brought about fear. From it sprung forth spiritual disease. And we carried it for a great many years. Then we hit bottom with it and had these experiences. Our experiences weren't the same, but the landing spots were similar.

As we shared our discovery with one another the need to

retaliate and cause one another pain went away. That part of our nature in our character cannot live in the place where God-consciousness and awareness are at the forefront of one's mind. We also made the discovery that when you live with this new awareness it irks others. It irks their demons, their trauma, their drama, and under the malaise of spiritual sickness, those who are irked will do whatever they have to do to protect *their* demons and *their* darkness.

I discovered that the result of trying to live a spiritual life and trying to not only repair the damages I have done but also deepen my understanding of God, He indeed rearranges our lives to better let us live by new principles. While I was trying to live by new principles, the same principles Papa tried to get me to live by, my life experienced major shifts. My mind was repaired and long held delusions were tossed aside. My physical life and its trappings were rearranged to better suit what needed to happen.

I had to learn to let go of all that did not serve me while living a new life based in God-consciousness. This was difficult. It's not easy for me to let go. I had to learn to do it without leaving claw marks.

The virtues attached to taking responsibility for oneself, attached to moving from pointing the finger at others while playing the role of victim to pointing that finger inward and uncovering our own deficiency, become the energy that keeps moving us forward. It is freeing and a required action. Living a spiritual life will always require action, the muscle of faith needs to be always exercised. There can be no rest for this muscle. If awakenings gained are not acted upon, they will indeed fade away like a decision does without the action to follow it up. It fails to become an accomplishment.

I tried, most times clumsily, to bring my discovery to my family with the effort of trying to begin the repair of all the damage I did over the years. They didn't want to hear it. The words fell on unbelieving ears. They didn't like it. Perhaps it irked them, their demons, their need to evade, their need to protect the insanity of generational trauma and drama. Just as the ego is offensive to others so too can the spirit of trying to flip the script. The spiritual side of things can be offensive to one who is ruled by resentment and fear or cemented in a place of fixed ideas and prejudice.

In a call to Rick one evening, I tried to explain all that I had found out about myself with the journey of facing destructive fears and resentments and how decrepit it was. How deficient and even how decrepit I became. He couldn't wait to get off the phone and wanted to dismiss the entire conversation. It was one of those "Cheers" moments.

My effort with my sister irked her demons and she became even more resentful. I threw my hands up. I paid off the debt owed to a family trust long after I waived any rights for myself and my children to it. I walked away and she gladly took what she could get for herself. I had moved to the place of not caring who won anymore. I wanted the decades-long war that my parents set in motion to end no matter the cost.

I even had to make an approach to my father and Pat to try to put right the wrongs I had done to them. It seemed to fall on deaf ears, but the demonstration was made.

In many ways the best I could do in the way of trying to make an amends to Nana and Papa would be by continuing to live a life free of resentments and fears, a life of God-consciousness.

The taxation placed on others with our trauma and drama can be heavy and damaging. The taxation placed on us by others can be equally heavy and damaging. The taxation placed on me by my parents and family was heavy. There is no doubt about this but all of it was necessary to bring me to where I am today. It had to be a part of my story. It most definitely has to be shared. The benefit placed on others by trying to live our life by spiritual principles can be life changing. The benefit placed on us by others who live by spiritual principles can be equally nourishing.

Pain and anger bring out the worst in us, but spiritual fitness brings out the best in us. This is guaranteed. It is law. Like energy seeks like energy as water seeks its own level. I spent a great deal of my life pissed off at God and His Plan but have found that it was all unfounded, and all-around damaging to me and those about me.

We do not know exactly how a prayer will be answered or what God will do and arrange for us. I have learned that all I need to do is trust in His Plan and all I need to know and remember is that His Plan will always be far better than any plan I might come up with. Better than any plan I might imagine.

I grew up in a place that was based in love that was weighed down with layers of conditions. Love was in truth offered by condition only. I never had the benefit of being shown the terms and conditions but was expected to live by them and pass them on. I simply grew to a place where I could no longer do it.

The ultimate ideal is to love without condition, but do we? In the totality of life lived I'll venture an answer of "Hardly." I have moments when it is so but always found myself falling into the trap of attaching some kind of terms and conditions to love. My lessons in love were always wrapped in abandonment and the fear of it. A natural consequence of shedding the fears puts me in a better position of being able to love without condition. It puts me in a better position of understanding what is healthy and nourishing to the soul and what is damaging.

As I carried out the terms and conditions placed at my feet which included abandoning others, I had to let this go too. But there was something else that came along. My effort to abandon others was always born out of judgment, playing God. As one learns to obey God, after a shift, judgment becomes discernment. There is a vast difference between the two for me and what came to replace abandonment was the natural healthiness of boundaries.

While God rearranges our lives by bringing forth others, and their stories, to add depth to ours, so does He take others away, removing their stories, and this also adds depth to ours. I have learned to simply let it happen. I have also learned that we must use God-consciousness and determine what is healthy for us and what is not. As a result of my past, I have come to see that the dependencies placed on others most times can be unhealthy. They damage us. As distasteful as it might seem we simply have to leave some people behind, and conversely, we must not pursue others.

My wife lost her Dad when she was young, and this has had a major bearing on her life. The greatest being the strength she was able to derive from it and then harness because of the circumstances happening at this time in her life. She was the one who found him at the moment these circumstances were set in motion.

At some level I can understand her loss as my father was never there but on some level I cannot. As much as she has tried to understand my abandonment issues there has always been a block to fully understanding it. To try to help her understand I have referred to her loss as having a sense of finality in it. Mine never did. I had to attend my father's funeral every day. I had to mourn the loss every day. I had to write his eulogy every day.

There are times when we are required to attend the funeral of those who are still alive. Relationships never fully form, or even heal, and a loss is felt even though the person is still in our lives. There are still other times when we are forced to end a relationship and attend its funeral. I had to do just this with many of the familial relationships in my life. It wasn't because they hurt me, or because I hurt them. It wasn't because they could possibly hurt me again or that I might possibly hurt them again. We simply didn't have anything in common outside of generational trauma and drama. As my station changed and theirs did not, as I was willing to walk away from the past and they were not, our journeys parted ways of their own accord.

A life lived based on mayhem and chaos, fully persuaded by generational drama, and the resultant damage I brought about because of it all, indeed has been painful. It has been equally painful to break away from it. Being on the other side of it is freeing and comes with peace though. It also comes with reminders as I can now clearly see where I was and for what it was but not only that I can see it in others and their stories, as those before me who were able to break free could see it in my story. While it may hurt to witness it in others, and though their inability to want to break free can disturb me at times, there is peace in knowing that *all* of it is clearly designed for reasons I may never know. That it is indeed God's plan. All I need to concern myself with most of the time is how I might be able to use my story to help another as others have used their story to help me.

Thirty-Five

"No Substitutions!"

The depth of experiences I've had always included the dynamics of others, and their stories. In other words, their stories have had a profound effect on me. Their guiding forces, especially their generational trauma and drama, have been instructive to and for me. I have had the fortune of learning so much from others who were outside of my family's orbit. People have come and gone over the years using that revolving door. Some have been in the background for but a moment going largely unnoticed but have held sway over me in major ways while others have been in the foreground in a pronounced manner dragging their manuals for living, their whiteboards covered with bullet points outlining their stories, and energy, before me. Always lending value to my awakenings.

Some of these relationships have been topical in nature and some extremely intimate. Over time their common denominator has become clear for me to see. They've held a persuasion in my stream of life. Some have had the effect of a pebble dropping into the water creating small gentle ripples, and some have had the effect of a launched cannon ball hitting the target with precision creating dramatic splashes and waves resulting in an inescapable undertow.

All my life I have been searching for answers. All my life I have been longing for that which I thought was lacking, that which I believed was missing, that which I *thought* I couldn't live without. Especially those familial relationships. I have wanted these relationships and to some extent I long for them even today. I have always wanted the perfection of the sitcom, especially as it relates to communication and solutions. I wanted a deep and meaningful relationship with Mom in a way that my imagination deemed it should be. I wanted the same in a relationship with Dad. I most certainly wanted this ideal relationship with my sister. It's only natural, right? Once I had a full understanding of what happened with Mom and the taking of my little brother, I yearned for this relationship as well. I dreamt of a meaningful camaraderie with my brother.

It is like this yearning and need was buried deep down inside of me going unnoticed and wholly ignored. I didn't know the bearing it would have on me as I navigated the stream of life. The mayhem and chaos obscured my vision and wouldn't allow me to see the complexity of this need, but this didn't mean it wouldn't be instrumental in the relationships I fell into. In fact, this buried need has had a subtle influence on so many relationships in my life. While these relationships have held instruction and had to be exactly as they were by divine design some of them grew to be as sick as the relationships within my family while still others instilled hope in me.

I come from a line of floral designers in my family. As a matter of fact, so many in my family have artistic abilities that are extraordinary. I am a third-generation floral designer by trade. After finding out that I was being erroneously led to believe by a florist that I was working for that they wanted to sell me their business I made the decision to leave there and take over a shop that was closing its doors. I quit my job on a Wednesday and began the work of resurrecting the new shop two days later as she was closing on the coming Monday if I didn't. The place and business were destroyed but I held the hope that it could be repaired. Many of my friends insisted that I change the name because of the damage done to it but I loved it and there was something about the name that resonated with me from deep within. The name was "Twigs" and with our children at such a young age and the place Mia and I landed in of wanting to flip the script for them I saw my own three children as twigs shooting off the larger tree. We didn't change the name.

The new place came with two employees who watched the previous owner run it into the ground. The driver Austin was an older fellow who agreed to continue with me. (A couple of months later I found out that he, as a bartender, used to serve Papa at the local social club many decades before. He even remembered Papa's regular drink. The floral shop was in the neighborhood where Papa grew up in. Small world, right?) Joanne needed a bit more convincing. She came from a family of floral designers as well. Her father and my great grandfather, Moo's father, were two of the largest design houses in our state in the past. I believe it was this commonality that became the catalyst for her to return to the shop after taking a couple of weeks off.

I had three terms of endearment for her.

"Jo Jo" was the one I used when she was there playing the role of friend. Though she was old enough to be my mother she was indeed one of the closest friends I've ever had. She knew me through and through and as an intuitive being she could read me even when I tried to keep the mask over what I didn't want to be seen.

"Joanne!!!" was the one I used as we worked together, as I

tried to be the "boss." It was the one I used with a raised voice that told her that I was nervous or anxious and when I did this she immediately moved to the person, the role, she was at her core. The comforter who always told you the blistering truth without any sugarcoating. The realist. The Mom in her came forth. (She was the "boss" by the way.)

"Mama." Here was the one I came to cherish the most. She came into my life when I was trying to break free from all the roles I had been exposed to in my family, the persuasion and traumas that laced my life, as I sought to create my own world free from these bondages with the hope that my own children might not have to experience the drag of them. She "adopted" me, and I "adopted" her. She called me her "adopted son." It used to blow her daughter's minds how much of a bond she and I shared. We shared this bond right up until her passing.

As the lost soul always looking for the answers, I had this uncanny way of trying to fit people into the roles that I came to believe were being executed in a deficient manner in my family. Though we used these terms of endearment with each other I didn't look at her as a substitute for my Mom. She was indeed a Mom to me and acted as the Mom for me on so many levels but there was this resistance within me in trying to firmly attach the role to her. Perhaps it was because there were those three terms of endearment and so many layers of relation to our relationship.

She was an incredible woman and even intimidated me at times, but it wasn't intentional. I believe it came from the way she lived her life. She was all about family. Truthfully it was all that she cared about. It was the most pronounced and admirable piece of her character. She held this unselfish and unconditional care for everyone in her family that was always laced with the truth, both soft and hard truths. She never minced words; she said it the way it was. She offered these observations from her own life experiences. And if she was wrong when you tried to protest or correct her? She didn't protest. She allowed you your opinion and took it into consideration.

She became a beacon of hope for me that added to the complex fabric of my existence at a time when I was asking all of those "life questions." She became my confidant and accepted me and my life's persuasions without that damaging judgment. She always employed this discernment that so many cannot bring forth. "Mama" was there through some of the toughest times in my life and always listened to the bit that was inside of me. She did this not only as a sage, but I believe to also show me how to do the same. To show me how healthy love is indeed without conditions attached. I always welcomed her endless counsel in every area of my life.

As a pall bearer I carried her to her final resting place but didn't leave the advice or lessons learned from this endless counsel at the graveyard. It has been instilled within me at depths that have taken root in a way that continues to push the false narrative out of its cemented place and into the Light.

Relationships can be viewed as either a lesson or a blessing but every one of them is indeed a blessing when seen through the prism of God-consciousness. I think a lot of times when someone mentions the "lesson or blessing" the vision is limited to "good or bad." The "good" being the "blessing," and the "bad" being the "lesson." I believe the irony here is that what we might perceive as bad, or a lesson, is in truth a blessing on an entirely different level. The lessons are always abundant and can contain layers of understanding. Most times these understandings are revealed and arrived at after a long period of time and consideration.

Though my ego craves all that would nourish it including

the incessant need to fill those "roles" it feels it needs to be present in the sitcom so it might feel okay this did not happen with "Jo Jo."

Our fledgling floral studio gained momentum with the needed attention and energy that we lent to it, and it grew over time. We have had the benefit of embracing not only the myriads of lessons in business and our craft, but the never-ending technological advances constantly presented to us.

A "friend" approached me and offered to take on the creation of our web presence with a website and other aspects. We had some of this in place but as an ego-driven being at this time I wanted "more." I always wanted "more." We entered into an agreement and a site was created. It went nowhere. Never gained any traction, and all that was promised never came to be. The "friend" bled us for thousands and thousands of dollars while subbing the work out to another fellow who never completed the background work because he wasn't paid with the thousands and thousands. In the madness of my ego, I was blinded by the madness of his ego. Blessing? Lesson?

During the Cold War the Soviets had a tactic they used where they would make a series of sharp turns with a submarine to have a look behind it. This movement was called a "Crazy Ivan" because of its dangerous nature and potential risk of collision and detection by both submarines. So many of the relationships in my life have had this same depth of tactical insanity attached to them. This relationship was one of them. A sudden turn away from that which is not fruitful, not nourishing.

One might see this as the lesson but indeed it held blessings that are still being uncovered more than a decade later. We ended this arrangement and relationship and after a failure or two of seeing the needs that he promised by still others fail I made the decision to take on the necessary technological work myself. The result has indeed been a blessing. We took control of the digital destiny of the studio.

Each lesson learned and uncovered comes with options. One of the most profound is the decision as to whether one will share the resultant learning that came with it or keep it to themselves. I have always been one who wants to share the result. I believe passing it on is wholly productive and expected. The spirit of altruism is most amazing when applied in practical and judicial and thoughtful ways.

At times I get restless, and my mind wanders to asking "What's next?" In one of these moments and with the intent and spirit of passing on what I came to know I thought to creating a coaching business related to the backbone structure of business models. Before I could launch this, I needed to see if it might be viable by practicing the art of passing it on. I needed to try it to see if it held the same level of satisfaction that working with others around breaking away from fears and resentments held.

I reached out to a few people who were in business or seemed to have plateaued in their business to inquire if they might be interested in taking the journey with me to reach for more. One of them agreed and we began the work. The result in her business was transformative and truly amazing. The practices applied propelled her business in monumental ways and put her on the map in a way she never dreamed of. We got close to one another and a bond was created between us that very much mirrored that of siblings. I would call her my "sister from another mister" and she would call me her "brother from another mother." It was an effective partnership until it wasn't.

Pride justifies and encourages the ego while the ego passively goads us into doing that which runs contrary to spirituality, God-consciousness. The ego is a hopeless romantic lulling us with an idealistic view and idealistic concepts but most times it is just so wrong and off base. Of all that I wanted to pass on in the way of coaching others in business, born out of the lessons learned in my own business and life it was this one part that I wished to make emphatically clear in the teachings. I wanted to pass this on as it was this exact thing that nearly destroyed me. It literally was at the base of the cause that brought me to trying to run my truck into a telephone pole. Ego.

When I began this work with this person there was only one condition that I placed on our endeavor. I simply expressed that when her ego showed up and began to rule her as I intuitively knew it might that I would end the lessons and coaching. I don't think she knew what I was speaking of when I spoke to this, but I had to bring this part to the table and have it in place.

The ego is a rapacious creditor and will use all that it has in cunningness to con its host and indeed this was what happened. The day arrived when her ego arrived on the scene in a pronounced manner, and she thoughtlessly trampled on my name. I had no choice but to walk away. All that I tried to teach and pass on in the way of remaining humble with successes couldn't be taught with words or by demonstration. Most times this lesson must come from personal experience, the same way I had to learn from personal experience.

What I never saw was that I had been unfairly trying to fill the role of sister with another. I wasn't trying to do this when we began our work together but as one's ego is in constant need of nourishment and will easily attach itself to the ego of another my ego found this to be the best avenue in which to regain some kind of relevance in my life again. Once discovered and seen for what it is the ego is like the Whack-a-Mole game you see in amusement parks. It rears its head, and we see it. We react by either ignoring it or allowing it to remain as a guiding force or we decide to abandon it. The decision to abandon it, whack it away, is easier when we have experienced the lessons of its destructive force. Thereby moving what might be seen as a lesson to taking the place of being seen as a blessing. It is an opportunity to recognize that we need something stronger than ourselves to combat it.

Our relationship began as an amazing journey that stretched each of our abilities and added depth to them in ways we never imagined. Her business was spiritual in nature but in the end, it seemed as though this was a form of a guise to hide the ego that easily attaches itself to our humanness and when I grew weary of the mental and emotional drain and felt that the relationship moved to a place where I was being used I "Crazy Ivaned." I made that sharp turn and abruptly cut all ties. Discernment allowed an effective decision to me made.

Another time a fellow came into my life and the similarities between us were wild. We seemed to speak the same language. We seemed to have a great deal in common with one another, especially as it relates to the familial persuasions we endure. We seemed to be on the same path with the same desires in life and willingness to work with others to see them transcend all the familial and societal drags that create the fertile ground for resentments and fears that become the prevailing winds against our sails as we navigate the stream of life.

We spent a few years working with one another via electronic platforms carrying the message of spirituality and God-consciousness with people around the world with those who would join us. This indeed was an effective partnership as well, until it wasn't.

Through a series of events, I came to see the depth at which I had been experiencing a sort of spiritual relapse. In a moment of duplicity where I made a faulty judgment, it appears my ego, always lying in wait, saw this as a chance to regain a bit of relevance in my life. I wouldn't come to see this for a couple of years and at that time I began to experience what seemed a spiritual atrophy. My God-consciousness took a hard hit, and I became lifeless though every area of my life couldn't be better. My vessel in the stream of life became listless.

My ego loves to eat crap. It typically finds darkness, deviousness, and derision to be its best source of energy. At times I think its satisfaction comes with my dissatisfaction. (Read that again.) My ego will take me to the edge of the cliff after fully convincing me to jump off and at the last moment will stop me. My ego wants to play God and will even convince me that I'm succeeding at this though the facts before me tell me otherwise. It is always a failure.

In this one moment of willful participation in duplicity I created a separation from God-consciousness. I allowed a lie to perpetuate because of the fear that I might lose this relationship. I did this selfishly without thinking of the consequences it might bring, especially to others. And then through a series of events with this individual my eyes were forced open, and I couldn't deny what came into view.

As I shared with him the revealing truths that I came to see he wasn't having any part of it. I knew in that moment that at the base of what I thought was an effective partnership had been the cunning persuasion of the ego that embraced the fear deep down inside of me to regain its relevance in my life. As I was trying to apologize and come clean for playing God, he accused me of playing God for recognizing these wrongs and speaking to them. The ego is a sneaky son of a bitch. I was forced to "Crazy Ivan" this relationship too.

When I entered these two toxic relationships, I didn't know where they would go. I didn't know if they would become enduring lifelong relationships or if they were going to be the fleeting variety. I did know that there were going to be deep lessons attached to them, that they were going to have a profound bearing on the guiding forces in my life. At their base all relationships have this power in them. It's like the power we find in our stories. The synergy between the power in our stories and the power in relationships is incredible with the constant of always being instructive.

I held the hope that the relationships would be healthy, the opposite of the relationships I had with my family members. But as someone who always longed for the deep and productive, the healthy and nourishing familial relationships, there was a part of me always wanting to call someone out of the dugout and into my game of life as a substitute for those I wanted a relationship with the most in my family. In other words, I became the person trying to check off the boxes when it came to some of the relationships that came into being in my part of the stream of life. I most times, unknowingly, tried to fit people into a box. In this respect, I tried to play God while feeding the false narrative and delusions. Unknowingly I was feeding my ego but suspected deep down inside that something was amiss, was corrupt.

The ego, that part of me that all the delusions I have ever lived by or created within myself, is the most cunning part of my being. My humanness. It seems to be looking for relevance and looking to ensure that it survives. It is as destructive as fear. It will use some of the relationships in my life as nourishment for its sick and twisted need to dominate. The ego easily attaches itself to the egos of others. There's this often-hidden corrosive nature about it. This is what happened with these two relationships.

The greatest combatant of this twisted mechanism is forgiveness. The ego, and even the relationship from one ego to another's ego, cannot live, endure, or survive the power that comes with forgiveness's nature. Forgiveness is the catapult that propels us away from not only the ego and the unhealthy relationships but to a place where we might find the freedom not only from our own bondage to our lower self but to another's self. But not only that, the bondage of another's deep need to remain sick. Their attachment to their own self. Their attachment to their own resentments and fears, their attachment to their need to play God. Forgiveness not only takes the place of resentment and fear, it erases it.

These two poignant relationships blew up in an explosive way. One day they were there and the next they were not. The incessant need to fit people into a box, to fit them into the dream of relationships with labels such as "sister" or "brother," clears as quickly as the fog does over the stream when soaked in the rays of God-consciousness. Forcing is futile but letting God hold sway does work. When forgiveness arrives and takes its place within us, we are then in a better place to have and hold the healthiest of relationships while the unhealthiest simply fade away. Most times the only thing that brings this clear understanding isn't only the open mind to see it or the willingness to see the truth or even the ability to be honest. It is the element of time. Time holds a powerful persuasion.

God-consciousness, along with forgiveness, allows not only our spirit and mind to be renewed. They usher forth a rearrangement of our physical life too. People, places and things are changed and rearranged as a natural consequence of our movement from one station to the other. Our task is to remain willing to let people, places, and things go. Perhaps with time, experience, and a deepened God-consciousness that affords us deeper and deeper levels of awareness those that we let go of are freed without those life-changing claw marks that we tend to leave on them. It is healthy to leave and healthy to leave others behind. Not everyone is going to want what you have and will have to battle through their own fears and resentments as they journey back to the Honeysuckle Dream.

We needn't be concerned whether we are in the background, or the foreground, of someone's process, progress, or experience. We need only be concerned with our own spiritual condition and leave the rest to God. We don't have the power that God has. Our spiritual condition determines the role God will assign to us.

We need only trust in His plan. The Divine Design.

Thirty-Six

Jean Nate

Mom passed away a few days before my 49th birthday. She was just shy of seventy-one years old. I had been writing my first book for a month and completed a couple of soft edits. I wanted something legible, and concrete, done for my birthday. Once I told her about it she became supportive and kept pushing me to finish it. When she asked questions and wanted to know more about it, I handed her very little information. I gave her bits and pieces. I wanted to answer those questions by handing her a copy of the manuscript on my birthday.

My birthday was on a Tuesday, and I worked feverishly trying to finish the edits to make it presentable. I spoke with her on the Sunday before my birthday. It would be the last time we spoke with one another. I told her I had a gift for her for my birthday and that I would get it to her on Tuesday. I printed the manuscript out and had it ready on Monday. I still have a copy of the manuscript with "Mom" written on the front page.

I collapsed on Monday night with exhaustion yet didn't sleep. I was restless, I tossed and turned until about three in the morning. Though I was exhausted my mind and body wouldn't allow me to sleep. I suppose my mind and body were too wired. Maybe I had a fear of what she might think of the book. It was a weird night for me. Eventually I landed on the couch downstairs.

When Mia woke, she let me sleep and went to the design studio to begin the day there. She thought I would show up a short time later. I didn't get to the studio until about two in the afternoon. When I eventually woke up, it was after one in the afternoon, and I felt horrible. I had this sinking feeling. Something wasn't right. Something was seriously off.

The first part was that I had wasted a day sleeping. I am not a fan of unproductive days. The second was the exhaustion that lingered with me that brought this deep sense of loss with it. My first instinct at the time was to try to evade it, to totally ignore it. I tried but couldn't escape it.

There weren't any missed calls from Mom.

She hadn't called or left a voicemail wishing me a "Happy Birthday."

After spending an hour trying to adjust to the exhaustion and trying to break free of it, I arrived at the studio to finish out the day with my wife. I told her I felt something was wrong. We tried to call Mom, but she wasn't picking up. I left her a voicemail. I called her repeatedly and still had no answer. With each unanswered call, the lies I tried to tell myself to get through the day wouldn't hold me with their weak power. I could not evade the reality of my senses.

Later that evening Mia and I went to Mom's house. The front living room was lit by the television that was on, it was the only sign of activity in the house. The outside of the house and the yard were lit by the bright moon. The doors were locked when we tried them. As I shivered in the cold, I pounded on the back door that I had come in and out of nearly my entire life. There was no answer. The only sound in the neighborhood was my frantic screaming "Mom please open the door!"

I knew she was in the house. I also knew she was gone.

I couldn't get in. I couldn't help her. I couldn't save her.

I went around the house climbing through the overgrown ewes that lined each side of the house trying to look in and couldn't see anything, all the while banging on them hoping that she was asleep and that I might wake her up. Might get her to come back.

When I made it to the front living room what I saw made my heart sink. It brought tears to my eyes. The reality of where Mom landed came crashing onto me as I watched her dog running through the house reacting to my cries. A few neighbors took notice and a relative that lived nearby *happened* to be driving by and stopped.

I called the fire department for assistance and as I was trying to get help my sister called me. I think the cousin called her or had someone call her. She brought all the venom she had for me with her on the call. I could certainly feel that energy as it mixed with my growing sense of powerlessness, loss, and increasing sadness. The call was interrupted when our car’s Bluetooth hijacked the call while I was standing outside of the vehicle. She thought I hung up on her and became even more venomous when the call reconnected.

The fire fighters gained access through Mom's bedroom window and opened the front door of the house from within. I was standing there waiting to bust into the house. They held me back as they blocked the door. They wouldn't let me in, wouldn't let me see her. They told me that I did not want to go in there and see her like this. They told me it would be best if I remained outside.

Mom was gone and had been gone for at least two days. I believe she passed away on the same day we last spoke with one another. I also believe she just couldn't do it anymore. In the end her life journey became all too painful for her and there was no peace and quiet in her stream of life anymore. Days later I would speak with someone on the job at the fire department and they told me that she didn't intentionally take her own life and that it looked like natural causes. I knew differently. While she didn't intentionally take her life the day she died, she had already made the decision to give up at deeper and deeper levels long before this. She had wanted to leave for quite some time and often expressed it to me.

The police arrived to secure Mom's house and when one of the officers approached me I asked him to help me in another manner. Before my sister arrived, I asked him to "play Switzerland" between us. After I explained a bit more to him, he agreed to try to keep the peace between us.

The coroner's office sent a couple of people, and they took Mom from the house. I felt nauseous as she was wheeled out and placed within the van. I wanted to run to her and tell her how sorry I was. How sorry I was for not being able to relieve the pain she could never break free of while she was here, but it was too late for that.

My sister arrived a short time after the fire fighters, and we remained as far apart as possible given the circumstances. The space between us leading up to this had been expansive for a great many years. We said as little as possible to one another and the police officer who I asked to help did indeed do just that.

The house was cleared, and we were allowed to enter. My sister didn't go in. I told her I was going in and was going to lock the doors. My sister held the key to the house up before my face with a menacing grimace on her face, much like Pat's indelible grimace so many years before as we passed her in the hallway in my father's apartment building. I didn't have a key to my mother's house. I surrendered it years before.

I went in through the front door while Mia sat in our car

with Mom's dog. I had to hold my shirt up to my nose and breathe through it. I had to use my shirt to help block the smell in the house. The smell was not from Mom's body. It was something else. The house was filled with garbage. Mom had become a hoarder, and it was bad.

With every holiday or celebration or just casual dinners we always invited Mom to join us, and she refused. She also refused to let me in her house. I could see why as I crossed the threshold into Nana and Papa's home that she inherited years before when Papa died.

As I walked into the living room, I had to dodge the piles of crap her dog left on the floor that Mom never cleaned up. They were like landmines in the path that was cut through the piles of garbage lined up against the walls. I followed the path into the dining room, the same dining room that appears so often in the old films of the family before Mom and Dad split. Although the lights the firefighters turned on were still on in all the rooms, the home seemed like a dark cave. The lights barely permeated the darkness. The place seemed so dim. It felt like that long hallway that I had created with all the locked doors that was my life.

I made it to the back of the house to the door that I had been pounding on behind the kitchen at the pantry. I looked up at the cabinets that once held all the canned goods that Nana left behind and thought to myself that what Mom was leaving behind held far more power in the way of lessons. I turned around and stood in the middle of the kitchen, the center of my grandparents' home growing up. I turned in a full circle drinking in the conditions before me as years and years of memories, and the images they held quickly played out through my mind with the same pace as the images that played out as my truck headed for that telephone pole years before.

My thoughts went to Mom. I apologized out loud to her for

not being able to help her transcend her pain. For not being able to take her pain away. I thanked her for my life and promised that I would tell her story, our story.

I couldn't give her a copy of the book for my birthday, but she gave me the gift of letting go of all that bound her. She was free of her body of pain. She was free of the generational drama.

I turned the light off in the kitchen and walked back into the dining room. I didn't go into the bedroom attached to the kitchen, the bedroom my sister and I shared growing up, my mother's bedroom as she grew up in Nana and Papa's house. I passed the bathroom on my left and then turned the light off in the dining room. I wanted to go into the basement to take a deep breath of the familiar musty smell and even the attic to catch one of the always dry air up there but I did not. I walked through the living room with a quickened step as the feeling that there was absolutely nothing left here washed over me. I didn't go into the other bedroom as this was where Mom had taken her last breath. I didn't want to see what was left behind in there. I turned off the last light and pulled the solid front door closed behind me.

I returned to my sister and handed her the key to the house. The house was now hers; my mother's prison cell was now hers. It was the last time that my sister and I were in each other's company and one of the last times that we would speak with one another. A key wasn't needed to lock the house and both my sister and I knew this. There was a twisted pleasure like her twisted pleasure she seemed to have in handing the key to Mom's house back to her.

Mom's house, and even her dog, became an extension of the absolute pain that she experienced in life. While her life here held as much value as anyone else's she never believed it did. She was filled with so much hope as she married my father. Her spirit was alive and buoyed. I see it in the films from that period in her life. The taking of her third child absolutely destroyed her. The resultant resentments and fears ate away at her, and her house showed me just how badly she suffered from them. She was absolutely powerless over them. They ruled every fiber of her being and she simply couldn't break free of them. They killed her and killed everything about her.

She taught me many lessons and one of the most important was that I must embrace every single part of myself, even the darkest parts. And that by embracing them and allowing them to be exposed to the Light they will indeed become some of the most powerful parts of my story.

Mom gave up. She simply grew tired and didn't want to be here anymore. I believe many people find themselves in this position at times and some even make the conscious decision to just let themselves go. This is what Mom did. She was beaten down by the currents in her stream of life. She didn't even want a life jacket when it was offered to her. She refused it. There was nothing that could bring her peace and comfort. Not even her grandchildren or a thought of them could break through the darkness she succumbed to.

She told Mia and I what she was going to do but I think there was a part of us that didn't believe her. Perhaps there was a part of us that knew deep inside that we were as powerless over her darkness as she was. She wouldn't accept our help as much as we offered it.

Mom gave up on her health years before as she fell into depression with her divorce from my father, especially after she lost that child. She became morbidly obese over time but kept lumbering though life the best she could. She did eventually leave the couch, she eventually went back to work, but there was always something missing. She always carried the feeling of defeat with her. She even remarried and seemed to be reborn for a time, but this too was short-lived and when her husband passed away, she was alone. She had no one. She didn't have me in her life when her husband died as we were estranged at this time and my sister didn't have the capacity to see past her own stuff to be of any real help to her. My sister had her own resentments against me and Mom that blocked any level of compassion and empathy in her to accept Mom. By all that she expressed I wholly believe she couldn't wait for Mom to be gone. By her own actions I believe she couldn't wait to take the leftover scraps.

Mom tried different medications to relieve the pain, but they didn't work. They masked the pain and eventually she would stop taking these. She went back and forth with the medications for years as she sought escape from reality. In the end she made the conscious decision to stop taking these meds, to let the darkness take her. She fell into seeking escape by watching all the classic films she always tried to use as a reprieve from the stream of life. This always allowed her to push reality off, to "think about it tomorrow" as she was fond of saying with her best Scarlett O'Hara impression.

She stopped taking the other medications that were helping to keep her physical body from failing. She chose how she was going to die, and it would come to match the suffering in her mind, her guilt, her shame and her remorse, that she endured for so long in her life.

Mom's body gave out because of her giving up. Her physical life, her house and even her car, came to match the disorder within her. The pain within her. The mayhem and chaos within her. Even her dog Bubba and his look and his way came to match the disorder.

When Mia and I returned home with him he was terrified. His fur had been neglected for so long that it was oily and overgrown. You could feel the dirt and grime on him. I could feel the mayhem and chaos of the end of Mom's life on him. I couldn't even see his eyes; they were buried with the overgrown fur.

We gave him a bath and he shook so badly as if it was torturing him. I found his eyes and could see the terror in them. The dirt pooled in the tub as I washed and rinsed him a few times. His nails were so overgrown that they were twisted around one another. We had to hold him down to free them up. I clipped the fur away from his eyes while we held him tight. You could see relief washing over him for a bit.

After he dried off, he fell asleep in Mia's arms on the couch. The care of him was enough to put him at ease. Isn't this the case with us as humans too? At times isn't the level of peace and comfort we achieve directly related to the level of care we feel from and even extend to others?

Our dependency on others comes in two forms. Healthy and unhealthy. Sick dependencies keep us sick while healthy dependencies inspire us to remain healthy or to get healthier. Dependency on human beings for our well-being and happiness will always be flawed as we are all fallible. We will always fall short of one another's sometimes unrealistic expectations. While I was able to break from these unrealistic expectations with and of Mom my sister simply could not. As I learned the futility of the resentments I had for Mom and learned to seek comfort in a Higher Parent, she could not.

The greatest of all the lessons Mom taught me, and still teaches me when I lapse into reflection, is that if I remain free of unrealistic dependencies on others and remain wholly dependent on God, I will be in the best position possible to enjoy every single part of the stream of life while I'm here. Even the dark ones.

Thirty-Seven

Lizzie-Ticjz

The dependency that I had on the generational trauma in my family knew no bounds. My lower self, the ego, certainly flourished off its darkness. This dependency, simply a layer of spiritual sickness and insidiousness, breeds an ignorance on unseen levels and from it stems an arrogance that we remain oblivious to while under its influence and the malaise of it.

Of course there are healthy dependencies in life, necessary dependencies in life. It is the harmful ones that we must be made aware of if we are to enjoy a break from spiritual sickness and a return to the Honeysuckle Dream. Some of the healthiest dependencies I have had have been on people in my life, and some of the wiliest dependencies have also been on people.

Mom and Dad, unknowingly and under the dependency of their generational trauma and spiritual illness, enlisted my sister and I in their never-ending war with one another. They set things in motion for us to begin our own personal war. We took their often-unspoken terms and conditions to places they never would have imagined. And when the two of us obliged them by doing this they were at a loss for any understanding of it. Dad simply drifted farther away if that was even possible. Mom tried to manage by playing the referee at times. She tried to keep that triangle from falling apart. Still other times she took sides. It got ugly. Eventually the triangle was permanently dismantled; it became a straight line only allowing two people at a time to engage with one another. And even this was put to death eventually.

Before Papa's passing away my sister insisted a trust be set up to benefit Mom and insulate any assets from her power to better preserve them ensuring she would be "taken care of in the best way." My sister and I were made co-executors of it. You're probably rightly imagining what happened. As money and worldly possessions do in many families it became the nail in the coffin that was the relationship between a brother and sister.

I used the assets in the trust for my selfish ends with the blessing of my sister. When I look back it feels like she was setting a trap for me. In a short time, her heart changed as I wasn't living my life by her standards, by the way she thought I should be. As I was always trying to actualize the false hope of having a relationship with my father, she caught wind that I was speaking with him, and this turned into its own war. She was pissed off that I was trying to have a relationship with him. She felt deceived and this got ugly. She demanded the assets be returned and this could not be done with a snap of my fingers. This exacerbated the situation even more.

We were trying to manage what amounted to a small trust while also trying to control one another and in the middle of this was Mom. She was trying to live her life and was remarried now. Battle lines were drawn. I resigned as co-executor of the trust and even waived any rights I might see from it as with the passing of Mom the assets would fall to my sister and me. I wrongly believed that if I waived my rights to it this might be enough to end the war. I wanted peace. That wasn't going to happen. My sister wouldn’t allow it.

My sister convinced Mom to bring me to Superior Court and file actions against me. They were successful as what my sister and I had done by removing the assets was indeed illegal. The orders required me to return the assets by a specific timeline. I agreed to do anything to stop the war. I was waving a white flag, yet my sister didn't see it. She saw the opportunity to move in with every piece of artillery she could summon to the battlefield.

As I waived my rights, she absolutely insisted that I waive the rights of my children as well. She wanted the natural line of inheritance created by the trust, the trust she had insisted on and created, to be changed so that she and her family would become the sole beneficiaries at the time of Mom's passing.

Sometimes we think that by eliminating people from our lives we believe it eliminates the situations or problems, or the resultant ripples in the stream that accompany them, but I have found it does not. Every little bit and piece that we experience is designed for one purpose. To move us from unconsciousness to consciousness. This is indeed what this situation did for me. I tried to eliminate the reason for the war or the escalation of it and it only increased it. My sister saw blood in the water and a gain for herself in not only what amounted to paltry assets but a gain in favor with my mother, and even my father. She mastered the triangle thing in my family as she tried to exercise control over our mother.

When she found out I was speaking with Dad she reached out to him, and she began speaking with him. I had to walk away from everybody at this point. The depth of insanity attached to it all, including my own, was simply too overwhelming. It brought the totality of my life, of the life we all had together and even the life we did not have together, front and center. I became deeply aware of the chemistry that had been in place from as far back as I can remember and when it was presented to me while being an adult with my own children, I had to run from it.

I waved that white flag but there was more to it. I gave up. I began the in-depth journey of trying to make sense of the madness with the commitment to myself that I would try to keep my children out of it. My sister tried to act the conscience for me while having no conscience. My father was still my father, he never changed. Mom went with the flow in the stream that she deemed would serve her best. At no other time did I feel like the black sheep in the family so deeply than at this time.

The thing about generational pain, and the ignorance that protects it, is that we try with all our might to protect it. We try to ensure that it continues, unknowingly most times. We will fight to the death to keep it relevant. We can't see the destructive forces within it all while in the midst of it. Though we may think we have power, we do not. At times we are wholly governed by it. Sometimes the only way to really see it all is to remove ourselves from it. This is not easy.

The generational trauma moves in a constant circle and drags in its orbit anything needed to feed it, to ensure it survives. It ends not only with our recognition of it but with our sincere desire to try to change it. This is where I landed. I wanted to be free and was willing to do whatever I could to gain that freedom.

As I hit my own personal bottom and began sifting through the ashes with that group of men who had done the same, I became aware of my part in all the trauma and drama that was my family. I saw the battles I fought, those I thought I had won and those I thought I had lost. With exhaustion and disgust, I left the battlefield but would constantly be invited to come back. Its gravitational pull tried to suck me back into its orbit over and over again.

Mom's husband died and she fell back into the familiar slumber she had been in for years. She fell deeper this time though. She really gave up and as she did my sister reacted in the same manner she had previously but also in deeper ways. She held Mom in contempt at deeper and deeper levels. At times she refused to speak with Mom or even deal with her, she left it to her husband who took to verbally abusing Mom and to placing the blame on me for circumstances set in motion by my sister's decisions and resultant consequences of her actions.

Here's just how delusional things had become. Long after I resigned as executor and waived my rights, and those of my children, thereby walking away, abandoning any future gain and handing it all to my sister, her husband called me and expected me to pay for half of the replacement of a furnace in the house even though technically it was theirs. When I refused and pointed this out, he was in disbelief that I wouldn't contribute. I wholly suspect he was not happy to be taking on my sister's responsibility.

One morning I arrived at the studio to receive a message from my answering service through the night. It was from Mom, and it simply said, "I forgive you." I reached out to her, and she explained what was happening. I was powerless. I couldn't help her. I had no power in the trust or sway over how it might benefit her. I had no fight left in me to battle my sister either. Mom was not only a prisoner in her home but was totally beholden to my sister who neglected her and her husband who had no respect for her.

My sister wanted Mom out of her own house, but Mom wanted to stay there. I knew that if I kept myself in contempt of the Superior Court order along with keeping the note on Mom's house that my sister could not sell her house. So, I refused to pay it off so that Mom could stay there. I continued to pay the taxes and insurance on her home though it was not mine nor would I see any personal gain from it. The only benefit would be Mom's security to live in her home without being abandoned to another place as my sister wanted. It was all I could do and Mom's refusal to pursue court orders ensured she could remain in her house.

After I went through the experience of sifting through all the fears and resentments and broke free of the spiritual sickness I had been under for nearly my entire life I had to try to clean up the wreckage I caused. While there were those about me that were at fault, under the influence of their spiritual sickness, it made no difference. I still had to do the necessary work of trying to repair the mess I left in my wake in the stream. This included approaching Mom and my sister.

My approach to Mom was readily accepted and as I said we grew to have some of the most amazing conversations and revelations with one another. We began the heavy work of uncovering the nastiness of the generational trauma and plainly speaking to it for what it was. My approach to my sister was not as welcomed or accepted. It was an imposition on her own reality, false and real. Though she agreed to meet with me, and I had the intention of trying to begin to make things right I could see from the moment we sat down that it was not going to work.

Beside her chair was a line of things that she had removed from Mom's house that I had abandoned in the basement at the workbench I built years before. She was displaying them as if they were trophies. As I witnessed the state of Mom's house and her hoarding as I walked through it that final time my mind was thrown back to this very moment in time and it simply sent the message that it was indeed over between my sister and me. I felt no hope for a relationship with her. The false hope was snuffed out as well.

Though we have always been at war at some level I tried with whatever resources I had within me whether it was false hope or even the briefest of moments when we saw eye to eye to be there for her. Not a bit of these efforts ever made a dent as I was vilified at every turn. While I left the battlefield she remained and continued in the mode of conquering and collecting.

While a note I held in place on my mother's house ensured she stayed there, and I agreed to pay the taxes on the house so the assets in the trust would not be depleted too quickly, I also held an insurance policy on the house. After Mom passed away my sister would continue her never-ending assault by filing bogus claims exceeding 50 thousand dollars against it to remodel Mom's house.

To further illustrate the absolute insanity, I was asked to cover the cost of the deductible I had in place on the policy. My sister and her husband were upset that I had a two-thousand-dollar deductible and their dream of realizing a great windfall from the insurance policy was being dimmed a bit.

Nothing made me more aware of the shame of my own existence than the constant war with my sister and her lack of shame when it came to the defense of and participation in the generational drama, the insanity we lived that I wanted to be free of.

The night my wife and I discovered that Mom had died would be the last time I looked into my sister's eyes and would be the last time I would see that grimace on her face. When I finally had the old 8mm films in the cans transferred to a disc and was able to watch them, I was floored by what I saw.

The contempt my sister held for me was evident and seemed to be in place long before I left the Honeysuckle Dream. We have always been like oil and water, impossible to mix with one another, even though the appearance seemed to be the opposite at times. Had we been twins in the womb instead of Irish twins she probably would've choked me with her umbilical cord.

We would have a couple of conversations in the days after Mom's passing related to Mom. Not one of Mom's wishes of what she wanted upon her death would be carried out. All that Mom ever wanted fell on deaf ears with my sister and I had no power to make any decisions. Not one thing that Mom possessed and wanted passed on to either me or my children was ever passed on to us.

We didn't have a service of any sort for Mom. Her life ended without a celebration of it. I do, however, get to celebrate it every day at some level. I get to celebrate the lessons learned by each of us. Individually and collectively. I came to see the body of pain we have to experience as humans that is perhaps set up to get us back to our childish faith we inevitably abandon. Mom did the same. She looked at it, relived it, came to terms with it, and gained freedom from it. She also knew that her time here was over and though her physical life and her trappings sent the message of mayhem and chaos when she left, I believe she had the last laugh as she departed here in peace with the comfort that she did the best that she could with what she had.

Mom and I came to discuss that some of the greatest lessons we have learned have always been offered by seeing just how badly we were *takers*. She was a taker, and I became one by extension and through her body of pain and lessons passed on. When the full realization is arrived at, clearly showing one that a life lived as a taker is futile then one gets to make the journey across the bridge to a different station. One is allowed to move from being a taker to being a giver. This same person comes to see those dependencies on people, and even on things, can easily be shed as the value changes from a selfish need to one of acceptance. We can move from being a victim to being held accountable and accepting responsibility. One gets to see that we no longer have to cling onto things. We can lose the fear of not getting what we want and the fear of losing what we have.

We come to know that once a dependency is shifted from people, places, and things to that ultimate Power that is God that He will indeed provide every single bit and piece needed for us to live not only in absolute freedom but in the freedom from the bondage of self, from the bondage of the lower self. We come to know that while our power was insufficient His Power would have and does provide everything. There is no freedom like that of deciding to walk away from the pain and trauma and then following it with the action required to get back to the Honeysuckle Dream. It can be so.

Thirty-Eight

Suck A Puddle

As I left Mom's house for the last time on the night we found her and began turning the lights off in the kitchen, passing through the house as I left, I came to realize that I had done the same with my father. I turned the lights off until the relationship fell into complete darkness. I had the opportunity to sit with him and Pat and come clean for all that I had done. I held a hope within that they might do the same. It was a false hope. It didn't happen.

As we sat together at this final time my father shared a story of a time with his own father. It was the one and only time he did this with me, and I knew as much as he might be capable of escaping his own generational trauma and childhood he simply could not let go. He couldn't let his past go. It was too heavy and held too much sway over his rudders and sails as he travelled along the stream of life. I fully suspect that his wife would never have let him.

Pat took a different approach this time when we were together. She didn't mince words when she said she never wanted me or my sister in her life, her actions always matched this, when she said she never wanted to love me, her lack of expressing love did the same. It matched. She confirmed what I always held as a belief deep in my heart. She didn't want to share our father with us, and we were expendable in her effort to see that we wouldn't.

By the time Mom had passed away I was already at the last light that illuminated the false hope of having anything at all in the way of a relationship with Dad. Like the relationship with my sister, too much water had gone over the dam and our vessels labeled “relationship” were already sunk. They could not be recovered. As much as I would have loved my father to reach out to me when Mom passed away that never happened. It was an impossibility. I was too far removed from the family and its nuances, and I suspect some of the family knew I wouldn't engage anymore when invited back to the battlefield.

In a conversation with my sister shortly after Mom was found dead, she revealed that when my father was told by his brother Rick that Mom had passed away, he simply said something to the effect of "Yeah, I saw that on social media." As my father grew older, he grew even colder.

Though he always fully expected me to come to him over the years and made no effort to return the favor I obliged. The day came when I had to stop. I simply couldn't do it anymore. When I was younger, he had a heart issue. I remember being taken to the hospital to see him and being told how lucky I was that he didn't die.

I was already acutely aware that we had nothing between us and years later when I recalled Mom describing the doctors trying to bring Nana back to life and how she didn't respond the thought crossed my mind containing the wish that this is what I wanted to happen to my father. That's harsh but so isn't the fear of abandonment, the thinking, and its attendant suffering, that is the exact result of it. Ugly!

Shortly before Mom passed away Rick called to tell me that

Dad had this rare form of Parkinson's and that the outlook wasn't good. It was the same old call to action to jump into the role of being a son to the father who was incapable of being a father. Rick said he just wanted to pass the information along and that I could do whatever I had to do with it. I couldn't run to Dad as I was forced to when he had a heart event years before. I didn't reach out. I simply let it go. The situation became another piece of reinforcement against the return to insanity.

When I sat with Dad that day and he told me the story about him and his father it held within it a parable of sorts. His body language expressed that he was forgiving me for the way I acted and retaliated over all the years. His look of horror as his wife spoke her truth to me showed me that deep down inside there was this piece of him that wanted to make its way to the surface but could not. His fundamental idea of God, his mustard seed-sized piece of faith, was buried by a mountain. There was no way he could surmount it. In that moment I saw in him what I had seen in Mom. It was defeat. It was a defeat felt and seen but without any solution to win a position over it. It seemed absolute.

I believe both Mom and Dad came to see what I have come to see. I just don't think they had the courage to fight and overcome it. That it was far easier to just continue to let their vessels drift along the stream at the whim of their storm.

I do not have the benefit of knowing the circumstances of my father's death as I intimately did with Mom's passing. He and I were fully estranged at this point. The phone calls about the weather and how many miles were on the car ended long before my false hope finally faded away. I do not know what he went through or if he came to any major realizations or awakenings. In fact, he became estranged from nearly everyone in the family. As much as I wanted to ask him the questions I tried to ask his sister, my aunt, I never had a clear opportunity.

The next-to-last conversation with my sister was the one when she called to tell me that Dad had passed away. It was short and cordial. She explained to me that Pat requested that she and I *not* be told that he passed away. Even in his death she did not want to share him with us. To this day I have not spoken with her, or her three daughters, and I don't imagine I ever will.

We use our stories in many ways but none more pronounced than to help others, or to even destroy them. My sister and I learned this lesson and the family lessons in profound ways. I believe that most times we weren't even aware that we were being taught them.

As I have commented to my wife on occasion when she speaks of the passing of her father and the finality of it, I always expressed that she was fortunate to a degree to have this finality. That the life lived with the fear of abandonment is a prison cell. The heart and the mind, the feelings and emotions, derived from it are as corrosive as acid.

I have always shared my *story* in an open way. Frankly after seeing the power of other people's stories and how they have led me to recover from so many things in my life I have come to see that there is more gained from sharing in an open manner than from hiding it behind a locked door in one of the rooms along that hallway that is our life.

A short time after Dad passed away and as I was trying to come to deeper understandings of how fear works versus courage, I posted something with depth on social media as it relates to this. I think we can all relate to the fear of abandonment at some level as we all experience the voluntary and involuntary removal and movement of people in our lives. If not this fear than many of the others that are closely associated with it.

The last conversation I had with my sister was when she

placed a call to me. Though we are not connected on social media I suspect she is always there looking at my profile which is public. She saw this post about abandonment, and I suppose it really resonated with her. She came upon the most pronounced and profound thing that we have in common with one another and to this day I do not know if she knows this. I had landed in the place of forgiveness and the full realization that many of us don't really know what we are saying and doing most times when fueled by fear and resentment, fueled by a lack of God-consciousness, when I engaged in the phone call with her.

I think she wanted to speak in depth to everything but was afraid to. I simply listened. She spoke to how she sold Mom's house, and I could feel her instant regret about bringing the subject up like she knew that she had gone too far with the gloating but that moment in the conversation quickly passed. She tried to speak to our common fear and experience but couldn't form cogent sentences. I suppose the charged emotions between us prevented her from doing that. She ended the conversation with a promise to reach out and the thought that maybe we could get together for dinner sometime which I intuitively knew would not happen. There was no way I could ever walk out onto that battlefield that was our life again. As we ended the conversation I added one thing.

"Hey Kim."

"What?"

"No matter what has happened and what will happen I do love you."

This was met with the same silence Mom extended to me when I told her she was in my first book.

Thirty-Nine

The Honeysuckle Dream - Found

There are many conditions that emanate from the person experiencing spiritual malaise and, in this respect, we are all indeed the same. As I expressed at the outset of our journey together it does not matter what race, color, or creed we are, nor does it matter what religion, philosophy, or persuasion we were brought up with. Or not brought up with. I believe we have one problem while here and it is the only problem that needs to be repaired. A solution *must* be found. Perhaps the reason for all of it is that simple.

We experience that absolute perfection in faith as a child, that Honeysuckle Dream, where we just intuitively know that God is. We have this belief, and all is well with us. Then the day arrives when we are pulled from the garden and thrown into the stream of life and begin to become aware of our senses in a different way. Fear and resentment present themselves and we haven't the *full* Power to resist. We begin our journey in a different manner and the lower self, the ego, is actualized and we begin our suffering unknowingly. Unbeknownst to us we also begin our search for God.

He is always there but that insidious lower self gets in the way, using the fears and resentments that we think are healthy in a wholly unhealthy way. The ego decimates us while decimating what little faith we carried out of the garden with us. We become mangled and in turn mangle those about us. Sometimes we go to great degrees with our body of pain to bring about pain to and in others. Yes, it is done intentionally at times.

It does *not* have to be like this. It does *not* have to be like this *at all.*

We can return to the Honeysuckle Dream anytime we want to if we are willing to put in the work of sifting through the ashes of what has been burned down around us by others and even ourselves. If indeed we can move or be moved to a place of having an open mind and becoming truly honest with ourselves in a strict manner.

Examine your senses and simply ask yourself if something is not right, does not feel right.

I grew up thinking and feeling just this. I knew something wasn't right. I knew it the moment I left the Honeysuckle Dream. I just couldn't define it. I knew it as Mom and Dad went to war and enlisted my sister and I in their war. I knew it as my sister and I gladly carried on with the war. I knew it when Dad remarried, and the marriage came with a new family. I knew it when Papa and Rick stepped up as fathers in my life. I knew it when Nana died. I knew it through my first marriage. I knew it as my life expanded and contracted. I knew it when my daughter was born. I knew it when I got remarried and suddenly had another daughter. I knew it when Hans was born. I knew it each time Mom and Dad came in and out of my life as an adult. I knew it when Moo died. I knew it when Papa died.

I knew it each time the thought to take my own life to kill the pain of my unbearable situation crossed my mind. I knew it as I dry fired the pistol into my mouth while biting the barrel and knew it when I would visit the many telephone poles I wanted to wrap my truck around.

While I knew it, I also knew that I didn't have the power to do anything about it. I was screwed here. Imagine believing in God but having so much fear of Him that you land at a place where you're also allowing that fear to prevent you from asking for help. This is where I was until I saw those who broke free from what I was experiencing.

Fear and resentment, the extension of spiritual disease, the disconnect from God, are as cunning as the ego. They lulled me into believing that they would take care of me and help me navigate the stream while in truth they were killing me. Their never-ending assault ensured that my faith, my intuition deep down inside, would remain buried. It would remain unusable while in a state of constantly screaming at me to wake up. By the time I removed all the debris that accumulated over the years from the generational pain in my family, its voice was weak and hoarse. My faith needed to be nourished back to health and needed to be made strong. As strong as it was in the Honeysuckle Dream, and then even stronger to navigate my effort to be rid of that body of pain wrapped around me like a wet t-shirt.

I truly believed that after Mom died, she would take all the pain we experienced together with her. It wasn't so. It lingered and I suppose it still does today to some degree. When I recall a memory with reflection, I can still run a finger along the scar tissue embedded in my soul and feel each and every nuance of it. All the sweet moments and realizations we came upon as well as all the pain she endured as she tried to return to the dream. I can feel the pain she was in at the end of her life when she let go. She fought to get back to the dream but could not fully recover. She was beaten down, weak, and truly spent when she left here.

Though some of it remains she took a great deal of the pain

that we had between us with her. Indeed, what she left me has become priceless. She left all the good behind. I can see all of it now with careful reflection. The endless resentments I had with her are all gone. I do not *refeel* the pain of them, or her pain, when my mind lapses into natural ruminations.

When Dad passed away, I mistakenly believed that he would take my fear of abandonment with him. That it would die with him and rule me no more. It simply wasn't so. As faith is a muscle that will either experience atrophy or strengthen while we are in the stream of life so indeed is fear. It is truly cunning and insidious. The fear of abandonment, and all the other fears I held, strengthened throughout my life.

I wrongly believed that if I removed the causes, the people, places and things, that it would go away. I was not only wrong about the cause. I was wrong about how fear is weakened and put to death. I did not understand that it needed to be its opposite, faith, that would do this work. I was convinced that my mind had the power to kill something that is, in reality, a very unnatural force. Yes, I said fear is an unnatural force.

My mind became soft and delusional through the years, and I continually tried to rely upon it to solve problems that it wasn't conditioned to solve. I simply had to have God's help with this.

As I left the pile of ashes behind me after thoroughly sifting through all of them and began my journey back to the Honeysuckle Dream, I left with a new Friend. I found God in the ashes. I came to see and know that He has indeed always been there. I could never fully make Him out through the fog that hung above the water in the stream of life, or the bridge, but He was there. I also came to see that I always wanted Him to be there. I just didn't know this either. The layers upon layers of fears and resentments prevented me from knowing it. I was playing hide and seek the whole time but needed to always be seeking.

As a child playing hide and seek, we don't want to be found, we want to win the game. But there is something in us that wants to be found, wants to be seen. As the seeker is looking for us while we are hiding in the "best hiding spot in the world" there is a part of us that wants to give our location away. Perhaps we make a sound. Perhaps we make some sudden movements calling their attention to us. It is the same with God. I believe many of us wish to be seen, wish to be found. But we don't know how to make this happen.

I have shared my *story* with you, and I think the part that I wish for you to take is the inspiration and impression that indeed God is real. And that God does indeed have all the Power that we lack to bring us home to Him. We need only ask. This asking must be followed up with the required effort of seeking Him. If our petition, our prayer, our asking, is laced with a willingness, a willingness that might be born out of desperation, half of the battle has already been won. We will be able to leave our battlefields with our wounds, cuts, scars, pains, and brokenness. We can undergo spiritual surgery. And fully recover from it.

God holds the scalpel and can remove whatever is blocking us from Him. He never makes the terms of healing and seeking Him too difficult. Indeed, it is not easy but then again what is? And isn't gaining anything of worth met with required effort? There is always a price to pay. For me it meant that I had to let go of everything. I had to let go of my position on the field. I had to retreat. I had to let go of all the crazy plans that I always carried with me onto the field. I had to drop them after seeing their deep levels of uselessness. I had to let go of all the dreams born out of delusion, my own running sitcom. I had to let go of all the fixed ideas that were attached to my family and the generational pain that we all lived in and used against each other.

I had to trust God. And I could only effectively do this after seeing my pitiful failure at trying to play God. My position, my station, had to change as I rolled down the tracks.

As I shifted from trusting and relying on my corrupted power to trusting and relying on God's Power and underwent this period of reconstruction I had to take this persuasion, this method, of self-examination and effort at trying to do the next right thing with me. I could no longer play by the same rules of engagement. This presented problems at first because I was afraid of losing what I had left in my life, but I had to be willing to have God rearrange everything which He indeed did. I had to stop letting the demons in me crucify the God in others. Or crucify what little faith they might have within them under the weight of their own body of pain, their own resentments and fears, their own generational trauma.

With each instance that a fear or resentment came to the forefront of my mind or heart I quickly came to know that as my power was always limited, I needed help from God to get through them. Indeed, they can lose their destructive force and become something entirely different. I now understand that fear and resentment are a subtle reminder that I am trying to play God again, that I am trying to hold sway over something by using the past or the future in a selfish manner. I have also come to see that they are of God in the manner of Him reaching out to me. They are that phone call or text message gently reminding me that I have taken my eyes off Him. I have removed my heart from Him.

My journey home to God required a great deal of prayer and careful reflection. Growing up I resented my father at deep levels for what we never had between us. We rarely spent time together. We didn't have a relationship. The same can be said for the relationship that I had with God while growing up. I never spent time with Him or seeking Him. I allowed the noises in my mind and those about me to take its place. To block me from Him.

If I want to have a relationship with another, I need to make the investment of dedicating time to and for it and the investment of getting to know the person. It is the same with God. The more time I spend in prayer with Him the deeper my faith becomes and the more I can see Him. The more I can see His Power. The more I can see His work about me. The more I can see Him in you. And with this comes the peace and comfort I have always craved. I can not only return to the Honeysuckle Dream, but I can also remain there. I can *hear* God.

Even when the stream of life gets crazy, the waves get higher and the undertow stronger, I can remain in the Honeysuckle Dream and simply watch it. I can stand there and smell the mint behind me while looking at the beauty of the flower and withstand the temptation to leave and engage with the fears and resentments that arise naturally. I can always remain with God while here on Earth.

Forty

I Found My Purple Socks

There is absolutely no doubt that what we are fed in life is what we become as there is no doubt that what we are given in life is truly a gift from God. I wholly believe what we do with it, with our *story*, is our gift to Him.

Few people may call themselves an expert in something and I rightly imagine it takes not only serious effort but a great deal of time to become an expert. I am indeed an expert in one thing. It is in the realm of spiritual disease, spiritual sickness. I became an expert in my lack of God-consciousness. With the never-ending guidance of my parents, I became an expert in the art of evading reality while embracing each fear they poured into me. I tried with all my might to use it all to my advantage, to play God myself, and the beginning of it, my departure from the Honeysuckle Dream, all came to an end when I returned home to God.

I didn't have to die as I wished when I asked God to come get me. I didn't need to die physically. I was allowed to die while still being alive and as this happened God-consciousness came to the forefront of every fiber of my being and permeated every aspect of my life. I became peaceful. I became free. Though it was painful, and I kicked and screamed like a newborn trying to get used to the move into life, the new vision I could see before me was far more nourishing than the dysfunction I grew up with and lived with behind me.

As an expert in that spiritual malaise, I came to know it intimately, and as I was able to break free from it, I quickly came to see that I must try to become an expert in being spiritually fit. I highly doubt that I will reach this perfection but to be able to hold that ideal as the center of life today is nourishing enough for me.

I can look the world in the eye. The place I was in so long ago as I walked on the beach in Puerto Rico with Rick with my gaze on the ground has finally been lifted upward. I can look you and life in the eye. While I tried to fill the empty spaces in my life that were the moments when I was alone, I can now be alone and at perfect peace and quiet. I am at ease. With my reconnection to God and that childish faith the fears began to dissolve as sugar does in warm water. I was able to move from fearing God and the belief that He didn't believe in me to being able to feel His nearness. He is always there, and I am never without Him. The space between us has been eliminated.

Even at my lowest points I had these beliefs that were spiritual in nature, yet they weren't enough to hold me. What I have now is an awakening that is spiritual in nature, and it expands more and more each day. Just when I think it cannot get deeper, better, it does. And this deepens my faith exponentially. The fears, especially the fear of abandonment, prevented me from placing my hand in God's hand as I was afraid that He might abandon me but today it is different. After seeing the blistering truth of my experience and most definitely that of my nature that became decrepit and finding God and experiencing a renewal I refuse to let go of Him.

The position in life, in my thoughts and resultant actions, that I enjoy today are not by my limited human power, they are powered by God. It is truly difficult to put into words what happened because of the willingness to let go and then having a God experience as a result of seeking Him. My words describing it will always pale in comparison to the actual experience. I needn't worry about that as I truly believe that while I do the best that I can to not pass on the generational trauma and drama I now have something that matches this desire and effort. It is and will be the way that I live my life. It will always be how I demonstrate my faith, and my understanding of God.

As I demonstrate this, I know that the position I have landed in is one where I might be able to represent God's Power. A profound change in character and personality brought about by this Power cannot be denied by those about me. It cannot go unnoticed and when asked what happened, how it happened, I am quick to say that God made it so, He made it possible. All I did was ask with a bit of blind faith. He answered the prayer. He provided the path to take, and I followed it.

Since this change in position phenomenal things have happened in my life. And by extension to those about me. While I watched my spiritual dysfunction bleed into everyone else's life who were closest to me I have also been able to witness the same effect as I sought to regain my spiritual fitness. I can now face life successfully and enjoy an arrangement in my mind that allows for peace and quiet. And so can those closest to me without the fear that "Mad Bob" will return.

Waking up with the fear of another day or even tomorrow is gone. Even the fear of what might be in the hereafter has been lifted. I needn't worry about it anymore. Faith keeps these fears at bay.

I loved my story while standing before the honeysuckle breathing in the scent of it and then quickly grew to hate my story. God made it possible for me to love my story again. He placed me in this new position. He showed me not only how to love my story and the better parts of it but how to love the deepest darkest parts of it as well. Those are the parts that seemed to be the most powerful and indeed they can be the most powerful as we transcend them and look upon them with a new perspective. It is in their power that we see how they might benefit others. How they might be of use, not only to us as a reminder, but to God as we carry the message of His Infinite Power and Grace by telling our own story to others.

I don't have to hate my story anymore. I don't have to hate Mom and Dad anymore. I don't have to hate my family anymore. I do not have the guilt, shame, and remorse anymore. All of the doors along that hallway that make up my life are wide open. Each space behind them is filled with Light. I do not want to or have to close the doors and try to lock them anymore. God-consciousness won't allow this. It does, however, allow me to take you into these rooms to show you around, and to love my story. This love, this appreciation, only deepened as I began to share my story with others. While it was amazing to have the light come back on in my eyes, to have that Light that was installed deep within me grow brighter each day, I have no choice but to do something with it. It is said that faith without any work is dead, and indeed this is the truth.

As my spiritual dysfunction was constantly fed and nourished with what seemed to be absolute darkness and grew into its own right as a monster-sized creature the same must happen with my faith. It needs constant recognition and as a muscle needs to be worked out daily to not only remain strong but to continue to gain strength. The most effective workout in the gym of life is the effort made in passing on what was so freely handed to me by others to still others that I might encounter. Including you.

God certainly did for me what I could never do for myself. God certainly did for me what others could not do for me. I quickly came to see that God pulled me out of the pit so I could go back in and get others out of it. As I came to see things differently, I came to see that I could return to the battlefield. It wasn't the area of the battlefield that I spent my entire life wandering around aimlessly without clear orders. I was now placed at the front lines, and I came to see that indeed I would now have to engage in spiritual warfare. I have met many out there who were once like me who found perfect peace and release from the darker side of human nature and their existence confirms that I am never alone.

I feel privileged to be able to meet with others who are stuck where I was stuck for so long and know that they are placed before me so that I might be able to help them get home. By doing so I am helping God. I am working for Him. There is no greater pleasure than to die of this world and being reborn to it with a different vision and to be able to pass that on to others and see their Light brightened as they return to the Honeysuckle Dream. To still see them move to loving their story and seeing the intrinsic value of it as they pass it on through continued effort and demonstration.

The most powerful thing I have ever done in my powerlessness was to let go absolutely.

And let God.

Forty-One

Nirvana - Heaven

Not a sunny day without a cloud in the sky passes that I do not recall that time spent before the honeysuckle when I was a child. Today I am blessed to be able to live in that Sunlight even on the cloudy days, even on the days when it feels like the storms that hover above the stream of life might capsize my vessel. I just know that God is there and no matter what happens I am safe. I am protected.

I have so very little in the way of possessions from my childhood. I have a few things that were my grandparents but have nearly nothing of Mom or Dad except for the memories. These memories have had the resentments and fears associated with them washed away. They are now sweet memories. I do not have to carry the resentments and fears with me, nor do I have to pass them on. With all the hope inspired by faith within me I believe that the generational trauma and drama can end with me. That I do not have to pass it on. More importantly I can not only see everything for what it was but can speak plainly to all of it with my wife and my children. Will I be perfect in the role of husband or father? The perfect friend? Hardly! But I can be perfect in showing it by admitting my imperfection and taking responsibility for it, always with a willingness to learn and grow and change.

I keep *reminders* about me. They are there to bring me, and my focus on life and the reason for living, back to God. To perhaps inspire me to always stay with God as this is where I am at total peace. I have these dice, each side is printed with the word "GOD," and I'm reminded that no matter how I rolled the dice or roll the dice it will always begin, and be, and end, with God.

When I reduce each and every bit and piece, every nuance of my journey, it always leads to and comes back to God. To faith in God. The fear was not real. It was unfounded, not based in fact. I have found that when I live a life based in God, in God-consciousness, life is indeed based in fact and that I can not only offer Him prayers and petitions, but I can also listen to and hear Him.

And this is as wonderful a sound as the birds that were singing as I stood before the sweet-smelling honeysuckle that day so many years ago.

Do not hesitate another moment to return to your version of the Honeysuckle Dream. Embrace your story, and let it set you free.

God is real.

He is there.

And He is waiting for you to return home to Him.

-

"Mom, I'm home!"

"Hi Honey Bunny! I've been waiting for you!!!"

"I know. I would have loved to have been here sooner, but I had to finish my business down below. I had to finish the act, complete the role. But there were a lot of times I really wanted to leave there and get back here." Of course, she already knew this.

"How do you think it went?"

"I think it went okay. There were so many moments while I was in the stream where I thought the ripples and currents caused by the human will stuff would stop my progress, but I believe I was able to effectively make a break from it all and move beyond it."

Mom met this with silence for a bit.

"Hey Mom." I spoke softly as I broke the silence.

"What babe?"

"Thank you! Thank you for always being there. Thank you for always trying, trying to transcend your pain, for fighting for me and believing in me. Thank you for all that you gave me and left me as you departed to come home."

"It was my contract in that life to do as I did. I did it not only for you and your sister and our family but for God. It was what He wanted and needed done. We always serve at His pleasure even when we don't think we are doing so."

"I know that your story had a profound effect on me while I was down there. Do you think mine might have the same on others?"

"What did you say to me when you were writing the first book?"

She went on to answer her own question.

"You told me that if it helped only one person then it would be a success."

"I hope my story and the way I lived my life touched just one person Mom." I expressed with a softness born out of exhaustion.

"It certainly touched me before I passed away. Not only that, but it also touched each and every person you came in contact with down there. Your story became a natural part of the synchronicity and synergy of everything as you lived it and travelled in the stream. We are all a part of the Whole and not one thing is wasted. It is all there for a specific reason.

You already know this though."

"Thank you, Mom. I love you!"

"I love you too Honey Bunny!"

"Mom?"

"Yes?"

"Where is Nana, Papa, Moo, and Dad?"

"They're all waiting for you to review all that we have accomplished in our roles that we played together."

"Can we go see them now?"

"Of course we can."

"Do you think I can go ..."

Epilogue

A Long Goodbye

I began this writing with a quote by Robert Bresson that speaks to the fact that if we can take what is hidden inside of us and bring it forth and expose it to the light then perhaps not only will it weaken its hold or sway on us it might become instrumental in someone else's life. Perhaps it will change their course in the stream of life.

This has been my hope throughout the entire process and my deeply held hope is that this book has helped you even if only in the smallest of ways. Whether you experienced a profound awakening and shift or simply a small ripple by becoming a part of my story I hope you are the better for it, I hope it helps to heal that which hurts inside of you. I hope you find your voice and that you can use it for good. I hope you use your story in an effective way.

As much as I wanted to share what will be written here as we close our time together at the start of the book, I was afraid it might have had too much of a bearing on how you might receive the narrative. I didn't want to set up any prejudices in you or collide with your own fixed ideas that were in place when we started.

To say that I have wanted to write this book for many years is an absolute understatement. There were two things in play long before I could begin typing it out. Of course, the question of how to tell it but then there was the question of when. I have tried numerous times to tell this story, to type it out. Each time that proceeded this effort in writing was met with a block. It wasn't there. I couldn't find the words or the cadence. I was trying to *force* it.

I always tried to tell my story from a place of the lower self, the angry little boy looking to exact revenge instead of the man who arrived at a place of forgiveness and acceptance. It is my deepest hope that you can see that the latter is where the book has emanated from. I offer all my story to you with profound love along with the hope that always comes from a place of acceptance and forgiveness. Indeed, it has taken me years to reach this station, to return to loving my story. It has taken me years to return to the Honeysuckle Dream.

There were many signs that led me to begin typing "one more time." I didn't want to as I had developed the fear that nothing would come of it. Each previous effort led to yet another failed attempt. As I moved to a place of understanding every nuance of my life, of forgiveness and acceptance of all that my life was, the channel that had been blocked suddenly became clear. The intuitive nudge grew stronger and stronger, and I was *pushed* by God to try yet one more time. This book has brought the age-old lesson to me yet once again that we must never lose hope, must never give up, on our efforts and dreams. Especially the Honeysuckle Dream.

I know that the spirit of Nana, Papa, Moo, and Mom, and even Dad, were with me as I told you my story. Especially Papa. When we moved into what is our dream home there was this small bedroom that I thought of using as a paint studio. That didn't happen. Instead, we turned it into what I began to call the "Writing Chamber." We didn't want it to be an "office." As I ordered furniture, I came upon the perfect desk that spoke to me. It was a part of the "Firth Collection" and Papa's last name was Firth. Though it took three years after the desk arrived to see my intent of telling my story come to life it was well worth the wait.

The quote I opened with was attached to a statue my wife and I purchased at an art festival. It was the meaning behind the statue. The artist created the statue, the piece of art, the expression of himself, from the quote. His life, an extension of his art, came from his story.

We have a few art festivals that are a part of the backbone of the art industry here in Rhode Island. Growing up there was one I never went to until just before this writing took place. My wife and I live in a coastal town and this festival takes place near our home during the summer. We had two of our dearest friends Bill and Claudia over for the afternoon on the Sunday with a plan to visit the art festival and then to have dinner. I'm always inspired by art and Claudia is an artist.

As we went up and down each row and viewed the different types of art, we came upon the artist that my wife and I have come to know and appreciate. We have a few of his paintings hanging in our home. Mia's spirits were buoyed as we saw a piece that would work for us. We bought the piece from Zach and would commission yet another to match it a day later.

Two tents away was an artist who worked in metals, a form of art that held no attraction for me. I've always respected this form, but I never felt a pull to it. He did have this one piece that wasn't a typical patina in metal, it was painted lime green. It drew your attention to the tent and to his art but as metal never did a thing for me, I kept walking. I didn't stop to look.

We walked the rest of the festival and when we were ready to leave we headed back to pick up the painting Mia and I picked out. As we approached Zach's tent and as I passed the metal artist, I felt this pull. I was being carried into his tent and at first I thought it was to see the lime green piece. I looked at it hanging on the wall of the tent and easily dismissed it. It didn't do a thing for me. I thought I was just curious.

As I turned from it, I couldn't help but look at the other pieces. They were truly amazing. Powerful in fact. They were loaded with expression and passion. My eyes fell upon a piece that really intrigued me. I had to know more about it. I wanted to know the *story* behind it.

This brilliant artist, Michael Alfano, was speaking with another couple and they soon backed away as my wife and I stood inside the tent. You could feel Michael's energy, you could feel his passion, you could feel his zest for living. You could feel the sense that he had arrived at a clear purpose and was now living it. It was powerful and it affected me deeply.

The piece my eye fell on was the silhouette of the front view of a face. It was nondescript, it could have been any one of us. There was a hand attached to the top of it and between the thumb and finger was a pencil. The pencil was a real pencil but everything else about the sculpture was metal. It held a yellow Ticonderoga number 2 pencil. This is in fact the only pencil I will use. I was beyond intrigued as I tried to understand and make sense of the sculpture.

As I arrived at my own interpretation of its meaning and value and as the other couple continued to back out of the tent, I asked him what it meant, how he came upon it. He began without hesitation. As my wife and I listened intently with Claudia and Bill behind us he spoke with passion, he got excited while telling *his* story and the story of how he came to land at the creation of this statue.

He explained that within each of us a story is written and that he believes it is our duty to tell the story, to express the story. That by telling our story others might be inspired to do the same or even change their story. The four of us were speechless and you could have lifted the jaws on the faces of my wife and I off the ground. We had tears in our eyes. We were blown away. Mia and I looked at one another. She said "Wow" and I said, "Holy shit."

It is needless to say that I have wanted to write this. My wife has wholly supported this in me for years and has even endured my madness and the madness of wanting to write this. I could not have been given a clearer sign that it was time to write, and my wife supported this quickly understood validation. We bought the statue, and it sits in the Writing Chamber with me as I type this manuscript.

This all happened on a Sunday.

Four days later we went to the local appliance store. We bought our dream home a few years back and have been making incremental changes to it to make it just the way we want it. This included getting a microwave to match the already updated appliances in the kitchen. We both love to cook.

We visited the store and made the purchase. As we did, we stood on one side of the counter. As we were finishing up, we moved to the other side of the counter. Once completed we fell to the “thank you's” and began to say goodbye to Leslie. I looked down to my left and saw a pamphlet on the lower part of the counter. It was a pamphlet from the artist we bought the metal sculpture from.

I picked it up and held it. I asked Leslie if she had visited the art festival over the weekend, if she had seen this artist. She said she didn't attend the festival but offered something that brought my thoughts to a standstill with an exclamation point. She said that she loved art and was an artist herself. She told us she was a writer and that she had published a book. I wanted to scream "I did too!!!" but have learned the art of letting someone finish their thoughts, their piece of their story. So, I listened. When she paused, I then offered that I had published a book as well. Our "thank you's" and "goodbyes" were delayed.

I asked what her book was about. She explained that it was about her experience of getting a divorce and her recovery from it. She stopped talking. I then explained that my first was about my recovery from alcohol and drugs and about finding God. Our books were different versions of this book. They held the essence of this book.

She then told us that she had finally begun her second book after experiencing many blocks and that she was excited to see it all happen. And here we were thinking we were going to the appliance store to get a microwave! Isn't this the Way though? Always? Indeed, it is. And if we can successfully clear the channel between God and ourselves, open ourselves up to Him, we will receive the clearest in guidance.

For so long I held onto everything that was blocking me and couldn't type this story but when it was time, when my channel was nearly fully cleared the *messages* could not be ignored. Action had to be taken.

A week before the art festival I landed at one of those "letting go" moments. For months I had been looking for a specific model of a vehicle that was becoming wildly popular and difficult to find. They were difficult to order as well. After six months of research and searching I woke up on a Saturday morning and the thought that ran through my head was "That's it. I give up."

As I opened my email there was a notification that a vehicle matching my exact search parameters was new to the market. It was not at a dealership of the same brand; it was at a different dealership. Before this, our new silver Labrador puppy Alice arrived in our lives after a few years without a dog. Six months previous we had met the breeder via a call to make the arrangements to get another Labrador. In the course of time, we came to know that her husband was the general manager at this same dealership that now had the vehicle I had been looking for.

I texted Jocelyn with the details and asked her if she could find out from her husband if the vehicle was indeed available and on the lot at the dealership. In no time she texted back and told me it was and that her husband would see me later that afternoon. This all took place the weekend before Independence Day. This bit of a nuance was not lost on me either.

The day before the holiday I drove away from the dealership in my dream vehicle. Sometimes it is the smallest of moments in our lives and sometimes the grandest that provides a shift in perspective, that validates the strides we make or have made. In this case it just happened to be a physical item, not the typical mental or emotional or spiritual happening that announced the shift.

As I drove onto the ramp to get onto the highway there was this sense of freedom that something was indeed going to happen that would come to match this dream achieved and realized. There was this *knowing* that I came to see and feel. With this came a message. I know it was of and from Mom as it arrived in her voice. She simply said, "Go tell the story, go see if there is just that one person out there who might benefit from it." I began to cry as the hot air from the wind whipped through my new Bronco and carried with it a new wind of change that I felt was coming. I had finally reached the comfortable place of acceptance. I had finally reached the place of forgiveness, forgiveness of others and of self, that would allow me to tell my story. I could now enjoy the same wild and unbridled freedom a bronco experiences.

As I began the writing different fears did present themselves and tried to exert their destructive forces on me. The typical "You're not good enough to do it," and the "Your family won't care for this," and the "You're not supposed to talk about the secrets like this." Of course it was false evidence trying to appear to be real. Thankfully the fears held no sway or bearing on me.

The process always seemed to be guided by something bigger than me. Clearly the signs were there, and clearly, I saw their exact message. All I needed to do was remain open. Remain open to the possibility that one person might be touched in a positive manner and remain open to not only God's Grace but His infinite direction. I had to take the result of lessons learned and sharpen my ability to listen to Him. I had to listen to my intuition like never before and keep my eyes open to every single nuance in my life as the writing took place. The experience at the art festival brought this persuasion upon me that allowed this to happen.

In no time the rhythm arrived as I began writing and the cadence was set into motion with this regularity that was easy to see. As easy as it can be to see and hear God after sustained practice. My eyes would open in the middle of the night in a pronounced way, and it felt as though I was being pushed. Pushed out of my bed. Pushed with the subject matter that needed to be typed out.

The first night this happened it felt surreal, but I soon came to trust in it, to rely on it. I would go into the Writing Chamber and put my headphones on and get lost in the ethereal music I always put on. My fingers would just move, and the words would appear, most times I didn't realize what was landing on the page until I printed it out and did a soft edit. It never ceased to amaze me how the story unfolded.

I would stop writing when it felt as though the words weren't there anymore. When it felt as though whoever was on the other side feeding them to me simply said "Okay. That's enough for today." I would listen to this direction. Besides, all previous efforts to not only force things in my life but also force efforts in writing led to futility. A uselessness that bore no fruit.

I would leave the chamber and go for a walk or begin to get ready for my day with a shower. There was always this reprieve of sorts. They stopped feeding me the information so I would stop the writing. There were many days when I would leave the chamber exhausted but fully rejuvenated. There was this relief coming over me. A natural catharsis that always takes place at some level, whether large or small, as a result of sharing our story. The reprieve would eventually end and a new stream of information, messages, would begin to flow across the plane of thought, bringing with them a new round of feelings that were always attached to them. Most days as I finished the writing there were tears that followed. Always a great indicator of healing that is happening whether mentally, emotionally, or spiritually.

Following the break from the writing and with the new flow of thoughts I quickly came to see that this was indeed the next chapter being presented to me. I began to journal. I jotted notes on post it pads and hung the pieces on the wall. I carried my leather-bound journal with me when away from the house and would scratch the information down in a fever. I kept legal pads about me to do the same. At the end of the day, I would make sure my laptop and any ruminations written down were back at my desk in the chamber and ready for me when I woke up the following morning.

I set my alarm for three in the morning, but my eyes always seemed to fly open before it went off. There were times when I was gripped with the fear that the messages and directions would stop coming to me. I wanted this book to be completed. I wanted to have my story out there with the hope that someone might be inspired by it as I had been inspired by the stories of so many people in my life.

This cycle became a daily rinse and repeat until every word that had to be typed or written was typed or written. The greatest element that was always at the center of this was prayer and meditation. Prayer of course being a petition to God and mine was simply "God please help me to tell my story in the most effective and complete way." This was followed by the thought and belief that He indeed was going to do just that. The meditation became the full in-depth reflection required to dig as deep as possible to remember all those things needed to effectively carry the message that we all have within us, the ability to fully awaken from the dreamy part of our story.

Writing this and getting it typed out was the easy part! At times the most difficulty I felt was in the period after I stopped writing when the messages began to present themselves. There were days when the flow of them was a slow and steady stream but the days that the stream of thoughts seemed so quick and rushed that they were stacking themselves upon one another were the days that I simply had to trust in the information being revealed. At first it would freak me out, but this soon turned into a wonder that kept me inspired to keep going.

The messaging received and the ability to keep my mind and heart open to not only the process and lessons of each life experience reviewed but to the messages set before me as I journeyed fed not only the need to do this, but the level of energy required to tell my story. At times when doubt appeared with the clear question of "Why bother?" I would receive the God shots.

As I pulled into the gym one day, thinking that perhaps there were too many words, a client called to place an order with our studio. When I asked if she wanted a copy of her request emailed, she offered her email address to me. It included the word "write" in it. She was a writer, and I shared that I had just crossed over 50 thousand words in the book I was writing.

Upon visiting a local garden center, I ran into one of their employees who is related to a local wholesaler that we used to do business with. She was excited to tell my wife and I that there was a marriage in her family over the weekend and was quick to bring up an image in her phone of her grandfather. Her grandfather is ninety-two years old, and Moo used to do business with him when she was a floral designer as he was starting out as a wholesaler doing business from his garage. He is wheelchair bound now but that didn't stop him from dressing in a full black tuxedo. If you knew anything about Moo she was always dressed to the nines, and most times in black. I *knew* Moo was with me at this moment cheering me on. I gave this young lady a huge hug which she gladly accepted and thanked her from the bottom of my heart for sharing this image with me. I explained that she didn't know what this meant to me but that I would return to tell her about it later.

Still another time as I knew I had to create this bridge in the writing and make a jump from the cataloging of details to how I was able to break free I didn't know how to do it. Of course I didn't have to figure this out. God always has a better plan than I can come up with. I was reminded of this as I began the work of creating floral designs for a family paying tribute to a loved one. It was a military service, like Papa's was a military service when he passed away. There were three pieces, and they had specific scripts on them specifying different terms of endearment. The sole grandson called his grandfather "Papa" and his piece was an open heart. These two things were not lost on me. My heart was open, and I know Papa has always been here with me in spirit since he left. One piece had the endearment of "Dad" on it, again not lost on me. The last sentiment was "Beloved" and perhaps was the most powerful in that it encompasses the feeling we hold closest to our heart. I not only held and still hold Papa close to my heart but have found a way to hold all that he was in a teacher and Dad along with his amazing strength and endurance in principles close to my heart.

I began writing this ending as I reached the middle of the book. Sometimes we get to put that cart before the horse. Beginning the writing of this ending of our time together helped to bring me back to what this book is all about. I was beginning to feel as though the book was too wordy, like one great big run on sentence. I was tempted many times to try to cut the writing. I wanted to fast track it and cut to the chase. I'm not sure if there was a mix of fear in there but I felt like I wanted it to end.

Amid the madness that became this effort in writing I had to cancel some sessions at the gym as exhaustion wouldn't allow me to workout. I had to listen to my body. My trainer Dan asked me if I was writing the *New Testament.* I told him I was writing *The Exorcist.*

As I wrote this story there were many awakenings and aha moments that took place. The greatest being that I indeed arrived at a place in my life where I fully accepted my past and my present, all with a peaceful look toward my future. Throughout my life I have been able to share those bits and pieces of my story and that was about all I could handle. The pain of it wouldn't allow me to spend too much time telling it or writing it. As I attempted to write this so many times it finally came to be. I could tell the story all in one shot.

As I wrote there were chapters that I did not want to write. I wanted to hold it back from you but could not. I have found a deep value in telling my story to others and this was the natural consequence of hearing other people's stories. Their courage and lack of fear in the face of being judged became inspirational to me. Their effort in telling their story allowed my effort to match theirs. Their faith that we can help one another bolstered my faith that I can do the same.

The last run-through and edit on my part came about after I threw the book away. I experienced some harsh difficulties with another soul that were heart-wrenching and eye-opening that became yet another one of those spiritual awakenings. It depleted my energy and my hope seriously waned. I threw the nine edited and revised copies away and decided to scrap the entire effort. Perhaps it was fear but there was something more.

It was indeed a bit more of the shedding of dependencies that were the result of this writing. The writing led to more and more awakenings. I simply needed to embrace them. I also needed to do a bit more shadow work related to a family member. I had to return to that beach and walk it once again. I had to see if I could walk it with my head lifted and gaze forward or if I was still looking down with my shoulders slumped.

I booked a week in Puerto Rico with my wife and took copy number ten of this book with me to finish it at last. To say "Good-bye" to old self in a pronounce manner. I read, and I walked the beach. I finished the job I began, and in the end, I could walk tall with my shoulders back and eyes forward gazing upward over the horizon. I continue to let go more and more each day.

With this hope inspired by faith I want to share another bit with you. My story is unique to me as yours is unique to you, even though there may be many similarities that allow us to relate and identify with one another. I wanted the telling of my story to include the repetition of certain parts to help drive home specific points that I thought were important. The hope in doing so was that this might break through any walls or fixed ideas you had within you, so you might be able to break free from the bondage of self and through the walls that are the natural defense system of the ego. In addition, the slow and steady descent into the depth of sickness and depravity was deliberate. I didn't want your soul or psyche to be assaulted in a harsh manner. The style of writing I chose was wholly deliberate as were the choice of descriptive words that were carefully considered and chosen. I sincerely hope that the editing process has not eliminated this element in the writing.

The telling of my story had nothing to do with me. It had everything to do with you. My life today seems magical, but the reality is that it is miraculous. I am not just surviving, I am thriving. The miracle is that by God's Grace I am free from the bondage of self and the fear of abandonment. So much so that I can share my story with you.

I thank you with all that is within me, and with all that is within my story, for being here. For being a part of my story and for allowing me to be a part of your story. Please go share your story and share it freely. Share it without fear. Share it with faith. Share it for you, share it for me.

Share it for God.

I bid you adieu. With love.

ABOUT ROBERT

Robert Ernest Bach writes with a focus on the emotional and psychological experiences that shape how we relate to ourselves and others.

His work explores themes of abandonment, connection, and the lasting impressions of memory—moving through both the weight of these experiences and the possibility of something beyond them.

Rather than offering conclusions, his writing invites reflection, allowing space for the reader to consider their own experience through a different lens.

ALSO BY ROBERT

Delusion Of Mind Strength Through Spirit